Cracking the

AP®

ENGLISH LITERATURE & COMPOSITION EXAM

2020 Edition

The Staff of The Princeton Review

PrincetonReview.com

Penguin
Random
House

The Princeton Review
110 East 42nd St, 7th Floor
New York, NY 10017
E-mail: editorialsupport@review.com

Published in the United States by Penguin Random House LLC, New York, and in Canada by Random House of Canada, a division of Penguin Random House Ltd., Toronto.

"In My Craft or Sullen Art" from *The Poems of Dylan Thomas* by Dylan Thomas. Copyright ©1952 by Dylan Thomas. Used by permission of David Higham Associates, London, as agents for the Trustees of Copyrights of Dylan Thomas.
Excerpt from *Libra* by Don DeLillo. Copyright © 1988 by Don DeLillo. Used by permission of Viking Books, an imprint of Penguin Publishing Group, a division of Penguin Random House LLC; Penguin Canada, a division of Penguin Random House Canada Limited; and Penguin Books Ltd., a division of Penguin UK.
Excerpt(s) from *White Teeth: A Novel* by Zadie Smith, copyright © 2000 by Zadie Smith. Used by permission of Random House, an imprint and division of Penguin Random House LLC. All rights reserved.
Excerpt from *Ultramarine* by Malcolm Lowry. Copyright © 1962 by Margerie Bonner Lowry. Published in 2005 by The Overlook Press, Peter Mayer Publishers, Inc. New York, NY. www.overlookpress.com. All rights reserved.

ISBN: 978-0-525-56823-0
eBook ISBN: 978-0-525-56861-2
ISSN: 1092-0099

Editor: Selena Coppock
Production Editor: Jim Melloan, Emma Parker
Production Artist: Gabriel Berlin
Content Developer: Rita Williams

Printed in the United States of America.

10 9 8 7 6 5 4 3 2 1

2020 Edition

Editorial

Rob Franek, Editor-in-Chief
David Soto, Director of Content Development
Stephen Koch, Student Survey Manager
Deborah Weber, Director of Production
Gabriel Berlin, Production Design Manager
Selena Coppock, Managing Editor
Aaron Riccio, Senior Editor
Meave Shelton, Senior Editor
Chris Chimera, Editor
Eleanor Green, Editor
Orion McBean, Editor
Brian Saladino, Editor
Patricia Murphy, Editorial Assistant

Penguin Random House Publishing Team

Tom Russell, VP, Publisher
Alison Stoltzfus, Publishing Director
Amanda Yee, Associate Managing Editor
Ellen Reed, Production Manager
Suzanne Lee, Designer

Acknowledgments

The Editor of this book would like to thank Rita Williams for her content development work on the revision of this book. Her imaginative ideas and improvements have vastly improved this, the 2020 Edition.

Contents

Get More (**Free**) Content
at **PrincetonReview.com/cracking**

As easy as 1•2•3

1 Go to PrincetonReview.com/cracking and enter the following ISBN for your book:

9780525568230

2 Answer a few simple questions to set up an exclusive Princeton Review account. (*If you already have one, you can just log in.*)

3 Enjoy access to your **FREE** content!

Once you've registered, you can...

- Find any late-breaking information released about the AP English Literature and Composition Exam

- Take a full-length practice SAT and ACT

- Get valuable advice about the college application process, including tips for writing a great essay and where to apply for financial aid

- Sort colleges by whatever you're looking for (such as Best Theater or Dorm), learn more about your top choices, and see how they all rank according to *The Best 384 Colleges*

- Access comprehensive study guides and a variety of printable resources, including bubble sheets for the practice tests in the book and a glossary of need-to-know literary terms

- Check to see whether there have been any corrections or updates to this edition

Need to report a potential **content** issue?

Contact **EditorialSupport@review.com** and include:

- full title of the book
- ISBN
- page number

Need to report a **technical** issue?

Contact **TPRStudentTech@review.com** and provide:

- your full name
- email address used to register the book
- full book title and ISBN
- Operating system (Mac/PC) and browser (Firefox, Safari, etc.)

Look For These Icons Throughout The Book

 ONLINE ARTICLES

 GOING DEEPER

 PROVEN TECHNIQUES

 APPLIED STRATEGIES

 TIME-SAVING TIP

 STUDY BREAK

 OTHER REFERENCES

Part I
Using This Book to Improve Your AP Score

- Preview: Your Knowledge, Your Expectations
- Your Guide to Using This Book
- How to Begin

PREVIEW: YOUR KNOWLEDGE, YOUR EXPECTATIONS

Your route to a high score on the AP English Literature and Composition Exam depends a lot on how you plan to use this book. Respond to the following questions.

1. Rate your level of confidence about your knowledge of the content tested by the AP English Literature and Composition Exam:

    A. Very confident—I know it all
    B. I'm pretty confident, but there are topics for which I could use help
    C. Not confident—I need quite a bit of support
    D. I'm not sure

2. Circle your goal score for the Exam:

    5   4   3   2   1   I'm not sure yet

3. What do you expect to learn from this book? Circle all that apply to you.

    A. A general overview of the test and what to expect
    B. Strategies for how to approach the test
    C. The content tested by this exam
    D. I'm not sure yet

YOUR GUIDE TO USING THIS BOOK

This book is organized to provide as much—or as little—support as you need, so you can use this book in whatever way will be most helpful to improving your score on the AP English Literature and Composition Exam.

*   The remainder of **Part I** will provide guidance on how to use this book and help you determine your strengths and weaknesses.

*   **Part II** of this book contains Practice Test 1, along with its answers and explanations. (Bubble sheets can be found in the very back of the book for easy tear-out.) We strongly recommend that you take this test before going any further, in order to realistically determine
    o   your starting point right now
    o   which question types you're ready for and which you might need to practice
    o   which content topics you are familiar with and which you will want to carefully review
    Once you have nailed down your strengths and weaknesses with regard to this exam, you can focus your preparation, build a study plan, and be efficient with your time.

- **Part III** of this book will
  - provide information about the structure, scoring, and content of the exam, including the most recent updates that were just announced by the College Board and will affect the course during the 2019-2020 school year and the May 2020 AP English Literature and Composition Exam
  - help you to make a study plan
  - point you toward additional resources

- **Part IV** of this book will explore various strategies, such as
  - how to attack multiple-choice questions
  - how to write effective essays
  - how to manage your time to maximize the number of points available to you

- **Part V** of this book covers the content you need to review and practice for the AP English Literature and Composition Exam.

- **Part VI** of this book contains Practice Test 2 and its answers and explanations. If you skipped Practice Test 1, we recommend that you do both (with at least a day or two between them) so that you can compare your progress between the two. Additionally, this will help to identify any external issues: if you get a certain type of question wrong both times, you probably need to review it. If you only got it wrong once, you may have run out of time or been distracted by something. In either case, this will allow you to focus on the factors that caused the discrepancy in scores and to be as prepared as possible on the day of the test.

- The final section of the book, **Part VII,** is a glossary covering all the literary terms you need to know for the exam.

You may choose to use some parts of this book over others, or you may work through the entire book. This will depend on your needs and how much time you have. Let's take a look at how you will make this determination.

Need Another Bubble Sheet?
Bubble sheets can be found in the back of this book for easy tear out, but if for some reason you need more, you can print them out from your online student tools.

HOW TO BEGIN

1. **Take a Test**

   Before you can decide how to use this book, you need to take a practice test. Doing so will give you insight into your strengths and weaknesses, and the test will also help you make an effective study plan. If you're feeling test-phobic, remind yourself that a practice test is a tool for diagnosing yourself—it's not how well you do that matters, but how you use the information gleaned from your performance to guide your preparation.

   So, before you read further, take Practice Test 1, which is found in Part II of this book. Be sure to do so in one sitting, following the instructions that appear before the test.

2. **Check Your Answers**

   Using the answer key on page 29, count how many multiple-choice questions you got right and how many you missed. Don't worry about the explanations for now, and don't worry about why you missed questions. We'll get to that soon.

3. **Reflect on the Test**

   After you take your first test, respond to the following questions:

   • How much time did you spend on the multiple-choice questions?

   • How much time did you spend on each essay?

   • How many multiple-choice questions did you miss?

   • Do you feel you had the knowledge to address the subject matter of the essays?

   • Do you feel you wrote well-organized, thoughtful essays?

4. **Read Part III of this Book and Complete the Self-Evaluation**

   Part III provides information on test content areas, structure, and scoring.

   As you read Part III, re-evaluate your answers to the questions above. At the end of Part III, you will revisit and refine the questions. You will then be able to make a study plan, based on your needs and time available, that allows you to use this book most effectively.

5. **Engage with Parts IV and V as Needed**

   Notice the word *engage*. You'll get more out of this book if you use it intentionally than if you read it passively and hope for an improved score through osmosis.

Strategy chapters will help you think about your approach to the question types on this exam. Part IV opens with a reminder to think about how you approach questions now and closes with a reflection section asking you to think about how/whether you will change your approach in the future.

Content chapters provide a review of the content tested on the AP English Literature and Composition, including the level of detail you need to know and how the content is tested.

6. **Take Practice Test 2 and Assess Your Performance**
   Once you feel you have developed the strategies you need and gained the knowledge you lacked, you should take Practice Test 2, which is found in Part VI of this book. You should do so in one sitting, following the instructions at the beginning of the test.

   When you are done, check your answers to the multiple-choice sections. See whether a teacher will read your responses to the free-response questions and provide feedback.

   Once you have taken the test, reflect on what areas you still need to work on, and revisit the chapters in this book that address those deficiencies. Through this type of reflection and engagement, you will continue to improve.

7. **Keep Working**
   There are other resources available to you, including a wealth of information on APStudents.org. You can continue to explore areas that can stand to improve and engage in those areas right up to the day of the test. Visit the following page for exam practice and information: **https://apstudent.collegeboard.org/apcourse/ ap-english-literature-and-composition**

More AP Info Online!
For short quizzes, high level AP course and test information, and expert advice, head over to www.princetonreview. com/college-advice/ advanced-placement-resources.

Part II
Practice Test 1

Practice Test 1

The Exam

AP® English Literature and Composition Exam

SECTION I: Multiple-Choice Questions

DO NOT OPEN THIS BOOKLET UNTIL YOU ARE TOLD TO DO SO.

At a Glance

Total Time
1 hour
Number of Questions
55
Percent of Total Grade
45%
Writing Instrument
Pencil required

Instructions

Section I of this examination contains 55 multiple-choice questions. Fill in only the ovals for numbers 1 through 55 on your answer sheet.

Indicate all of your answers to the multiple-choice questions on the answer sheet. No credit will be given for anything written in this exam booklet, but you may use the booklet for notes or scratch work. After you have decided which of the suggested answers is best, completely fill in the corresponding oval on the answer sheet. Give only one answer to each question. If you change an answer, be sure that the previous mark is erased completely. Here is a sample question and answer.

Sample Question

Sample Answer

Chicago is a
(A) state
(B) city
(C) country
(D) continent
(E) village

Ⓐ ● Ⓒ Ⓓ Ⓔ

Use your time effectively, working as quickly as you can without losing accuracy. Do not spend too much time on any one question. Go on to other questions and come back to the ones you have not answered if you have time. It is not expected that everyone will know the answers to all the multiple-choice questions.

About Guessing

Many candidates wonder whether or not to guess the answers to questions about which they are not certain. Multiple choice scores are based on the number of questions answered correctly. Points are not deducted for incorrect answers, and no points are awarded for unanswered questions. Because points are not deducted for incorrect answers, you are encouraged to answer all multiple-choice questions. On any questions you do not know the answer to, you should eliminate as many choices as you can, and then select the best answer among the remaining choices.

GO ON TO THE NEXT PAGE.

ENGLISH LITERATURE AND COMPOSITION

SECTION I

Time—1 hour

Directions: This section consists of selections from literary works and questions on their content, form, and style. After reading each passage or poem, choose the best answer to each question and then completely fill in the corresponding oval on the answer sheet.

Questions 1–15. Choose your answers to questions 1–15 based on a careful reading of the following passage.

A green and yellow parrot, which hung in a cage outside the door, kept repeating over and over:

"*Allez vous-en! Allez vous-en! Sapristi!* That's all right!"

Line He could speak a little Spanish, and also a language
(5) which nobody understood, unless it was the mocking-bird that hung on the other side of the door, whistling his fluty notes out upon the breeze with maddening persistence.

Mr. Pontellier, unable to read his newspaper with any degree of comfort, arose with an expression and an
(10) exclamation of disgust.

He walked down the gallery and across the narrow "bridges" which connected the Lebrun cottages one with the other. He had been seated before the door of the main house. The parrot and the mockingbird were the property of
(15) Madame Lebrun, and they had the right to make all the noise they wished. Mr. Pontellier had the privilege of quitting their society when they ceased to be entertaining.

He stopped before the door of his own cottage, which was the fourth one from the main building and next to the
(20) last. Seating himself in a wicker rocker which was there, he once more applied himself to the task of reading the newspaper. The day was Sunday; the paper was a day old. The Sunday papers had not yet reached Grand Isle. He was already acquainted with the market reports, and he glanced
(25) restlessly over the editorials and bits of news which he had not had time to read before quitting New Orleans the day before.

Mr. Pontellier wore eye-glasses. He was a man of forty, of medium height and rather slender build; he stooped a
(30) little. His hair was brown and straight, parted on one side. His beard was neatly and closely trimmed.

Once in a while he withdrew his glance from the newspaper and looked about him. There was more noise than ever over at the house. The main building was called
(35) "the house," to distinguish it from the cottages. The chattering and whistling birds were still at it. Two young girls, the Farival twins, were playing a duet from "Zampa" upon the piano. Madame Lebrun was bustling in and out, giving orders in a high key to a yard-boy whenever she got
(40) inside the house, and directions in an equally high voice to a dining-room servant whenever she got outside. She was a fresh, pretty woman, clad always in white with elbow

sleeves. Her starched skirts crinkled as she came and went. Farther down, before one of the cottages, a lady in black was
(45) walking demurely up and down, telling her beads. A good many persons of the *pension* had gone over to the *Chênière Caminada* in Beaudelet's lugger to hear mass. Some young people were out under the wateroaks playing croquet. Mr. Pontellier's two children were there—sturdy little fellows of
(50) four and five. A quadroon nurse followed them about with a faraway, meditative air.

Mr. Pontellier finally lit a cigar and began to smoke, letting the paper drag idly from his hand. He fixed his gaze upon a white sunshade that was advancing at snail's pace
(55) from the beach. He could see it plainly between the gaunt trunks of the water-oaks and across the stretch of yellow camomile. The gulf looked far away, melting hazily into the blue of the horizon. The sunshade continued to approach slowly. Beneath its pink-lined shelter were his wife, Mrs.
(60) Pontellier, and young Robert Lebrun. When they reached the cottage, the two seated themselves with some appearance of fatigue upon the upper step of the porch, facing each other, each leaning against a supporting post.

"What folly! to bathe at such an hour in such heat!"
(65) exclaimed Mr. Pontellier. He himself had taken a plunge at daylight. That was why the morning seemed long to him.

"You are burnt beyond recognition," he added, looking at his wife as one looks at a valuable piece of personal property which has suffered some damage. She held up her
(70) hands, strong, shapely hands, and surveyed them critically, drawing up her fawn sleeves above the wrists. Looking at them reminded her of her rings, which she had given to her husband before leaving for the beach. She silently reached out to him, and he, understanding, took the rings from his
(75) vest pocket and dropped them into her open palm. She slipped them upon her fingers; then clasping her knees, she looked across at Robert and began to laugh. The rings sparkled upon her fingers. He sent back an answering smile.

"What is it?" asked Pontellier, looking lazily and amused
(80) from one to the other. It was some utter nonsense; some adventure out there in the water, and they both tried to relate it at once. It did not seem half so amusing when told. They realized this, and so did Mr. Pontellier. He yawned and stretched himself. Then he got up, saying he had half a mind

GO ON TO THE NEXT PAGE.

(85) to go over to Klein's hotel and play a game of billiards.

"Come go along, Lebrun," he proposed to Robert. But Robert admitted quite frankly that he preferred to stay where he was and talk to Mrs. Pontellier.

"Well, send him about his business when he bores you, *(90)* Edna," instructed her husband as he prepared to leave.

"Here, take the umbrella," she exclaimed, holding it out to him. He accepted the sunshade, and lifting it over his head descended the steps and walked away.

"Coming back to dinner?" his wife called after him. *(95)* He halted a moment and shrugged his shoulders. He felt in his vest pocket; there was a ten-dollar bill there. He did not know; perhaps he would return for the early dinner and perhaps he would not. It all depended upon the company which he found over at Klein's and the size of "the game." *(100)* He did not say this, but she understood it, and laughed, nodding good-by to him.

Both children wanted to follow their father when they saw him starting out. He kissed them and promised to bring them back bonbons and peanuts.

───────────

Excerpt from *The Awakening* by Kate Chopin (pp. 1–6).
Copyright © 1899 by Herbert S. Stone & Co.

1. The tone of the beginning of the passage is

   (A) cacophonous
   (B) whimsical
   (C) brooding
   (D) satirical
   (E) pastoral

2. In line 6, the word "his" is referring to

   (A) the parrot
   (B) Mr. Pontellier
   (C) Mr. Lebrun
   (D) the mocking-bird
   (E) Mr. Klein

3. Lines 8–10 establish Mr. Pontellier as

   (A) fastidious and officious
   (B) intolerant and judgmental
   (C) restless and volatile
   (D) surreptitious and untrustworthy
   (E) ambitious and corrupt

4. The parrot's chatter made at the beginning of the passage helps to establish

   (A) the unpleasantness of the setting
   (B) Mr. Pontellier's restlessness and discomfort
   (C) the tension between Mr. Pontellier and Robert
   (D) the tension between Robert and Mrs. Pontellier
   (E) a sense of unease between man and nature

5. In line 26, the word "quitting" means

   (A) finishing
   (B) leaving
   (C) giving up
   (D) dismissing
   (E) setting free

6. Mr. Pontellier's attitude toward his companions on Grand Isle could be characterized as

   (A) aloof
   (B) curious
   (C) mistrustful
   (D) warm
   (E) antagonistic

7. In line 49, the word "sturdy" helps to establish

   (A) Mr. Pontellier's self-satisfaction with his children
   (B) the children's ability to withstand Mr. Pontellier's neglect
   (C) parallels between the children and their mother
   (D) suspicion that Mr. Pontellier is not the children's biological father
   (E) a contrast between the Pontellier children and the rest of the island's inhabitants

GO ON TO THE NEXT PAGE.

8. In lines 52–66, which word complements our understanding of Mr. Pontellier's personality?

    (A) Smoke
    (B) Idly
    (C) Gaunt
    (D) Folly
    (E) Plunge

9. The use of "the sunshade" to refer to the approach of two people is an example of

    (A) metonymy
    (B) apostrophe
    (C) hyperbole
    (D) personification
    (E) synecdoche

10. Lines 58–66 reveal:

    I. Mr. Pontellier's dislike of Robert
    II. Mr. Pontellier's contempt toward his wife
    III. Mr. Pontellier's self-righteousness

    (A) I only
    (B) II only
    (C) III only
    (D) I and III
    (E) II and III

11. In line 67, Mr. Pontellier uses which literary device to provoke a reaction from his wife?

    (A) Hyperbole
    (B) Onomatopoeia
    (C) Assonance
    (D) Understatement
    (E) Apostrophe

12. Lines 67–78 serve to introduce

    (A) Mrs. Pontellier's unattractive appearance.
    (B) an indication that the relationship between Mr. and Mrs. Pontellier is strained.
    (C) a suggestion that Robert is uncomfortable around Mr. Pontellier.
    (D) Mrs. Pontellier's dominant position in the marriage.
    (E) Mr. Pontellier's protectiveness toward his wife.

13. In line 87, the phrase "quite frankly" serves the purpose of

    (A) establishing Robert's stubbornness
    (B) elaborating on Robert's animosity toward Pontellier
    (C) contrasting Robert's contentment with Pontellier's ambivalence
    (D) accentuating Pontellier's alienation from the residents of Grand Isle
    (E) revealing Robert's social status in comparison to that of Pontellier

14. The description of the interactions between Mrs. Pontellier and Robert convey a tone of

    (A) unapologetic intimacy
    (B) passionate longing
    (C) polite tolerance
    (D) underlying antagonism
    (E) conspiratorial secrecy

15. Lines 86–90 serve to further clarify

    I. Mr. Pontellier's indifference toward his marriage
    II. Mr. Pontellier's disdain for his children
    III. Mr. Pontellier's fear of Robert's influence over his wife

    (A) I only
    (B) II only
    (C) III only
    (D) I and II
    (E) I and III

GO ON TO THE NEXT PAGE.

Questions 16–27. Choose your answers to each of the following questions based on careful reading of the following poem by Christina Rossetti.

Passing away, saith the World, passing away:
Chances, beauty and youth sapped day by day:
Thy life never continueth in one stay.
Line Is the eye waxen dim, is the dark hair changing to gray
(5) That hath won neither laurel nor bay?
I shall clothe myself in Spring and bud in May:
Thou, root stricken, shalt not rebuild thy decay
On my bosom for aye.
Then I answered: Yea.

(10) Passing away, saith my Soul, passing away:
With its burden of fear and hope, or labor and play;
Hearken what the past doth witness and say:
Rust in thy gold, a moth is in thine array,
A canker is in thy bud, thy leaf must decay.
(15) At midnight, at cockcrow, at morning, one certain day
Lo the bridegroom shall come and shall not delay:
Watch thou and pray.
Then I answered: Yea.

Passing away, saith my God, passing away:
(20) Winter passeth after the long delay:
New grapes on the vine, new figs on the tender spray,
Turtle calleth turtle in Heaven's May.
Tho' I tarry, wait for Me, trust Me, watch and pray.
Arise, come away, night is past and lo it is day,
(25) My love, My sister, My spouse, thou shalt hear Me say.
Then I answered: Yea.

16. How many speakers does the poem directly present?

   (A) One
   (B) Two
   (C) Three
   (D) Four
   (E) Five

17. "Laurel" and "bay" (line 5) are allusions to

   (A) flowers highly prized for their rarity which bloom
        briefly and beautifully and then die
   (B) spices which add flavor to food and, metaphorically,
        to life
   (C) leaves traditionally woven into wreaths to honor
        poets
   (D) traditional symbols for Homer and Ovid,
        respectively
   (E) traditional symbols for true faith and pious conduct,
        respectively

18. Lines 6–7 suggest that

   (A) the principal narrator is faced with a choice between
        the afterlife that true faith offers or the physical
        corruption that awaits the unbeliever
   (B) although the World has regenerative powers, the
        principal narrator of the poem does not
   (C) paradoxically, life can sometimes emerge
        from death
   (D) there is a natural cyclical pattern of renewal that the
        principal narrator has forsaken
   (E) the principal narrator is gravely ill and certain to die
        before the spring

19. Which of the following lines contains an image NOT
   echoed closely elsewhere in the poem?

   (A) Line 6
   (B) Line 7
   (C) Line 13
   (D) Line 14
   (E) Line 21

20. Which of the following choices best characterizes
   the speaker's attitude in each of the poem's three
   stanzas, respectively?

   (A) Realization of death's inevitability; fear of physical
        decay; passive acceptance of what cannot
        be escaped
   (B) Nostalgia for the earthly world that must be
        left behind; fear of physical decay; welcome
        acceptance of the afterlife
   (C) Realization that death will come before one's
        ambitions have been achieved; dismay over the
        visible signs of physical decay; supplication for
        the healing powers of divine intervention
   (D) Sorrow and mild surprise at the arrival of early
        death; deepening awareness of death's certainty;
        hopefulness for a place in the afterlife
   (E) Acknowledgment of death's inevitability;
        understanding of the need to prepare oneself;
        happiness at the prospect of union with the divine

GO ON TO THE NEXT PAGE.

21. In the context of the poem "a moth is in thine array" (line 13) is intended to imply that the

    (A) narrator's attire is being eaten by moths
    (B) narrator's body is being consumed by cancer, or a cancer-like disease
    (C) narrator's soul contains a destructive element which, unless the narrator takes some action, will render it unworthy of the afterlife
    (D) narrator's soul is corrupted with sin that only death can purge
    (E) narrator's soul is getting ready for decay

22. Lines 15 and 16 suggest that

    (A) the principal narrator's final hour will come, despite the small uncertainty of knowing exactly what hour that will be
    (B) the bridegroom mentioned in line 16 will arrive at three distinct times
    (C) the hour when a deadly illness first infects the principal narrator cannot be avoided
    (D) a mysterious and evil stranger will arrive at some time between midnight and morning
    (E) the principal narrator's soul prophesies that she will eventually meet the man who will become her beloved husband

23. In the third stanza "winter" can be taken to represent

    (A) long disease
    (B) earthly life
    (C) the coldness of the grave
    (D) mental despair
    (E) aging and loss of vigor

24. Which of the following statements most accurately characterizes the relationship of the imagery in the third stanza to that of the first and second stanzas?

    (A) The third stanza weaves together the wedding-day imagery of the second stanza and the springtime imagery of the first stanza, thereby reconciling those earlier stanzas' differing views.
    (B) Through its imagery, the third stanza further develops the themes which were advanced by the first stanza and then questioned by the second stanza.
    (C) The third stanza echoes much of the first two stanzas' imagery, but recasts that imagery so that what earlier had been likened to decay is instead characterized as renewal.
    (D) By echoing the imagery of the earlier stanzas, the third stanza reaffirms and repeats the views advanced by those stanzas.
    (E) By introducing the terms "love" and "sister," the third stanza continues the progression by which each stanza proposes its own unique central metaphor around which to further the poem's exploration of the themes of death and renewal.

25. Lines 7 and 8 provide an example of

    (A) apostrophe
    (B) doggerel
    (C) enjambment
    (D) mixed metaphor
    (E) simile

26. In context, the word "spray" (line 21) most nearly means

    (A) tree
    (B) blanket
    (C) a small branch
    (D) a liquid mist
    (E) a holy spirit

27. The grammatical subject of the sentence that begins at line 24 is

    (A) "Arise"
    (B) "night is past and lo it is day"
    (C) "My love, My sister, My spouse"
    (D) "thou"
    (E) "Me"

GO ON TO THE NEXT PAGE.

Questions 28–40. Read the following passage carefully before you choose your answers. The selection is an excerpt from the novel *Barchester Towers* by Anthony Trollope.

It is not my intention to breathe a word against Mrs Proudie, but still I cannot think that with all her virtues she adds much to her husband's happiness. The truth is that in
Line matters domestic she rules supreme over her titular lord, and
(5) rules with a rod of iron. Nor is this all. Things domestic Dr Proudie might have abandoned to her, if not voluntarily, yet willingly. But Mrs Proudie is not satisfied with such home dominion, and stretches her power over all his movements, and will not even abstain from things spiritual. In fact, the
(10) bishop is henpecked.

The archdeacon's wife, in her happy home at Plumstead, knows how to assume the full privileges of her rank, and express her own mind in becoming tone and place. But Mrs Grantly's sway, if sway she has, is easy and beneficent. She
(15) never shames her husband; before the world she is a pattern of obedience; her voice is never loud, nor her looks sharp; doubtless she values power, and has not unsuccessfully striven to acquire it; but she knows what should be the limits of a woman's rule.

(20) Not so Mrs Proudie. This lady is habitually authoritative to all, but to her poor husband she is despotic. Successful as has been his career in the eyes of the world, it would seem that in the eyes of his wife he is never right. All hope of defending himself has long passed from him; indeed,
(25) he rarely even attempts self-justification; and is aware that submission produces the nearest approach to peace which his own house can ever attain.

One other marked peculiarity in the character of the bishop's wife must be mentioned. Though not averse to the
(30) society and manners of the world, she is in her own way a religious woman; and the form in which this tendency shows itself is by a strict observance of Sabbatarian rule. Dissipation and low dresses during the week are, under her control, atoned for by three services, an evening sermon
(35) read by herself, and a perfect abstinence from any cheering employment on the Sunday. Unfortunately for those under her roof to whom the dissipation and low dresses are not extended, her servants namely and her husband, the compensating strictness of the Sabbath includes all. Woe
(40) betide the recreant housemaid who is found to have been listening to the honey of a sweetheart in the Regent's park, instead of the soul-stirring discourse of Mr Slope. Not only is she sent adrift, but she is so sent with a character, which leaves her little hope of a decent place. Woe betide the six-
(45) foot hero who escorts Mrs Proudie to her pew in red plush breeches, if he slips away to the neighbouring beer-shop, instead of falling in the back seat appropriated to his use. Mrs Proudie has the eyes of Argus for such offenders. Occasional drunkenness in the week may be overlooked, for six feet on
(50) low wages are hardly to be procured if the morals are always kept at a high pitch, but not even for grandeur or economy will Mrs Proudie forgive a desecration of the Sabbath.

28. Which of the following descriptions is an example of the narrator's use of irony?

(A) "It is not my intention to breathe a word against Mrs Proudie" (lines 1–2)
(B) "the bishop is henpecked" (lines 9–10)
(C) "doubtless she values power, and has not unsuccessfully striven to acquire it" (lines 17–18)
(D) "it would seem in the eyes of his wife he is never right" (lines 22–23)
(E) "a perfect abstinence from any cheering employment on the Sunday" (lines 35–36)

29. Mrs Proudie's authoritarian character is shown most pointedly in the phrase

(A) "not satisfied with such home dominion" (lines 7–8)
(B) "knows how to assume the full privileges of her rank" (line 12)
(C) "submission produces the nearest approach to peace" (line 26)
(D) "the soul-stirring discourse of Mr Slope" (line 42)
(E) "has the eyes of Argus for such offenders" (line 48)

30. The use of the word "titular" in line 4 is an example of

(A) hyperbole
(B) metonym
(C) onomatopoeia
(D) zeugma
(E) irony

31. In the context of the passage, the phrase "if not voluntarily, yet willingly" (lines 6–7) is used to show Dr Proudie's attitude toward

(A) the duties that the clergy are expected to assume
(B) entering the institution of marriage
(C) strict Sabbatarianism
(D) granting his wife some power
(E) the hiring of domestic help

GO ON TO THE NEXT PAGE.

32. The description of Mrs Grantly serves to

    (A) provide another example of the power of
        the aristocracy
    (B) prove that Mrs Grantly henpecks her husband
    (C) imply specific faults of Mrs Proudie
    (D) suggest a rivalry between her and Mrs Proudie
    (E) assert why women should be seen and not heard

33. The narrator's attitude toward Mrs Proudie can best be
    described as one of

    (A) pity
    (B) objectivity
    (C) emotional judgment
    (D) sardonic condemnation
    (E) jaded disgust

34. Which of the following best describes Dr Proudie's
    relationship to his wife?

    (A) Morally devoted
    (B) Completely servile
    (C) Awkwardly tender
    (D) Thoroughly uxorious
    (E) Bitterly tyrannical

35. The author attributes Dr Proudie's attitude and behavior
    most clearly to

    (A) ambition
    (B) pride
    (C) pacifism
    (D) spirituality
    (E) feudalism

36. In context, the word "character" (line 43) is best
    interpreted as meaning

    (A) dubious personage
    (B) reference
    (C) antagonist
    (D) conscience
    (E) footman

37. What is the effect of the repetition of the phrase "Woe
    betide…" in the final paragraph?

    (A) It retards the tempo of the prose.
    (B) It satirizes the fate of the servants.
    (C) It highlights the drama of the situation.
    (D) It changes the point of view of the narrator.
    (E) It emphasizes the moral consequences of the action.

38. In context, the adjective "recreant" (line 40) is best
    interpreted as meaning

    (A) unfaithful and disloyal
    (B) engaging in a pastime
    (C) refreshing
    (D) craven and cowardly
    (E) depraved

39. Which of the following best describes the effect of the
    last paragraph?

    (A) It suggests a cause of Mrs Proudie's
        moral transformation.
    (B) It introduces Mr Slope as an observer
        of Mrs Proudie's actions.
    (C) It illustrates how Mrs Proudie's religious
        beliefs reflect her character.
    (D) It counters speculations about Mrs
        Proudie's character.
    (E) It shows how hard it is to hire household servants.

40. The style of the passage as a whole can best be
    described as

    (A) humorless and pedantic
    (B) effusive and subjective
    (C) descriptive and metaphorical
    (D) terse and epigrammatic
    (E) witty and analytical

GO ON TO THE NEXT PAGE.

Questions 41–55. Read the following poem by Amy Lowell carefully, and then choose answers to the questions that follow.

You—you—
Your shadow is sunlight on a plate of silver;
Your footsteps, the seeding-place of lilies;
Your hands moving, a chime of bells across a windless air.

Line
(5) The movement of your hands is the long, golden running of
    light from a rising sun;
It is the hopping of birds upon a garden-path.

As the perfume of jonquils, you come forth in the morning.
Young horses are not more sudden than your thoughts,
(10) Your words are bees about a pear-tree,
Your fancies are the gold-and-black striped wasps buzzing
    among red apples.
I drink your lips,
I eat the whiteness of your hands and feet.
(15) My mouth is open,
As a new jar I am empty and open.
Like white water are you who fill the cup of my mouth,
Like a brook of water thronged with lilies.

You are frozen as the clouds,
(20) You are far and sweet as the high clouds.
I dare to reach to you,
I dare to touch the rim of your brightness.
I leap beyond the winds,
I cry and shout,
(25) For my throat is keen as is a sword
Sharpened on a hone of ivory.
My throat sings the joy of my eyes,
The rushing gladness of my love.

How has the rainbow fallen upon my heart?
(30) How have I snared the seas to lie in my fingers
And caught the sky to be a cover for my head? How have you
    come to dwell with me,
Compassing me with the four circles of your mystic
    lightness,
(35) So that I say "Glory! Glory!" and bow before you
As to a shrine?

Do I tease myself that morning is morning and a day after?
Do I think the air is a condescension,
The earth a politeness,
(40) Heaven a boon deserving thanks?
So you—air—earth—heaven—
I do not thank you,
I take you,
I live.
(45) And those things which I say in consequence
Are rubies mortised in a gate of stone.

41. Overall, the speaker's attitude toward the subject of the poem is one of

(A) reverence and need
(B) devotion and fear
(C) love and anger
(D) uncertainty and exultation
(E) piety and amazement

42. The phrase "I drink your lips,/I eat the whiteness of your hands and feet" (lines 13–14) serves to

(A) describe the antagonistic interactions of the speaker and her subject
(B) point out the beauty of the poem's subject
(C) make clear that the speaker's relationship to her subject is more physically based than it is emotionally significant
(D) underscore the speaker's delight in the physical characteristics of her lover
(E) provide a figurative contrast between the speaker and her subject

43. In the last stanza, the relationship between the speaker and her subject is most directly implied to be

(A) better than breathing or eating in the opinion of the speaker
(B) as expensive and rare as gemstones
(C) a heavenly experience
(D) encompassing everything else in the world, including the air, heaven, and earth
(E) necessary to the author's survival

44. Which of the following best conveys the meaning in context of "How have I snared the seas to lie in my fingers/ And caught the sky to be a cover for my head?" (lines 30–31)?

(A) The speaker is impressed with the physical feats she can perform now that her relationship has blossomed.
(B) The speaker is impressed with how attuned her lover is to the natural world.
(C) The speaker cannot believe her good fortune at being in such a wonderful relationship.
(D) The sea and sky, representing the relationship, are protecting the speaker from harm.
(E) The speaker feels amazement at how beautiful the world around her looks because of the new perspective granted by her relationship with her lover.

GO ON TO THE NEXT PAGE.

45. The use of repetition and punctuation in the first line of the poem could be interpreted to suggest

    (A) the speaker's amazement at the existence of her subject
    (B) the difficulty that the speaker has communicating with the poem's subject, even though they are in love
    (C) the speaker's inability to make her sentiments clear
    (D) that the speaker's thoughts are being interrupted by everyday life or other concerns
    (E) that the speaker wants to be very clear in terms of who her subject is and who she is speaking to within the context of the poem

46. The speaker compares her beloved to all of the following EXCEPT

    (A) the clouds
    (B) bees buzzing among fruit
    (C) heaven, the earth, and the air
    (D) the perfume of flowers
    (E) the clear water of a brook

47. The third stanza of the poem principally suggests that

    (A) the speaker of the poem is fragile, like a jar made out of pottery or glass
    (B) the speaker is ready and waiting to receive the experiences and emotions that her relationship and/or her lover provides for her
    (C) the speaker loves the flowers of which her lover reminds her
    (D) the poem's speaker is similar to many of nature's treasures, such as the lilies in the brook
    (E) the speaker is unable to resist her lover's advances even when she would like to do so

48. The phrase "Compassing me with the four circles of your mystic lightness" (lines 33–34) indicates that the speaker is

    (A) metaphorically surrounded by her lover
    (B) lost in the beauty of the metaphorical light provided by her lover
    (C) letting her lover set her direction in life
    (D) unsure where to go without her lover's presence
    (E) connecting with her lover on a spiritual level

49. Which word is a metaphor for the poem itself?

    (A) Sun
    (B) Perfume
    (C) Morning
    (D) Rubies
    (E) Sword

50. Which stanza most suggests the religious level of devotion felt by the poem's speaker?

    (A) 2
    (B) 3
    (C) 4
    (D) 5
    (E) 6

51. "As the perfume of jonquils, you come forth in the morning" (line 8) is an example of

    (A) personification
    (B) metaphor
    (C) simile
    (D) hyperbole
    (E) metaphysical conceit

52. The poem's final stanza suggests which of the following?

    I. The speaker needs her lover in order to live.
    II. The speaker's lover is similar to the morning.
    III. The speaker is thankful for the gift of heaven.

    (A) I only
    (B) III only
    (C) I and II only
    (D) I and III only
    (E) I, II, and III

53. Grammatically, the word "hone" (line 26) is a

    (A) verb
    (B) adjective
    (C) direct object
    (D) noun
    (E) preposition

GO ON TO THE NEXT PAGE.

54. The poem states or implies which of the following?

    I. The speaker believes that heaven is necessary to her well-being.

    II. The speaker's lover is far away from her.

    III. The speaker shows reverence for the natural world.

  (A) I and III only

  (B) II only

  (C) I and II only

  (D) I only

  (E) I, II, and III

55. Which of the following best describes the use of rhetorical questions in the poem?

  (A) The author uses them to imply that the speaker is questioning her religious beliefs.

  (B) The author uses them as a juxtaposition with the poem's many similes and metaphors.

  (C) The author uses them to emphasize that the speaker is overwhelmed by her love.

  (D) The author uses them to introduce new aspects of her characterization of the lover.

  (E) The author uses them to convey the speaker's wonder at her situation and at her lover.

STOP
END OF SECTION I

**IF YOU FINISH BEFORE TIME IS CALLED, YOU MAY CHECK YOUR WORK ON THIS SECTION.
DO NOT GO ON TO SECTION II UNTIL YOU ARE TOLD TO DO SO.**

This page intentionally left blank.

ENGLISH LITERATURE AND COMPOSITION

SECTION II

Total Time—2 hours

Question 1

(Suggested time—40 minutes. This question counts as one-third of the total essay score.)

In the following poems by Samuel Taylor Coleridge and William Blake, the speakers explore infancy. Read the poems carefully. Then, in a well-written essay, analyze how the authors use poetic elements and techniques such as imagery to reveal their attitudes toward infancy.

To an Infant

Ah cease thy tears and sobs, my little life!
I did but snatch away the unclasped knife:
Some safer toy will soon arrest thine eye,
Line And to quick laughter change this peevish cry!
(5) Poor stumbler on the rocky coast of woe,
Tutored by pain each source of pain to know!
Alike the foodful fruit and scorching fire
Awake thy eager grasp and young desire:
Alike the good, the ill offend thy sight,
(10) And rouse the stormy sense of shrill affright!
Untaught, yet wise! mid all thy brief alarms
Thou closely clingest to thy mother's arms,
Nestling thy little face in that fond breast
Whose anxious heavings lull thee to thy rest!
(15) Man's breathing miniature! thou mak'st me sigh—
A babe thou art—and such a thing am I!

To anger rapid and as soon appeased,
For trifles mourning and by trifles pleased;
Break friendship's mirror with a tetchy blow,
(20) Yet snatch what coals of fire on pleasure's altar glow!

Oh thou that rearest with celestial aim
The future seraph in my mortal frame,
Thrice holy Faith! whatever thorns I meet
As on I totter with unpractised feet,
(25) Still let me stretch my arms and cling to thee,
Meek nurse of souls through their long infancy!

—Samuel Taylor Coleridge

Infant Sorrow

My mother groaned, my father wept;
Into the dangerous world I leapt,
Helpless, naked, piping loud,
Like a fiend hid in a cloud.
Line
(5) Struggling in my father's hands,
Striving against my swaddling bands,
Bound and weary, I thought best
To sulk upon my mother's breast.

—William Blake

GO ON TO THE NEXT PAGE.

Question 2

(Suggested time—40 minutes. This question counts as one-third of the total essay score.)

The following excerpt is from Don DeLillo's novel Libra (1988). In this passage, we are given a fictional treatment of the young Lee Harvey Oswald, who as an adult would assassinate President John F. Kennedy. Read the passage carefully. Then, in a well-written essay, analyze how DeLillo uses literary elements and techniques such as diction, imagery, and point of view to portray the subject and the substance of the portrait itself.

He returned to the seventh grade until classes ended. In summer dusk the girls lingered near the benches on Bronx Park South. Jewish girls, Italian girls in tight skirts, girls with
Line ankle bracelets, their voices murmurous with the sound of
(5) boys' names, with song lyrics, little remarks he didn't always understand. They talked to him when he walked by making him smile in his secret way.

Oh a woman with beer on her breath, on the bus coming home from the beach. He feels the tired salty sting in his eyes
(10) of a day in the sun and water.

"The trouble leaving you with my sister," Marguerite said, "she had too many children of her own. Plus the normal disputes of family. That meant I had to employ Mrs. Roach, on Pauline Street, when you were two. But I came home one
(15) day and saw she whipped you, raising welts on your legs, and we moved to Sherwood Forest Drive."

Heat entered the flat through the walls and windows, seeped down from the tar roof. Men on Sundays carried pastry in white boxes. An Italian was murdered in a candy
(20) store, shot five times, his brains dashing the wall near the comic-book rack. Kids trooped to the store from all around to see the traces of grayish spatter. His mother sold stockings in Manhattan.

A woman on the street, completely ordinary, maybe fifty
(25) years old, wearing glasses and a dark dress, handed him a leaflet at the foot of the El steps. Save the Rosenbergs, it said. He tried to give it back thinking he would have to pay for it, but she'd already turned away. He walked home, hearing a lazy radio voice doing a ballgame. Plenty of room, folks.
(30) Come on out for the rest of this game and all of the second. It was Sunday, Mother's Day, and he folded the leaflet neatly and put it in his pocket to save for later.

There is a world inside the world.

He rode the subway up to Inwood, out to Sheepshead
(35) Bay. There were serious men down there, rocking in the copper light. He saw, beggars, men who talked to God, men who lived on the trains, day and night, bruised, with matted hair, asleep in patient bundles on the wicker seats. He jumped the turnstiles once. He rode between cars, gripping
(40) the heavy chain. He felt the friction of the ride in his teeth. They went so fast sometimes. He liked the feeling they were

on the edge. How do we know the motorman's not insane? It gave him a funny thrill. The wheels touched off showers of blue-white sparks, tremendous hissing bursts, on the edge of
(45) no-control. People crowded in, every shape face in the book of faces. They pushed through the doors, they hung from the porcelain straps. He was riding just to ride. The noise had a power and a human force. The dark had a power. He stood at the front of the first car, hands flat against the glass. The
(50) view down the tracks was a form of power. It was a secret and a power. The beams picked out secret things. The noise was pitched to a fury he located in the mind, a satisfying wave of rage and pain.

GO ON TO THE NEXT PAGE.

Question 3

(Suggested time—40 minutes. This question counts as one-third of the total essay score.)

"When a true genius appears in the world, you may know him by this sign, that the dunces are all in confederacy against him."

—Jonathan Swift
"Thoughts on Various Subjects, Moral and Diverting"

Either from your own reading or from the list below, choose a work of fiction in which th main character finds himself in conflict with the social or moral values of his environment. Then, in a well-written essay, analyze how that tension contributes to an interpretation of the work as a whole. Do not merely summarize the plot.

The Awakening	*Long Day's Journey Into Night*
As I Lay Dying	*Love Medicine*
Catch-22	*Man's Fate*
Crime and Punishment	*Marat/Sade*
The Duchess of Malfi	*Medea*
Hamlet	*Miss Lonelyhearts*
A Handmaid's Tale	*Native Son*
Heart of Darkness	*Nausea*
Hunger	*One Flew Over the Cuckoo's Nest*
I Know Why the Caged Bird Sings	*The Scarlet Letter*
The Idiot	*The Turn of the Screw*
The Iliad	*Waiting for Godot*
Invisible Man	*Wuthering Heights*
King Lear	

STOP
END OF EXAM
IF YOU FINISH BEFORE TIME IS CALLED, YOU MAY CHECK YOUR WORK ON THIS SECTION.

Practice Test 1:
Answers and
Explanations

PRACTICE TEST 1 ANSWER KEY

1.	A	21.	E	41.	A
2.	D	22.	A	42.	D
3.	B	23.	B	43.	E
4.	B	24.	C	44.	C
5.	B	25.	C	45.	A
6.	A	26.	C	46.	B
7.	A	27.	D	47.	B
8.	B	28.	A	48.	A
9.	E	29.	C	49.	D
10.	E	30.	E	50.	D
11.	A	31.	D	51.	C
12.	B	32.	C	52.	C
13.	C	33.	D	53.	D
14.	A	34.	B	54.	D
15.	A	35.	C	55.	E
16.	D	36.	B		
17.	C	37.	C		
18.	B	38.	A		
19.	C	39.	C		
20.	E	40.	E		

PRACTICE TEST 1 EXPLANATIONS

Questions 1–15

This passage is from *The Awakening* by Kate Chopin, published in 1899. It is considered an early feminist novel and delves into the themes of gender roles and social constraint.

1. **A** Like many questions on the exam, this question is essentially a sophisticated vocabulary question. The key to understanding it is to note the unpleasant noises made by the birds at the outset. There is no sense of the playfulness of whimsy, (B), and though it isn't a lighthearted start, it is too lively and raucous to be brooding, (C). There is no humor intended to be satirical, (D), and there is none of the idyllic romantic depiction of nature in pastoral imagery, (E). It's all about the noise.

2. **D** This is a fairly easy question if you don't get too caught up in the idea of the parrot. The parrot, (A), speaks words in various languages; the "fluty notes" come from the mockingbird on the other side of the door.

3. **B** Although the passage is written in third person, there is a clear sense of Mr. Pontellier's distaste for his environment. He doesn't know what he wants, but it's not this. We do see an "exclamation of disgust" in the text, which might suggest volatility, (C). Though he may share some of the pettiness of the truly officious, (A), we do not see him as being particularly tidy, organized, or neat, nor do we see any signs of a fiery temper, so you can eliminate (C). Choice (D) can also be eliminated because he is transparent almost to a fault, and there is no evidence that he has any passion for power, as suggested in (E). Phrases like "expression and exclamation of disgust," along with the tendency for people to "cease to be entertaining," show his judgmental and intolerant nature.

4. **B** Though Mr. Pontellier does not seem particularly happy or comfortable in his environment, we have no reason to believe that this retreat at Grand Isle is anything but pleasant, so eliminate (A). At this point, we haven't been introduced to Robert or Mrs. Pontellier, which means neither (C) nor (D) can be correct. And while there is initial annoyance at the various birds mentioned, this is not a consistent nature motif that goes beyond the beginning of the passage. Therefore, eliminate (E). The passage does depict Mr. Pontellier as being restless, unsatisfied, and out of place throughout, as exemplified by such words as "maddening," "restlessly," and referring to his "disgust" at his lack of "any degree of comfort." Choice (B) is the correct answer.

5. **B** The writers of the exam love to include words with many viable definitions and then ask the reader to choose the best one. This can be tricky if the word is used in an unconventional or dated manner as it is here. It is up to the reader to decipher the definition based on the context. In this situation, Mr. Pontellier is speaking about his time in New Orleans prior to arriving at Grand Isle. Choice (B) is the best option because it makes sense that he did not have time to read the paper prior to leaving the day before.

6. **A** Mr. Pontellier appears completely devoid of any meaningful connection to humanity. He doesn't hate people, but he doesn't seem to like anyone, either. He shows no signs of curiosity, (B), warmth, (D), or antagonism, (E), toward others, and his ambivalence toward his wife's friendship with Robert does not connote mistrust, (C). Indeed, people often "cease to be entertaining" to him, and he easily walks away from them when they become tiresome, making (A) the best answer.

7. **A** Though Mr. Pontellier doesn't seem to care much for humanity, he apparently takes pride in having robust children. We may hope that the children have the necessary thick skin to tolerate their father, but we do not know whether he is neglectful, so get rid of (B). We receive surprisingly little physical description of Mrs. Pontellier, so (C) is likely incorrect. Although Mr. Pontellier is portrayed as being of "medium height" and "slender build," we have no evidence that the children are not his, nor does he express any suspicion of this, so eliminate (D). We know almost nothing of the physical features of the island's inhabitants other than that there are "a good many persons of the *pension*" along with "young" Robert, "fresh, pretty" Mrs. Lebrun, two young twins, Mrs. Pontellier, and others; therefore, (E) is incorrect. To call his children "sturdy" is downright effusive coming from Mr. Pontellier, but it is the only possible answer. Choice (A) is correct.

8. **B** If you are stumped by the wording or intent of this question, you might be able to use your sense of diction to figure out the answer. One of these words is not like the others. Choice (A), smoke, implies something noxious or implies the presence of fire—neither of which are evident in Pontellier's depiction. Choice (C), gaunt, may describe his appearance somewhat, but not his personality. Pontellier's use of "folly" gives us the impression that he wouldn't know a good time if it bit him, so eliminate (D). Choice (E), plunge, is far too active of a verb for this idle man. Choice (B) is correct.

9. **E** Here's a question that rewards students for studying their literary terminology. Metonymy, (A), is a thing or concept that is not called by its own name, but by the name of something intimately associated with that thing or concept. This is often confused with synecdoche, as they're both part/whole concepts, but the key here is common association. Robert and Mrs. Pontellier are not commonly associated with a sunshade. Apostrophe, (B), is when a speaker addresses a person or object in a rhetorical manner, not expecting an answer, and is not used in this passage. Hyperbole, (C), the purposeful use of exaggerated speech, is not related to the "sunshade" episode. Had the sunshade been referred to as "walking" or "crawling its way across the lawn," then personification, (D), would be correct. As it is, the sunshade is used to refer to not only itself, but the two people carrying it up to the house as well, which is an example of synecdoche. Study the glossary if this question gave you trouble!

10. **E** If you are familiar with this work already, you may be inclined to think (I) is correct. But in this passage, there is no evidence of any animosity on Mr. Pontellier's behalf toward Robert, so (I) is not true. Mr. Pontellier's scolding of his wife and his judgment of her looks as "property that had suffered some damage" clearly illustrates contempt, so (II) is correct. Further, his mocking of two adults committing the "folly [of bathing] at such an hour in this heat" in juxtaposition to his pride in having gone swimming at dawn shows how much he likes himself and congratulates himself for his choices—in other words, his self-righteousness. Therefore, (III) is also true, and (E) is the answer.

11. **A** Again, we have a literary term identification question. Onomatopoeia, (B), is when a word imitates the sound it makes, like "crack" or "boom." Assonance, (C), uses vowel-sound repetition to create internal rhyme. Understatement, (D), occurs when a speaker uses less intensity or enthusiasm to

express something than the occasion or feeling warrants. Mr. Pontellier's charged and scolding statements toward his wife are, essentially, the opposite of this. Apostrophe, (E), is when a speaker addresses a person or object in a rhetorical manner, not expecting an answer to their addressing of it, and though Robert and Mrs. Pontellier do not respond to Mr. Pontellier's braying, he was, likely, expecting a response from them. Hyperbole is exaggeration for effect, and, since Mr. Pontellier recognizes his wife and Robert, one can assume that they are not literally "burnt beyond recognition."

12. **B** The description of Mrs. Pontellier's "strong, shapely hands" does not make her sound unattractive, eliminating (A). There is no suggestion that Robert is uncomfortable around Mr. Pontellier, (C). In fact, Robert seems oblivious to him, focusing only on Mrs. Pontellier. The characterization of Mrs. Pontellier as a "piece of personal property" (lines 68–69) in her husband's eyes does not support the idea that she is the dominant one in their relationship, so (D) is incorrect. Mr. Pontellier's "burnt beyond recognition" comment (line 67) does not reflect concern or protectiveness when coupled with that same "personal property that has suffered some damage" attitude, which eliminates (E). A strained relationship (B) is supported throughout the selection: in Mr. Pontellier's criticism and way of looking at his wife, in her trip to the beach with Robert and in her exchange of laughter with him.

13. **C** To be "frank" is to be plainly honest with someone. However, when someone says the phrase "quite frankly," in conversation, there is an implied attitude of annoyance, challenge, or rebuke. So, what do we think when the phrase is used in narration? Since we have no evidence that Robert is annoyed with, defying, or threatening Pontellier, then we have to take the phrase at face value— that he refuses to join Mr. Pontellier in a polite but certain manner. Eliminate (A) and (B). Choice (D) is a bit tricky, as Mr. Pontellier seems to not have any close friends on Grand Isle. However, there are many references throughout the passage to Pontellier's social interactions, most notably the billiards games over at Klein's. What is striking is Robert's contentment juxtaposed with Mr. Pontellier's restlessness and lack of passion or enthusiasm for anything. Choice (C) is correct.

14. **A** Once again, if you have read the novel, you could get into trouble here. Later on in *The Awakening*, there is quite a bit of passion, conflict, and secrecy, but none of this is evident in the opening chapter, eliminating (B), (D), and (E). While the interactions between Mrs. Pontellier and Robert relegate Mr. Pontellier to awkward "third wheel" status, the slowness of their stroll from the water, the way they sit facing each other, and the "answering smile" she gives Robert all indicate a closeness that eliminates (C), leaving (A) as the answer.

15. **A** Though Mr. Pontellier seems to criticize nearly everyone and everything, he does not extend this attitude toward his children, so (II) cannot be true. On the contrary, though Mr. Pontellier does not allow his children to follow him to Klein's, he does "kiss them and promise to bring them back bonbons and peanuts." If Pontellier is concerned about his wife's friendship with Robert, he certainly doesn't show it. On the contrary, he encourages his wife to spend time with him until "he bores you." Therefore, (III) is also not accurate. When his wife asks him whether he'll be returning for dinner, his response is very indicative of his character and thus his attitude toward his marriage: he shrugs. This means that (I) is true, and (A) is the answer.

Questions 16–27

The passage is by Christina Rossetti (1830–1894), and was written when she was in her early thirties. The poem's spiritual, death-haunted theme is typical of Rossetti, who was beset with ill health her entire, and relatively long, life.

The Rossettis, Christina and her brothers, William Michael and Dante Gabriel, were at the center of an influential mid-nineteenth-century arts movement called the Pre-Raphaelite Brotherhood. Pre-Raphaelite painting and writing were concerned with medieval themes, romance (often tinged with self-destruction or death), nature, nostalgia, vivid imagery, and color.

Christina's brother Dante (arguably the leader of the Pre-Raphaelite movement) is guilty of one of the truly cheeseball acts of narcissism in literary history. When Dante Gabriel Rossetti's wife died, the painter-poet buried the manuscripts of several of his poems in the casket with her. Ah, love. Seven years later he decided maybe it wasn't such a good idea and had the mess dug up so he could get his poems back. The last laugh, however, is on Dante, whose reputation is waning. His sister Christina, however, has acquired a growing respect from the literary world after many years spent in her brother's shadow.

The poem on the test (like almost everything Christina Rossetti wrote) is a meditation on the transience of life and the inevitability of death. When, in the third stanza, God promises to come for the poet when her hour arrives, the poem becomes an avowal of faith.

Although the bulk of the poem's meaning is accessible to most readers, the questions asked on the test lay several traps for the unwary. When reading and interpreting poetry, be on guard against making assumptions that can't be justified. Several questions have incorrect choices that suggest the principal narrator is on her deathbed. You should not reason that the poem's intense contemplation of death indicates the speaker is gravely ill or about to die; those are unwarranted assumptions. Do not assume or infer anything that is not very close to what is actually written in the passage. (And this goes for reading sections on any standardized test!)

Another difficulty you face when answering the questions on the Rossetti passage is that the questions ask about some of the poem's subtler points. There are several questions, for example, about the important shift in the recurrent nature imagery that occurs in the poem's final stanza. Complications also rise from the presence of multiple speakers in the poem.

This long-standing tradition of conversing with the spiritual forces of the cosmos may seem a hopelessly old-fashioned device, but poets up to the present day continue to create interesting and important works using this convention. The Rossetti poem, however, not only has the speaker in dialogue with the metaphysical world, but takes matters a degree further in the second stanza by having the Soul speak with the voice of the past. Following the line "Hearken what the past doth witness and say:" the Soul presents what the past has to say about human mortality. You needed to understand that in this stanza the past is *not* being directly presented as a speaker. In fact, the past is probably not even being quoted; the Soul is interpreting the past for the benefit of the principal narrator. This is a tangled piece of rhetorical construction and causes most students some problems.

Overall, the passage, taken together with its questions, is at the difficult end of the spectrum of work you will see on the AP English Literature and Composition Exam.

16. **D** As noted in the passage description, this is a tough question. Most students choose (E), five. But the past is not a speaker. The past is being interpreted for the principal narrator by the Soul. Another choice that sophisticated readers sometimes pick is (A), one. The reasoning behind choosing (A) is usually that only the poet is speaking; the Soul, World, and God represent elements and ideas within the poet. In this reading, the poem is a kind of internal monologue in which the poet sorts out her feelings about death and the afterlife. This interpretation is absolutely plausible. (Rossetti certainly did not intend for you to think she had actually held a conversation with the World or with God.) The problem is that it is an *interpretation*. The question asks, "How many speakers does the poem directly present?" The emphasis is on what the poem presents, not what the poem might suggest. The question is not asking for an interpretation but simply for what the poem presents. It presents four speakers, so (D) is the correct answer.

17. **C** This is one of the relatively rare knowledge questions on the test. You either know it or you don't. Eighty to ninety percent of the test is about your ability to understand the material you read, both the details and the larger picture. But there are some facts which the test writers feel they can expect you know. They expect you to know the basic terminology of literary criticism and form (for example: simile, metaphor, sonnet, couplet), and they occasionally ask about those literary historical references a well-read individual should recognize. This question is an example of the latter.

In ancient Greek and Roman society, a garland of laurel and bay leaves was awarded in recognition of triumph in sports, war, or poetry. The original "gold medal" of the Olympics was a laurel wreath, as is that wreath you always see framing Julius Caesar's bald pate. The reason the answer specifically mentions poets is that laurel (bay is a variety of laurel) was the symbolic flower of Apollo, patron God of poetry. Even today, when people are honored as the national poet their title is *poet laureate*. Speaking of honors, graduation from college with a bachelor's degree will mean that you have earned your bacca*laureate*, a term derived from the medieval university tradition of crowning graduates with laurel.

18. **B** The lines in question here, "I shall clothe myself in Spring and bud in May: / Thou, root stricken, shalt not rebuild thy decay," contrast the cyclical progress of the seasons with the linear trajectory of human life. Line 7 is a troublemaker line for many students, who frequently pick up on "root stricken" as indicating that the principal narrator is deathly ill. What root stricken refers to is the fundamental presence of death in human life. The author and humans in general are "root stricken" in the sense that death is imminent from birth; or to use another plant metaphor, we carry the seed of death within us from conception.

19. **C** The incorrect answers all make use of imagery that draws on living things, especially plants, and of the changing seasons. In line 13, the image of "Rust in thy gold" is the one image of the poem that draws neither on the seasons nor on living things.

20. **E** The key to answering this question correctly is Process of Elimination (POE), which we'll talk about later in this book. Be methodical by checking each of the answer choices' explanation with the first stanza. This should help you get rid of (B) and probably (D) as well, since a surprise does not seem to be found in the stanza. Choice (A)'s explanation of the second stanza doesn't fit, so you

can eliminate it right there. Choice, (E), with its expression of happiness, fits the third stanza better than (C), in which "supplication for divine intervention" doesn't adequately convey the idea that the speaker in the stanza is actually God.

21. **E** The question shouldn't have given you too much trouble. Basically, you were asked what "a moth in thine array" is meant to signify metaphorically. The image is yet one more description of the natural aging process. The incorrect choices offer various misreadings, either seeing illness where none is present or spiritual anxieties that neither the line in question, nor the poem as a whole, is concerned with.

22. **A** Understanding the lines in question is not as much about the lines themselves as it is about letting them make sense in the overall context of the poem. If you understood the bulk of the poem, then this question shouldn't have been difficult. If the poem itself gave you trouble, this question might have as well. The incorrect choices offer various misreadings and overinterpretations. Don't get too bogged down. Try Process of Elimination, and if you're still stuck, take a guess and move on.

23. **B** Always return to the passage. The third stanza presents a dramatic reversal in the poem's meaning and direction by refiguring imagery from the previous stanzas with an antithetical meaning. In the first two stanzas, Spring and the imagery of Spring are used to represent youth, energy, and life. You might easily think, then, that Winter, as Spring's opposite, represents aging and loss of vigor, (E), or perhaps the coldness of the grave, (C), that is death itself. But the question asks for the meaning of Winter in the *third* stanza. In this stanza God says that now "Winter passeth after the long delay." What follows are images of spring now clearly tied to death and the afterlife. Spring in the final stanza is a metaphor for the joy of reunion with God. In the final stanza, God offers death as a joyous springlike occasion. It is earthly life, separate from the Maker, which is the long Winter.

24. **C** As with all questions with longer answers, you must read carefully and eliminate when an answer is partially correct. "Partially correct" means "wrong." Otherwise, the reasoning behind this question is fully covered in the explanation to question 23.

25. **C** This is another terminology question. If it gave you any trouble you should refer to our glossary of literary terms (found on page 277) for the AP English Literature and Composition Exam. Also, remember to use Process of Elimination to get rid of those answers you are sure are wrong and guess with what's left. No blanks!

26. **C** This is essentially a vocabulary question, but chances are you were unfamiliar with the passage's usage of the word "spray." Figure out the meaning from the context. None of the incorrect answer choices makes sense in context except possibly (A), and we hope that between (A) and (C), you chose (C).

27. **D** You are certain to see a question (or two or three) like this one on your test. If you got this question wrong, brush up on your skills with our section on grammar for the AP English Literature and Composition Exam (page 90). As outlined in that section, the best way to figure out the construction of the kind of sentence the test writers like to ask about is to rewrite the sentence (in your mind—you shouldn't need to actually write it down) into a more natural form. The sentences are never straightforward "subject, verb, direct-object, indirect object" sentences like "Jack threw the ball to me." The sentence that begins on line 24, "Arise, come away, night is past and lo it is day,/ My love, My sister, My spouse, thou shalt hear me say," should be rewritten:

"Thou shalt hear me say, 'Arise, come away, night is past and lo it is day,

My love, My sister, My spouse.'"

Notice we've put quotation marks around what God reports he will say. This is how the sentence would normally be punctuated. If you rewrite it in this manner, you should be able to see that "Thou" is the subject, so (D) is your answer.

Questions 28–40

This passage is from Anthony Trollope's novel *Barchester Towers*, the second of his Barsetshire novels. It was written in 1857 and unlike many Victorian novels was more concerned with the topics of the day than the recent past. However, like the Victorian prose you are apt to see on the test, the sentences can be somewhat convoluted, with multiple negations and other forms of twisted syntax. Tone isn't always easy to discern. Close reading is essential.

28.　**A**　The narrator states, "It is not my intention to breathe a word against Mrs Proudie," but then spends several paragraphs doing just that. Choice (B) is a colloquialism derived from figurative language describing a domineering wife. Because domineering is precisely what Mrs. Proudie is said to be, there is no irony here. Choice (C) is the juxtaposition of Mrs. Grantly, the archdeacon's wife, but there isn't enough said about her to know if this is ironic or not. Choice (D) might be construed as hyperbole, but it certainly is not the opposite of the author's intended meaning. Choice (E) is close; one might detect some sarcasm, also known as verbal irony, but the author doesn't mean the opposite of what he has stated, so (A) is the best answer.

29.　**C**　Although (C) describes Dr. Proudie, it does so in the context of how Mrs. Proudie's despotic behavior has cowed him. While tempting, (A) refers much more closely to Mrs. Proudie's ambitions and how they extend beyond the normal sphere of the wife of a bishop. Choice (B) refers to Mrs. Grantly, not Mrs. Proudie. Choice (D) refers to something Mrs. Proudie expects those under her roof to submit to, but it is not as pointed an example of her authoritarian nature as (C) is. Choice (E) uses a mythological allusion to a watchful, not authoritarian, character.

30.　**E**　Dr. Proudie is, in name, or title ("titular"), the lord of Mrs. Proudie but as the passage explains in great depth, it is Mrs. Proudie, in actuality, who lords over her husband. The situation is the opposite of what it is in name. Choice (A) doesn't have much going for it, other than a big word that students who aren't adequately familiar with literary terms won't understand. Hyperbole is exaggeration, which does not apply here, so eliminate (A). Choices (B) and (D) do much the same thing, but with even fancier words. Choice (C) might appeal to a student who knows that onomatopoeia has something to do with how words sound, and "titular" does sound funny—but it's not a noun or verb, so it can't really sound like the noise made by the thing it describes.

31.　**D**　The phrase states that in domestic matters, he would not have offered the power to his wife but was happy to cede it. Choices (B) and (E) are based on careless reading of the phrases "domestic" or the vague memory that the passage was about his marriage. Choices (A) and (C) take deceptive language from elsewhere in the passage.

32. **C** In the context of the passage, which is devoted to describing Mrs. Proudie's character, the example of Mrs. Grantly, the archdeacon's wife, is used to describe Mrs. Proudie by contrast. Mrs. Grantly's virtues are laid out, and the transition into the subsequent paragraph, "Not so Mrs Proudie," makes the author's intention clear. Choice (A) is a trap answer designed to snare the careless reader who sees the words "the full privileges of her rank," which actually pertain to her role as a clergyman's wife. Choice (B) is another use of deceptive language. The transition into the paragraph, "In fact, the bishop is henpecked," refers to Dr. Proudie, not the archdeacon, Mrs. Grantly's husband. Choice (D) is probably the most evil of all trap answers, one designed to catch the rare student who may have read this novel or its sequels—in particular, *Framley Parsonage*, in which the rivalry of Mrs. Grantly and Mrs. Proudie is given substantial attention. It certainly is not the author's intention to suggest a rivalry, although he may have intended to foreshadow it. Choice (E) has some merit. From the description of Mrs. Grantly, it certainly seems as if the author favors women who exert their power domestically and privately. The passage states, "before the world she is a pattern of obedience; her voice is never loud…she knows what should be the limits of a woman's rule." Nevertheless, the language in the answer choice, "assert why women should be seen and not heard," suggests that the author provides evidence for a position stronger than the one he actually takes.

33. **D** Choice (A), pity, is best used to describe how the author feels toward Dr. Proudie, "her poor husband." Although the narrator may feign an appearance of objectivity, his opening comments make it clear that what he presents is his subjective opinion, so eliminate (B). Given that, (C), emotional judgment, might be tempting, but his language is strong enough to justify (D), sardonic condemnation. He is certainly mocking Mrs. Proudie, and his judgment of her does condemn her behavior. Choice (E) is too extreme for the passage.

34. **B** We do not get a sense of Dr. Proudie's devotion to his wife or of his moral compass, no matter what we might want to infer from knowing his profession, so (A) is out. Choice (B) is supported by the text of the third paragraph. Choices (C) and (D) suggest a happy and loving marriage, not the picture painted by this paragraph. Choice (E) might describe Mrs. Proudie's relationship to her husband, but not the reverse.

35. **C** He is described as "aware that submission produces the nearest approach to peace which his own house can ever attain." Choice (A) refers most nearly to a quality best attributed to Mrs. Proudie. Choices (B) and (E) are not supported by the text. Choice (D) is a trap answer for those who read quickly and saw that the passage was about the clergy and religious matters.

36. **B** Even if you weren't familiar with the Victorian use of "character" as shorthand for "character reference," you could derive the meaning from the context of the passage—the maid has been dismissed and because of this "character," she is unable to find decent employment. Choices (A), (C), and (D) all prey on a reader's familiarity with the dictionary definitions of the word, as opposed to the contextual meaning. Choice (E) is a trap for the reader who sees "character" and "foot" near each other in the passage and overinterprets—perhaps thinking that the footman is sent to escort the housemaid from the premises.

37. **C**   The repetition of the phrase "Woe betide" accentuates the seriousness of the servants' situation. It neither slows down the prose, as in (A), nor satirizes or mocks the servants' fate, as in (B). The phrase is consistent with the narrator's attitude throughout the rest of the passage, so (D) is incorrect. Choice (E) is too extreme.

38. **A**   The maid in question has been unfaithful to her duty. As is par for the course on a single phrase or word question, the primary dictionary definition, (D), is offered as an answer choice, as is a word it kind of sounds like, (B). The other choices have no merit whatsoever.

39. **C**   The point of the paragraph is to illustrate Mrs. Proudie's hypocrisy. The paragraph does so by showing how strict she is in applying the rules to others when it comes to this single point of religious belief, although she is given to "[d]issipation and low dresses" the rest of the time. Choice (A) might be tempting because of the religious aspect, but in no place does this paragraph suggest a transformation for the domineering Mrs. Proudie. Choice (B) also has its merits, as this paragraph is where Mr. Slope is introduced, but no mention is made of him observing Mrs. Proudie (quite the contrary, one is expected to observe Mr. Slope). For similar reasons—the mention of religion—(D) might be attractive but as mentioned above, it doesn't counter speculation about her despotic reign. Rather, it extends it beyond her husband to her household staff—which she might have a hard time hiring, as (E) suggests, but that would not be the point of the paragraph.

40. **E**   The author analyzes Mrs. Proudie in an amusing way, mocking her cleverly by first pointing out her flaws in contrast to a social equivalent, then by exposing her hypocrisy. Most of the other answers fall into the half-right, half-wrong category, and using Process of Elimination will save the day here. Choice (A) is wrong on both counts—the passage is neither humorless nor pedantic. Although the passage is certainly subjective, it is hardly emotional, so as long as you know the definition of effusive, you can eliminate (B). Choice (C) starts out stronger; the passage is certainly descriptive. Alas, a few metaphors do not a metaphorical passage make. If you chose (C) or even kept it on your first pass through the answer choices, don't kick yourself. Close answer choices are one of the ways a question can be made more challenging. Lacking both terseness and epigrams, though, (D) should be an easy candidate for elimination for this particular passage.

Questions 41–55

This poem was written in 1922 by Amy Lowell, one of the leading female poets of her day, who was known for her frank and emotion-filled depictions of relationships, sensual love and for being at the forefront of imagism, a literary movement of the early twentieth century.

Amy Lowell has sparked recent critical interest because of her interesting use of language and sensual themes. The title ("In Excelsis") refers to the Latin exclamation of praise that is a part of the Catholic Mass. In this poem, the rejoicing is due to the speaker's lover, whom she talks about throughout. A challenging part of this poem is keeping track of what Lowell is referring to with each of her many uses of figurative language, particularly simile and metaphor. If you've done that successfully, you probably won't have too much trouble with most of the questions. Using Process of Elimination carefully will definitely help you spot the small differences between answer choices that are often key to picking the correct one.

41. **A**   Figuring out which answer choices are half wrong will help you use Process of Elimination (as discussed in Chapter 4) effectively. The first stanzas indicate reverence, or deep respect, and at the end of the poem, the author compares her beloved to the things she needs to live. Therefore, both words in (A) are supported. Choices (B) and (C) can be eliminated because each has one word that fits and one that does not; the speaker does not show fear or anger. Choice (D) might look promising because of the author's use of rhetorical questions to her subject, but she's not actually showing uncertainty—they really are rhetorical. Choice (E) has "piety," which looks good if you caught the religious subtext of the poem. However, the author isn't actually saying she is religious or faithful, which is the definition of piety (though she does use some subtle religious imagery).

42. **D**   The interactions cannot be described as antagonistic, (A), and there's no contrast—figurative or otherwise—in this part of the poem, so you can also get rid of (E). The other three choices all look tempting because all have to do with the physicality of the speaker's lover, who is the subject of the poem. However, you can't justify the idea that the relationship is more physical than emotional— that's too much reading into the lines. Eliminate (C). Choices (B) and (D) are similar, but the lines go beyond pointing out the beauty and, with their action verbs ("eat" and "drink"), imply that the speaker is having some interaction or feeling about the physicality of the person she's talking about. That makes (D) the better answer, but this is definitely a tough one!

43. **E**   The speaker draws a comparison between the existence of her relationship and other things she needs, like food and air, so (E) is correct. Choice (B) looks promising because of the mention of rubies in the passage, but the relationship is not described as "expensive," therefore, get rid of (B); nor is a comparison made in which the relationship is better than breathing or eating. It is arguably as necessary, but you can't support "better" without overreading, so eliminate (A). Choice (C) is a trap for those who saw the word "heaven" throughout the poem and in this stanza in particular, and (D) simply isn't what the stanza says, although those words are mentioned.

44. **C** The meaning of the given phrase is actually fairly straightforward, so the key is to not read too much into it. Choice (A) is a bit too literal an interpretation, and we don't learn about the lover in these phrases, so (B) is out as well. Choice (D) is certainly a possible interpretation, but it strays a bit far from the words themselves—it might be appropriate to write in an essay, but not in a multiple-choice question. Choice (E), with its interest in the physical world (the sea and sky) is a bit too literal again, just like (A).

45. **A** The speaker repeats "you" with a dash like that almost as if she can't believe that her lover even exists, and this fits tonally as well as in terms of the content with the rest of the poem. (Remember to keep your answers consistent!) No difficulty, (B), or inability, (C), is expressed anywhere else, and while the use of the dashes might suggest (D), there's no evidence for that in the poem either. Choice (E) is also incorrect, as the speaker gives no indication that she is worrying about not being clear—or knows about anything else, for that matter!

46. **B** This question requires a bit of close reading. Choices (A), (D), and (E) were probably fairly easy for you to spot (and, therefore, to eliminate, since we're looking for the thing that is NOT supported by the passage here!). However, eliminating (C) requires an understanding of the last stanza, in which the comparison made is less obvious: The speaker draws that comparison to say that her lover is as necessary to her as those other things which one takes for granted. Make sure to keep your answers consistent, and if question 42 made sense to you, this one should too! Choice (B), by the way, is a comparison drawn in the poem, but it's a comparison to the lover's "fancies," or ideas, not to a lover's personal characteristics, so it is the odd one out.

47. **B** The speaker is comparing herself to a jar that will be filled, which fits with the language of (B). The same comparison is mentioned in (A), but that choice gets the point of the comparison wrong. Choices (C) and (E) are not supported by the passage. Choice (D) looks good, except that it's the subject of the poem, not the speaker, who is referred to with those comparisons. Make sure you read the answer choices as carefully as you do the poem!

48. **A** Getting this question right depends on noticing that the word "compassing" is being used like "encompassing," not like a compass that shows direction. This realization helps one eliminate (B), (C), and (D), all of which play with the other definition of compass. Choice (E) isn't bad, but it ignores the verb altogether and focuses only on the word "mystic"—that's not a good reading of the whole phrase. Choice (A) is what's left, and it uses the correct definition of that tricky first word.

49. **D** All of the choices are metaphors used in the poem, but (A), (B), and (C) are all about either the speaker's lover or her relationship. Choice (E) is what the speaker compares her own voice to. Choice (D) gets at the thrust of that last stanza: it's the "things which [she] say[s]" that are compared to rubies—and the poem itself is what she's saying.

50. **D** The use of the word "shrine," at which the speaker will kneel, is your major clue here. The other stanzas suggest devotion, certainly, but other than the title and maybe some coded references to Jesus imagery (which the test won't expect you to pick up on), there's nothing else here that's religious.

51. **C** This question relies on your knowledge of the terms in the glossary, so study them if you had trouble. Since this is a comparison using the word "as," it is a simile, not any of the other terms listed. Choice (E), a metaphysical conceit, would be associated with John Donne and his era, and because this poem was written in the twentieth century, it definitely doesn't apply.

52. **C** Check the Roman numerals with this question rather than each answer choice. This approach will always save you time! Statement (III) is untrue: the speaker is actually using heaven as an example of something she takes for granted, rather than something she is thankful for. Rule out (B), (D), and (E). Both (A) and (C) contain (I), so it must be correct. Statement (II) is correct in that neither the morning nor her lover are things that the author feels the need to thank the universe for: they're both simply things she needs to survive. Don't forget Consistency of Answers (a strategy we explain in Chapter 4), which can help you see that (II) is correct!

53. **D** "Hone" is usually a verb, but in this case, Lowell uses it to mean the whetstone or object on which the blade of her throat is sharpened. If you had trouble with this, you might not have read the choices closely—in which case you went for (A), the trap! Or you may need to see the grammar review earlier in this book.

54. **D** Consistency of Answers (see Chapter 4) should help you identify (I) as correct, especially at this point when you've done so many questions in this passage. Statement (III) looks tempting, but it mixes up parts of the passage: it's her lover that the speaker is reverential toward, not nature. Statement (II) might also look good, but it refers to a figurative, not literal, idea expressed in the poem. Her lover isn't really as far away as the high clouds. In fact, we don't know that the lover is actually any place in particular at all. Therefore, (D) is the answer.

55. **E** The speaker asks all these questions in a sense of disbelief that she has been so lucky as to become involved with the subject of the poem. Choice (C) is close to being correct, but "overwhelmed" is a little too strong to be adequately supported by the poem. The other answer choices are all based on various misreadings: Choice (A) makes too much of the poem's religious references, (D) may be true of some of the questions but not all of them, and (B) is simply fancy-sounding language that doesn't fit with the meaning of the poem—there's no juxtaposition there.

Part III
About the AP English Literature and Composition Exam

- The Structure of the AP English Literature and Composition Exam
- How the AP English Literature and Composition Exam Is Scored
- Overview of Content Topics
- How AP Exams Are Used
- Other Resources
- Designing Your Study Plan

THE STRUCTURE OF THE AP ENGLISH LITERATURE AND COMPOSITION EXAM

Ahoy there, student! You may remember in the first few pages, we urged you to register the book, in part to find out any late-breaking information on the AP English and Composition Exam. As we went to press, we heard a rumor that two types of multiple choice questions, vocabulary in context and identification, might no longer appear.

But it was only rumor—and you know what Shakespeare said about rumors (that they stuff the ears with false reports). The minute we have verified information to fill your ears with true reports, you'll find it in your online Student Tools. If you haven't already, you can register for those items at **PrincetonReview.com/cracking** and we will keep you updated. Be sure to check periodically so you go into the exam with the most up-to-date information.

Test Date: Early May
Total Time: 3 hours (usually administered at 8:00 A.M.)

Section I: Multiple Choice (60 minutes)—
45% of your grade
Total number of questions: 55

Section II: Free Response (120 minutes)—
55% of your grade
Three Essays:
1. Poetry Analysis (40-minute essay on a single poem or comparison of two poems, which will be provided to you)
2. Prose Fiction Analysis (40-minute essay on a story, novel excerpt, or essay that is provided to you)
3. Literary Argument (40-minute essay on a given literary topic, supported by the student's own reading)

The Big Six and You

The AP English Literature and Composition course description content reflects content from the AP course, including the big ideas that undergird the questions you ask of all the literature you study. We're going to call the six big ideas the Big Six. The Big Six are concepts that enable you to study and understand literature – and to write about it. Five of the Big Six are elements of literature. The sixth is how you take the five elements and analyze literature yourself.

Let's review the Big Six. They are:

Character – Characters in literature show a wide range of values, beliefs, assumptions, biases, and cultural norms, and provide an opportunity to study and explore what the characters represent.

Setting – Settings and the details associated with them represent a time and place, but also convey values associated with the setting.

Structure – Structure refers to the arrangements of sections and parts of a text, the relationship of the parts to each other, and the sequence in which the text reveals information. These are all choices made by a writer that allow you to interpret a text.

Narration – Any narrator's or speaker's perspective controls the details and emphases that readers encounter, so affects how readers experience and interpret a text.

Figurative language – Comparisons, representations, and associations shift meaning from the literal to the figurative. Figurative language can include word choice, imagery, and symbols. Simile, metaphor, irony, personification, and allusions are all examples of figurative language.

Literary argumentation – How do you write about literature yourself? You develop your interpretation (using the first five of the Big Six!) and then communicate it. You need to develop a thesis – a defensible claim – and support it with textual evidence.

The multiple choice section of the AP Literature and Composition exam will be testing your knowledge of the Big Six. Each one is weighted a certain amount in the multiple choice questions.

You are evaluated on your knowledge of the Big Six throughout the exam. For the multiple choice section, for example, you are evaluated on seven skill categories that map very closely to the Big Six. (Two of the skill categories, 5 and 6, are covered under Figurative Language, one of the Big Six.) The weighting is shown below.

Skill Category	Exam Weighting
1: Explain the function of character	16–20%
2: Explain the function of setting	3–6%
3: Explain the function of plot and structure	16–20%
4: Explain the function of narrator or speaker	21–26%
5: Explain the function of word choice, imagery, and symbols	10–13%
6: Explain the function of comparison	10–13%
7: Develop textually substantiated arguments about interpretations of part of all of a text	10–13%

Who Writes the Exam?

The initial content for the exam is generally gathered by an AP Development Committee that is made up in equal parts of high school and college teachers. This ensures that the material presented on the test falls within the range of topics associated with the course itself. Once those topics and questions have been written, however, they are often fine-tuned by professional test designers who work to keep the test, especially the multiple-choice section, similar to previous administrations. This is actually an asset to you, since that stability also adds a degree of predictability to the ways in which questions are shaped and wrong answers are selected. On multiple-choice tests, knowing how the wrong answers are written and how they can be eliminated is key. We'll discuss this topic in detail in Part IV, Chapter 4.

HOW THE AP ENGLISH LITERATURE AND COMPOSITION EXAM IS SCORED

What Your Final Score Means

After taking the test in early May, you will receive your scores sometime around the first week of July, which is right about when you've just started to forget about the whole experience. Your score will be, simply enough, a single number from 1 to 5. Here is what those numbers mean:

Score (Meaning)	Percentage of test takers receiving this score	Equivalent grade in a first-year college course	Credit granted for this score?
5 (extremely qualified)	6.2%	A	Most schools (contact admissions department to verify)
4 (well qualified)	15.9%	A–, B+, B	Most schools (contact admissions department to verify)
3 (qualified)	28.0%	B–, C+, C	Some do, but some don't (contact admissions department to verify)
2 (possibly qualified)	34.3%	N/A	Very few do (contact admissions department to verify)
1 (no recommendation)	15.6%	N/A	No

The data above are from the College Board website and based on the May 2019 test administration and the College Board AP English Literature and Composition Course and Exam Description, effective Fall 2019.

Your Multiple-Choice Score

In the multiple-choice section of the test, you receive one point for each question you answer correctly. You receive no points for a question you leave blank or answer incorrectly. That is, the famous "guessing penalty" on some standardized tests does not exist here. So, if you are completely unsure, guess. However, it is always best to use Process of Elimination (POE, as discussed in Chapter 4) to narrow down your choices and make an educated guess.

Your Essay Score

Each AP essay in the Free-Response section is scored on a scale from 0 to 9, with 9 being the highest score. The scores of each essay are added together and this total, anywhere from 0 to 27, is your Essay section score. A Reader (a high school or college-level English teacher) goes through your essay and gives you a score based on an overall evaluation. This process is called "holistic" scoring. We will go into the details of essay scoring in Chapter 5, but here is the general outline of the 0 to 9 system: A "9" essay answers all facets of the question completely, making good use of the passage to support its points, and is "well written," which is a catch-all phrase that means sentences are complete, properly punctuated, clear in meaning, show an educated vocabulary, and are spelled correctly. Low-scoring essays are deficient in these qualities to a greater or lesser degree. If the essay receives a score of 0, the student has written what amounts to gibberish (misspelled gibberish). If you write in perfect medieval Latin, or Esperanto, or perhaps write a funny, publishable, prize-worthy story about your AP teacher, you will receive a "—." This score is the equivalent of 0.

The essay Readers do not award points according to a standardized predetermined checklist. The essays are scored individually by individual Readers. Each reader scores essays for one type of question. The institution that scores the test, the Educational Testing Service (ETS, in the 'biz) says that the Reader of your literary argument will be familiar with the work about which you write. If, for your literary argument on mistaken identity, you chose to write about Sophocles' *Oedipus Rex*, then your essay Reader would have read that work. (Of course, you could choose something stunningly obscure and mess with their heads, but we don't recommend it.) If a certain test has an essay on a poem by John Donne, an essay on a prose extract by Jean Toomer, and an literary argument on the topic of mistaken identity in a novel or play of your choice, there will be three distinct Readers: a Reader for your Donne essay, a Reader for your Toomer essay, and a Reader for your literary argument. Each will give you a score based solely on the essay she or he reads. The other Readers will not see your other essays or know how you were scored on them, nor will they know how you performed on the multiple-choice section.

Your Final Score

Your final 1 to 5 score is a combination of your section scores. Remember that the multiple-choice section counts for 45 percent of the total and the essays count for 55 percent. While this proportion makes them almost equal, they are not entirely equal. A somewhat convoluted mathematical formula is applied to arrive at your score.

Neither you nor the colleges you apply to will ever know what your individual section scores are. ETS doesn't tell. You get a final score between 1 and 5, and that's it.

Does this mean you don't need to think about how your multiple-choice and essay scores combine? No. You should get a feel for how your multiple-choice score affects your final, total score.

Look at the overall test as two separate assessments:

> Multiple Choice: 55 questions; 45% of the overall score
>
> Free Response: 3 essays, each scored on a 0 to 9 scale; 55% of the overall score

Updates Online
At the time of this book's printing, only scoring rubrics for the Free-Response Questions had been posted online. Be sure to visit your online Student Tools and/or the College Board's website for any additional rubrics or updated rubrics.

The cutoff point for each grade varies from year to year and is set only after all the multiple-choice sections and essays have been scored. Regardless, a good bottom-line goal is to get at least 30 questions right on the multiple-choice sections and to earn at least 15 points on the essays. These two scores will net you a final passing grade of 3. Increases in either category can increase your final scores. The grading scale for the AP English Literature and Composition Exam looks something like this:

Essay Points	15	18	21	24	27
MC Points					
20	2	3	3	4	5
25	3	3	4	4	5
30	3	4	4	5	5
35	3	4	4	5	5
40	4	4	5	5	5
45	4	5	5	5	5
50	5	5	5	5	5
55	5	5	5	5	5

Conclusions

1. The bottom-line goal on the multiple-choice section is 30, or a little more than half. The bottom-line goal on the essays is the minimum passing score on each essay, 5 (3 × 5 = 15).
2. Set realistic goals for yourself. Look what happens if your multiple-choice score stays at 30 while you raise your essays one point each (from a 15 to an 18): You go from a 3 to a 4!

The average score is a 3, but earning a 5 is possible, even if you only scored within the 20 to 35 range on the multiple-choice section.

Now let's start practicing ways for you to get your best possible score.

Pacing Chart for AP English Literature and Composition Exam				
My Score on Practice	Shooting for Minimum of	Time Spent	Must Get Right	Guess
_____	30 of 55	60 mins	30	25

The AP English Literature and Composition Exam is unlike other AP Exams in one other factor: time. The multiple-choice section is always one hour long. At the time of this book's printing, only scoring rubrics for the Free-Response Questions had been posted online. Be sure to visit your online Student Tools and/or the College Board's website for any additional rubrics or updated rubrics.

When you are getting the feel of the passage and the kinds of questions, take all the time you need. Your purpose, after all, is different at this stage, as you are familiarizing yourself with the process. Later, when you are practicing for the real experience, limit your time to precisely one hour.

Remember—you can guess. Look at it this way:

Time: 1 hour
Practice Test of 55 questions

Passage	Number of Questions	Number To Get Right	Number To Guess On
1	15	8	25 (from any section)
2	14	8	
3	11	6	
4	15	8	
		30	

Use a chart like this one to evaluate your performance when practicing:

The Time Factor			
Time Evenly Divided	Time I Spent	Time Shooting For	Number to Get Right
_____	_____	_____	_____

OVERVIEW OF CONTENT TOPICS

There is not a required reading list for the AP English Literature and Composition Exam, but the College Board provides a list of authors and poets with whom you should be familiar and whose work is of the caliber and density that you are expected to understand. They can be works written in, or translated into, English. These lists include the following:

Poetry

- W. H. Auden
- Elizabeth Bishop
- William Blake
- Anne Bradstreet
- Edward Kamau Brathwaite
- Gwendolyn Brooks
- Robert Browning
- George Gordon, Lord Byron
- Lorna Dee Cervantes
- Geoffrey Chaucer
- Lucille Clifton
- Samuel Taylor Coleridge
- Billy Collins
- H. D. (Hilda Doolittle)
- Emily Dickinson
- John Donne
- Rita Dove
- Paul Laurence Dunbar
- T. S. Eliot
- Robert Frost
- Joy Harjo
- Seamus Heaney
- George Herbert
- Garrett Hongo
- Gerard Manley Hopkins
- Langston Hughes
- Ben Jonson
- John Keats
- Philip Larkin
- Robert Lowell
- Andrew Marvell
- John Milton
- Marianne Moore
- Sylvia Plath
- Edgar Allan Poe
- Alexander Pope
- Adrienne Rich
- Anne Sexton
- William Shakespeare
- Percy Bysshe Shelley
- Leslie Marmon Silko
- Cathy Song
- Wallace Stevens
- Alfred, Lord Tennyson
- Derek Walcott
- Walt Whitman
- Richard Wilbur
- William Carlos Williams
- William Wordsworth
- William Butler Yeats

Drama

- Aeschylus
- Edward Albee
- Amiri Baraka
- Samuel Beckett
- Anton Chekhov
- Caryl Churchill
- William Congreve
- Athol Fugard
- Lorraine Hansberry
- Lillian Hellman
- David Henry Hwang
- Henrik Ibsen
- Ben Jonson
- David Mamet
- Arthur Miller
- Molière
- Marsha Norman
- Sean O'Casey
- Eugene O'Neill
- Suzan-Lori Parks

Drama (continued)

- Harold Pinter
- Luigi Pirandello
- William Shakespeare
- George Bernard Shaw
- Sam Shepard
- Sophocles

- Tom Stoppard
- Luis Valdez
- Oscar Wilde
- Tennessee Williams
- August Wilson

Fiction (Novel and Short Story)

- Chinua Achebe
- Sherman Alexie
- Isabel Allende
- Rudolfo Anaya
- Margaret Atwood
- Jane Austen
- James Baldwin
- Saul Bellow
- Charlotte Bronte
- Emily Bronte
- Raymond Carver
- Willa Cather
- John Cheever
- Kate Chopin
- Sandra Cisneros
- Joseph Conrad
- Edwidge Danticat
- Daniel Defoe
- Anita Desai
- Charles Dickens
- Fyodor Dostoevsky
- George Eliot
- Ralph Ellison
- Louise Erdrich
- William Faulkner
- Henry Fielding
- F. Scott Fitzgerald
- E. M. Forster
- Thomas Hardy
- Nathaniel Hawthorne
- Ernest Hemingway
- Zora Neale Hurston
- Kazuo Ishiguro

- Henry James
- Ha Jin
- Edward P. Jones
- James Joyce
- Maxine Hong Kingston
- Joy Kogawa
- Jhumpa Lahiri
- Margaret Laurence
- D. H. Lawrence
- Chang-rae Lee
- Bernard Malamud
- Gabriel García Márquez
- Cormac McCarthy
- Ian McEwan
- Herman Melville
- Toni Morrison
- Bharati Mukherjee
- Vladimir Nabokov
- Flannery O'Connor
- Orhan Pamuk
- Katherine Anne Porter
- Marilynne Robinson
- Jonathan Swift
- Mark Twain
- John Updike
- Alice Walker
- Evelyn Waugh
- Eudora Welty
- Edith Wharton
- John Edgar Wideman
- Virginia Woolf
- Richard Wright

Expository Prose

- Joseph Addison
- Gloria Anzaldua
- Matthew Arnold
- James Baldwin
- James Boswell
- Jesús Colón
- Joan Didion
- Frederick Douglass
- W. E. B. Du Bois
- Ralph Waldo Emerson
- William Hazlitt
- bell hooks
- Samuel Johnson

- Charles Lamb
- Thomas Macaulay
- Mary McCar hy
- John Stuart Mill
- George Orwell
- Michael Pollan
- Richard Rodriguez
- Edward Said
- Lewis Thomas
- Henry David Thoreau
- E. B. White
- Virginia Woolf

More Great Books

For more information on colleges, you might want to check out some of our guide books, which include *The Best 385 Colleges, The Complete Book of Colleges, Paying for College Without Going Broke,* and many more!

HOW AP EXAMS ARE USED

Different colleges use AP Exam scores in different ways, so it is important that you go to a particular college's website to determine how it uses AP Exam scores. The three items below represent the main ways in which AP Exam scores can be used.

- **College Credit**. Some colleges will give you college credit if you score well on an AP Exam. These credits count toward your graduation requirements, meaning that you can take fewer courses while in college. Given the cost of college, this could be quite a benefit.
- **Satisfy Requirements**. Some colleges will allow you to "place out" of certain requirements if you do well on an AP Exam, even if they do not give you actual college credits. For example, you might not need to take an introductory-level course, or perhaps you might not need to take a class in a certain discipline at all.
- **Admissions Plus**. Even if your AP Exam will not result in college credit or even allow you to place out of certain courses, most colleges will respect your decision to push yourself by taking an AP course or even an AP Exam outside of a course. A high score on an AP Exam shows a mastery of more difficult content than is taught in many high school courses, and colleges may take that into account during the admissions process.

OTHER RESOURCES

There are many resources available to help you improve your score on the AP English Literature and Composition Exam, not the least of which are your **teachers**. If you are taking an AP class, you may be able to get extra attention from your teacher, such as obtaining feedback on your essays. If you are not in an AP course, reach out to a teacher who teaches AP English Literature and Composition and ask whether the teacher will review your essays or otherwise help you with content.

Another wonderful resource is **AP Students**, the official site of the AP Exams. The scope of the information at this site is quite broad and includes the following:

- course descriptions, which include details on what content is covered and sample questions
- reading and writing study skills tips
- essay prompts from previous years
- information about exam fees and reductions
- tons of practice content: multiple choice, passages, and more

The AP Students home page address is **http://apstudent.collegeboard.org**

The page where you can find gobs of information about AP English Literature and Composition is: **https://apstudent.collegeboard.org/apcourse/ap-english-literature-and-composition**

Finally, The Princeton Review offers tutoring for the AP English Literature and Composition Exam. Our expert instructors can help you refine your strategic approach and add to your content knowledge. For more information, call 1-800-2REVIEW.

DESIGNING YOUR STUDY PLAN

In Part I, you identified some areas of potential improvement. Let's now delve further into your performance on Practice Test 1, with the goal of developing a study plan appropriate to your needs and time commitment.

Read the answers and explanations associated with the multiple-choice questions (starting at page 27). After you have done so, respond to the following questions:

- How many days/weeks/months away is your AP English Literature and Composition Exam?

- What time of day is your best, most focused study time?

- How much time per day/week/month will you devote to preparing for your AP English Literature and Composition Exam?

Go Online!

If you're looking for additional resources to prepare for the AP Exam, remember to visit the course home page on AP Students. Here you can find more information about the exam, including sample questions and scoring details.

Another Course? Of Course!

If you can't get enough AP English Literature & Composition and want to review this material with an expert, we also offer an online Cram Course that you can sign up for here: https://www. princetonreview.com/ college/ap-test-prep.

Time Well Spent

If you're not sure how to best spend your time, register this book and log into your online Student Tools so that you can download our helpful, free study guide for this book.

- When will you do this preparation? (Be as specific as possible: Mondays and Wednesdays from 3:00 to 4:00 P.M., for example.)

- Based on the answers above, will you focus on strategy or content or both?

- What are your overall goals in using this book?

Part IV
Test-Taking Strategies for the AP English Literature and Composition Exam

PREVIEW

Review your responses to the questions in "Reflect on the Test" on page 4, and then respond to the following questions:

- How many multiple-choice questions did you miss even though you knew the answer?

- On how many multiple-choice questions did you guess blindly?

- How many multiple-choice questions did you miss after eliminating some answers and guessing based on the remaining answers?

- Did you find any of the essays easier/harder than the others—and if so, why?

HOW TO USE THE CHAPTERS IN THIS PART

For the following Strategy chapters, think about what you are doing now before you read the chapters. As you read and engage in the directed practice, be sure to appreciate the ways you can change your approach. At the end of Part IV, you will have the opportunity to reflect on how you will change your approach.

Chapter 1
Basic Principles of
the Multiple-Choice
Section

WHAT ARE THE BASIC PRINCIPLES OF CRACKING THE EXAM?

As with any multiple-choice test, there will come a time when the studying is over, and you are as prepared as you are ever going to be. You will be sitting at your desk with a sealed exam booklet and an answer sheet in front of you. The proctor, droning on at the front of the room, will finally finish reading the instructions and say, "You may break the seal and begin the test."

At that moment, what you know isn't going to change. Your head will be crammed with knowledge, and you might wish you knew even more, but your score will depend on getting what you know onto that answer sheet.

Imagine your exact double sitting at the next desk. In terms of English literature, your double knows exactly what you know. Will you and your double's scores be the same? *Well, if you know how to beat the test, your score will be better.* You will squeeze every possible drop of what you know onto that answer sheet while your double will struggle to bring all his or her knowledge to the table. The scores will reflect the difference.

The multiple-choice section of the AP English Literature and Composition Exam is just like any other standardized test in that you should have three serious considerations:

1.) Time management is crucial.
2.) Process of Elimination is necessary for narrowing answers to more viable options.
3.) You must answer EVERY question. Leave NOTHING blank.

Have a Plan

In order to do your best on the AP Exam, you need a plan. Stop worrying about doing things the "right way" and start concentrating on answering every question most efficiently. Blank bubbles have no chance, but even random bubbled answers have hope. Go into test day with a plan for answering questions you don't know and a plan for managing your time.

The Plan
Here's an outline of what you should do on the multiple-choice section:

1. Note the Time and Number of Passages
When the test begins, make note of the time. The proctor might put the start time on the board; most rooms have a clock, but don't count on either. Your best bet is to take a wrist watch and set it to 12:00. It's easy to read how much time you have left if you have everything in even increments. This is a good trick for taking any timed test.

Because you'll be faced with four or five reading passages, you can bet on about 12–15 minutes per passage with questions. Keep track of time. Don't rush, but try not to dedicate too much time to any one passage or question.

2. Pick a Passage to Complete First
Some passages may be a bit easier than others. There is no order of difficulty on the test, but you know yourself and your skills best. If you see twentieth-century literature and seventeenth-century poetry, choose the one that makes you most comfortable. Reading the passage that is easiest for you will help you to start the test confidently and efficiently. Then you reserve time for harder passages to come.

3. Pick a Passage to Complete Last
Scan the passages for one that looks harder (to you) than the others. Save this one for the end so that you can use any extra time on it. If you complete the other passages faster than the 12–15 minutes, you can dedicate the remaining time to the reading and questions that will be most difficult. Remember, this passage is one where you may have to guess because you don't know the answers or you're running out of time, but that's okay. If you answered the easier passages with more consideration, it won't hurt you as badly to miss a few here.

4. Work the Passage
Note our verb choice: *work*, not *read*. You'll see what we mean when we get to the next chapter.

5. Answer the Questions Using Planned-Ahead Strategies
All passages are not created equal. Because you can't count on easier passages first and more difficult passages later, you have to rely on your instinct and prior knowledge to assess the situation and go confidently in the direction of the test.

Letter of the Day (LOTD)
One such automatic strategy is to pick a "letter of the day" (LOTD) from A to E in advance. If you run into a situation where you can't eliminate any answers or

No Order of Difficulty
Unlike some other exams, questions on the AP English Literature and Composition Exam are not arranged in order of difficulty. Passages deemed "easy" or "difficult" by the test writers could appear earlier or later.

simply don't have time to look at the remaining questions, you can just bubble in that answer. (Remember, you are not penalized for wrong answers!)

This is a quick and easy way to make sure that you've answered every question. And theoretically, if the questions are evenly distributed across all five choices, being consistent in your guesses should help to pick up a couple of freebie points.

TIME MANAGEMENT

A key factor on standardized tests is time management. You have to answer roughly 50–55 questions in 60 minutes, and that means there's no time to waste. The more questions you answer, the better chance you have of correct answers—LEAVE NOTHING BLANK.

Analyze yourself as a test taker and determine how to tackle the test in the best way for you. We can present general guidelines to get you going, but you have to come up with your own personal plan for test day.

Do It Your Way

Don't listen to other kids say how "easy" that test was or how "it was so hard I didn't even get to everything!" If you worry about how others are testing, you won't be confident in your own abilities. Remember that the first thing you should do is look over the passages to determine your approach.

If you can get to all the passages and answer all the questions with five minutes left over, great, but don't count on it. Plan ahead. There's no law that says you have to do the passages in order. Don't.

As we've already mentioned, the first thing you should do as soon as the multiple-choice section begins is look over the passages—this is definitely allowed. Decide which passage to do first, but much more important—decide which passage to do last.

The object is to find the most difficult passage and put off doing it until the end. There are a couple of reasons for doing this. First, if you're going to run out of time, why not run out of time on the passage where you might miss a lot of questions anyway? Second, a more difficult passage is undoubtedly going to take the most time. You don't want to get into a situation where you have to rush just to finish three out of four passages. This is such a simple technique. All you have to do is remember to use it.

A Word of Advice
We recommend that you save the passage (and questions) you find most challenging for last. This strategy ensures that you answer all of the questions you know before moving on to the ones you may not know and which, therefore, might cost you valuable time.

You Can Skip a Passage and Still Get a Good Score

It's true. It is completely possible to get a final score of 5 without doing all the passages. No, it isn't easy. It calls for excellent essays and accurate answers on the passages you do attempt. If you'd be satisfied with a final score of 4 (and you should be; it's an excellent score), and if you know that reading comprehension questions are tough for you, then you should definitely consider skipping a passage. Of course, skipping a passage does not mean leaving questions blank. When you get to questions that are too time-consuming or that you don't know the answer to (and you can't eliminate any options), use your letter of the day (LOTD).

ACTIVE READING

With five prose fiction and poetry analysis passages and 55 questions to do in an hour, you need a strategy to make the most of your reading time. It's called active reading, and it will help you wring information from the passage quickly.

Steps in active reading

1. Preview the questions—just the stems, not the answer choices. This technique works well for some people and not for others. The passages in this book give you plenty of opportunity to try it a couple of times. If it works for you—if you can retain most or even some of the information you'll need to find in order to answer the questions—then you'll be one step ahead when you start reading the passage.
2. Identify the main point of each paragraph or stanza *before* you allow yourself to move on to the next one. This will force you to concentrate intensely and will avoid that lost, "what did I just read?" feeling that comes from skimming through a passage. It might help you to make a quick note of a key word or two for each part of the passage.
    Don't let this step slow you down, though. If a sentence or stanza really doesn't make sense to you, stop and close your eyes for a couple of seconds, look at it again, and, if necessary, just move on. It might make sense later in the context of one of the questions.
3. Ask questions constantly as you read. Why is the author talking so much about snowflakes? Why doesn't John want to go to the beach with his family? What is the red truck supposed to symbolize? Why does the author use "despondent" instead of "sad"? Why is this dream sequence here? Tear the prose fiction selection or poem apart instead of simply letting it flow into you as written. This step forces you to engage with the passage instead of letting it slip past you.
4. Identify the main point of the whole passage. There—you've got the theme and the author's purpose.

Once you master active reading techniques, you'll probably find them useful far beyond the exam.

Spacing Out?
If you feel your eyes glazing over at any point during the test, stop, take a deep breath, and get yourself to re-focus. We know it's easier said than done, but sharp concentration is a key to test success!

Why Is This Wrong? Half Bad = All Bad

The key is to take each answer a word at a time. Don't fixate on what's right about the answer; if any part of the answer is wrong, then eliminate the answer. **Half bad equals all bad**. In fact, one-tenth bad equals all bad. Read the following excerpt from Zadie Smith's *White Teeth* and the question that follows.

Types of Answer Choices

1. All true but one word or phrase

If part of the answer is wrong, then the whole thing is wrong. Read the entire answer choice to determine whether the answer is appropriate for what the question is asking.

2. Distractor/Absolute Wrong Answer

This is the answer that just cannot be the answer based on what you read in the passage. Through process of elimination, you should be able to spot this answer pretty quickly.

3. Key/Right or Best Answer

This is the answer that is most suitable in response to the question. The Key may be similar to other answer choices; however, all parts of this answer fulfill the question and align with the passage.

4. Irrelevant Details/Information

Sometimes you'll see details and think, "ooh! I read that," but you have to be careful that this doesn't throw you from the true focus of the question. Some answer choices will include some relevant details but will also include speculative details or things that just aren't in the passage. Read the entire answer choice before seeing one small detail and making an incorrect choice.

Early in the morning, late in the century, Cricklewood Broadway. At 0627 hours on January 1, 1975, Alfred
Line Archibald Jones was dressed in cor-
(5) duroy and sat in a fume-filled Cavalier Musketeer Estate facedown on the steering wheel, hoping the judgment would not be too heavy upon him. He lay in a prostrate cross, jaw slack, arms
(10) splayed on either side like some fallen angel; scrunched up in each fist he held his army service medals (left) and his marriage license (right), for he had decided to take his mistakes with him.
(15) A little green light flashed in his eye, signaling a right turn he had resolved never to make. He was resigned to it. He was prepared for it. He had flipped a coin and stood staunchly by the results.
(20) This was a decided-upon suicide. In fact, it was a New Year's resolution.

....

While he slipped in and out of consciousness, the position of the planets, the music of the spheres, the
(25) flap of a tiger moth's diaphanous wings in Central Africa, and a whole bunch of other stuff that Makes Shit Happen had decided it was second-chance time for Archie. Somewhere, somehow, by
(30) somebody, it had been decided that he would live.

1. Lines 3–16 of the passage best describe the author's portrayal of Alfred Archibald Jones as

(A) A harshly condemnatory treatment of a coward
(B) A sympathetic portrayal of a man who regrets his life
(C) A farcical portrayal of an attempted suicide
(D) A mock heroic portrait of a vintage car enthusiast
(E) A darkly ironic treatment of an overly sensitive man

(A) You may say "'harsh,' 'coward'? It strongly implies he has failed in life because he means to take "mistakes" with him, and the mistakes are both military service and marriage, major events in the lives of most men. That's support for it's being a harsh view. He is not described as cowardly, though, but as someone who "stood staunchly" by coin-toss results. If one part of the question is wrong, then the choice is wrong. Eliminate this answer.

(B) While the tone is somewhat arch, the description of him as "like some fallen angel" and laying "in a prostrate cross" indicate some sympathy for him. It is certainly not *un*sympathetic. Hold on to this one.

(C) We are told that he plans to commit suicide in the passage, so the last part of this answer is correct. But is the tone farcical? While there is some irony involved in saying that a "bunch of other stuff that Makes Shit Happen" decides his fate, "farcical" is too strong a word. Half bad is all bad, so eliminate this one.

(D) Is the passage mock heroic? Again, he "stood staunchly" by his decision and his "army service medals" indicate military service, which may lead you to associate him with heroism. But there's no indication he's particularly heroic in the passage. As for vintage car enthusiasm, you don't have an indication of whether his car—the "Cavalier Musketeer Estate" of lines 5–6—is an old classic or not. Don't be distracted by a detail that may appear in the passage but does not provide the information needed to answer the question.

(E) There seems to be some irony in the passage, and an attempted suicide may lead you to conclude that it's dark. But you cannot be sure whether he's overly sensitive.

Eliminate the Obvious and Come Back

That leaves choices (B) and (E).

Ask yourself if the portrait is sympathetic. The author doesn't exactly seem to be shedding tears for him, so you're not sure. But neither is he condemned. You are also not clear about what the word "ironic" means. What should you do? Be brave.

Process of Elimination (POE)

Pick (B). You couldn't find anything wrong with (B).

Don't be afraid to pick answers you aren't sure are right. Sometimes that's necessary. Just make sure you don't pick answers that you think are probably wrong. We know that sounds obvious, but students do pick weak answers and they know they're doing it. Why? Because one answer was kind-of-but-not-really-right while the other was totally unfamiliar. The student thinks the unfamiliar answer might be right but then again, it might be embarrassingly wrong. The student picks the kind-of-but-not-really-right answer and loses points but thinks that's okay because at least it wasn't the embarrassing answer. Relax! You can't embarrass yourself on this exam. The multiple-choice questions are scored by a machine. No one—not your AP teacher, not your classmates, not the AP essay Readers—knows or cares which answer you pick. Be fearless. If POE leaves you with two or three answers you aren't sure about—*pick one.*

In the example above, (B) was correct. Don't let unclarity on the definition of "ironic" mislead you into thinking material is darkly ironic when another answer might be more appropriate for the passage. Often irony takes the form of a subtle kind of humor when what is said is different from what is meant. **Irony** is an important term, both for the test and for the study of literature in general. We give it a full treatment in the glossary at the back of this book. But this is just one example, and irony comes in dozens of colors and flavors.

POE Summary

- When in doubt, narrow down the choices by looking for wrong answers.
- Eliminate what you can and then look more closely at what's left.
- Half bad = all bad.
- Don't leave any question blank, ever.

A PREVIEW OF COMING ATTRACTIONS

There's one more time management technique that you absolutely have to know. It's called the "Art of the Seven-Minute Passage." We'd like to tell you about it now, but unfortunately the full technique won't make sense until we've outlined the general principles of reading prose fiction or poetry analysis passages and shown you examples of the kinds of questions you'll see on the AP Literature Exam. You'll find our explanation of the Art of the Seven-Minute Passage in Chapter 8.

Summary

Have a Plan

o   Note the time and the number of passages.

o   Pick a passage to do first.

o   Pick a passage to do last.

o   Work the passage. Use active reading techniques.

o   Answer *all* the questions on the passage, using our techniques.

Time Management

o   Guess aggressively.

o   Pick a passage to do last based on what you consider your greatest weakness.

o   Skip a passage, guess, or use your Letter of the Day (LOTD) on *all* the questions in that passage, and still get a good score.

o   Learn the Art of the Seven-Minute Passage and use it.

POE

o   Guess aggressively.

o   Use POE (Process of Elimination).

o   The best way to use POE is to look closely at the wording of each answer choice for what is wrong, and eliminate.

o   Bubble an answer for *all* questions, even if it's just your LOTD.

Chapter 2
Using Time
Effectively to
Maximize Points

BECOMING A BETTER TEST TAKER

Very few students stop to think about how to improve their test-taking skills. Most assume that if they study hard, they will test well, and if they do not study, they will do poorly. Most students continue to believe this even after experience teaches them otherwise. Have you ever studied really hard for an exam and then blown it on test day? Have you ever aced an exam for which you thought you weren't well prepared? Most students have had one, if not both, of these experiences. The lesson should be clear: Factors other than your level of preparation influence your final test score. This chapter will provide you with some insights that will help you perform better on the AP English Literature and Composition Exam and on other exams as well.

PACING AND TIMING

A big part of scoring well on an exam is working at a consistent pace. The worst mistake made by inexperienced or unsavvy test takers is that they come to a question that stumps them and rather than just skip it, they panic and stall. Time stands still when you're working on a question you cannot answer, and it is not unusual for students to waste five minutes on a single question (especially a question involving a graph or the word *except*) because they are too stubborn to cut their losses. It is important to be aware of how much time you have spent on a given question and on the section you are working. There are several ways to improve your pacing and timing for the test:

- **Know your average pace.** While you prepare for your test, try to gauge how long you take on 5, 10, or 20 questions. Knowing how long you spend on average per question will help you identify how many questions you can answer effectively and how best to pace yourself for the test.
- **Have a watch or clock nearby.** You are permitted to have a watch or clock nearby to help you keep track of time. However, it's important to remember that constantly checking the clock is in itself a waste of time and can be distracting. Devise a plan. Try checking the clock every 15 or 30 questions to see whether you are keeping the correct pace or whether you need to speed up. This will ensure that you're cognizant of the time but will not permit you to fall into the trap of dwelling on it.
- **Know when to move on.** Since all questions are scored equally, investing appreciable amounts of time on a single question is inefficient and can potentially deprive you of the chance to answer easier ones later on. You should eliminate answer choices if you are able to, but don't worry about picking a random answer and moving on if you cannot find the correct answer. Remember, tests are like marathons; you do best when you work through them at a steady

pace. You can always come back to a question you don't know. When you do, very often you will find that your previous mental block is gone and you will wonder why the question perplexed you the first time around (as you gleefully move on to the next question). Even if you still don't know the answer, you will not have wasted valuable time you could have spent on questions that come easier to you.

- **Be selective.** You don't have to do any of the questions in a given section in order. If you are stumped by an essay or multiple-choice question, skip it or choose a different one and come back. Also, you probably do not have to answer every question correctly to achieve your desired score. Select the questions or essays that you can answer and work on them first. This will make you more efficient and give you the greatest chance of getting the most questions correct.

- **Use Process of Elimination (POE) on multiple-choice questions.** Many times, one or more answer choices can be eliminated. Every answer choice that can be eliminated increases the odds that you will answer the question correctly.

Remember, when all the questions on a test are of equal value, no one question is that important and your overall goal for pacing is to get the most questions correct. Finally, you should set a realistic goal for your final score. In the next section, we will break down how to achieve your desired score and how to pace yourself to do so.

GETTING THE SCORE YOU WANT

Depending on the score you need, it may be in your best interest not to try to work through every question. Check with the schools to which you are applying to determine your needed score.

AP Exams in all subjects no longer include a "guessing penalty" of a quarter of a point for every incorrect answer. Instead, students are assessed only on the total number of correct answers. A lot of AP materials, even those you receive in your AP class, may not include this information. It's really important to remember that if you are running out of time, you should fill in all the bubbles before the time for the multiple-choice section is up. Even if you don't plan to spend a lot of time on every question or even if you have no idea what the correct answer is, you need to fill something in. Use your LOTD, as we discussed earlier.

TEST ANXIETY

Everybody experiences anxiety before and during an exam. To a certain extent, test anxiety can be helpful. Some people find that they perform more quickly and efficiently under stress. If you've ever pulled an all-nighter to write a paper and ended up doing good work, you know the feeling.

However, too much stress is definitely a bad thing. Hyperventilating during the test, for example, almost always leads to a lower score. If you find that you stress out during exams, here are a few preemptive actions you can take.

- **Take a reality check.** Evaluate your situation before the test begins. If you have studied hard, remind yourself that you are well prepared. Remember that many others taking the test are not as well prepared, and (in your classes, at least) you are being graded against them, so you have an advantage. If you didn't study, accept the fact that you will probably not ace the test. Make sure you get to every question you know something about. In either scenario, it's best to think of a test as if it were a game. How can you get the most points in the time allotted to you? Always begin with questions you can answer easily and quickly before tackling those that will take more time.
- **Focus on what you can control.** Don't stress out or fixate on what you don't know. Even if you've underprepared (which shouldn't be the case since you're using this book), you can still improve your score by maximizing the benefits of what you do know.
- **Try to relax.** Slow, deep breathing works for almost everyone. Close your eyes, take a few, slow, deep breaths, and concentrate on nothing but your inhalation and exhalation for a few seconds. This is a basic form of meditation that should help you to clear your mind of stress and, as a result, concentrate better on the test. If you have ever taken yoga classes, you probably know some other good relaxation techniques. Use them when you can (obviously, anything that requires leaving your seat and, say, assuming a handstand position won't be allowed by any but the most free-spirited proctors).
- **Eliminate as many surprises as you can.** Make sure you know where the test will be given, when it starts, what type of questions are going to be asked, and how long the test will take. You don't want to be worrying about any of these things on test day or, even worse, after the test has already begun.

The best way to avoid stress is to study both the test material and the test itself. Congratulations! By using this book, you are taking a major step toward a stress-free AP English Literature and Composition Exam.

REFLECT

Respond to the following questions:

- How long will you spend on multiple-choice questions?

- How will you change your approach to multiple-choice questions?

- What is your multiple-choice guessing strategy?

- How much time will you spend on the first essay? The second? The third?

- What will you do before you begin writing your essays?

- How will you change your approach to the essays?

- Will you seek further help, outside of this book (such as from a teacher, tutor, or AP Students), on how to approach multiple-choice questions, the essays, or a pacing strategy?

Chapter 3
Advanced Principles:
Reading the
Multiple-Choice
Passages

READING THE PASSAGES IN THE MULTIPLE-CHOICE SECTION

Because of the time constraints, you'll want to make sure that you go about reading the passages in the most efficient way possible. You might also want to use a slightly different approach depending on whether the passage is prose fiction or poetry analysis, but there are a few things you should keep in mind regarding both types of passage.

- You are reading in order to answer questions, not for enjoyment or appreciation. As you read, ask yourself, "Do I understand this well enough to answer a multiple-choice question about what it means?"
- You can come back to the passage anytime you want, and you *should* go back to the passage in order to answer the questions.

Both of these points address the same issue. The passages are on a test, but you don't do most of your reading on tests. Generally when you study for an English test, you read the works your teacher assigned and have to answer questions from memory; however, on the AP Literature and Composition Exam, the passages will likely be unfamiliar, which can be a tad daunting. The test writers deliberately select works that aren't typically taught in schools. The writers are great, familiar authors, but the works are more obscure.

The good news is that it's unlikely anyone else taking the test has seen the work before either; therefore, you're all starting with a similar level of knowledge. The best news is this is an open-book test. You don't have to read the passage in the same way you read for English class. You're not looking to memorize information —you can use the passage to your advantage while answering the questions. Soak up the basic structure of the passage, but don't stress over remembering every little detail. Only focus intently on what the questions are asking you, and find the parts of the passages that will help you answer appropriately.

Reading Prose Fiction Passages

The right way to read prose fiction passages in the multiple-choice section is simple. It's the method that works for YOU. Bear in mind that this is a timed test, so while we stand by the Active Reading tools provided in Chapter 1, you may want to modify or supplement those skills with the following. As you work through the practice drills and tests, make a point of trying different methods so that you can identify the one that's most efficient for you. It does you little good to fully understand a passage if that means you only have time to read and answer half the questions.

1. Preview the Questions

For some students, a quick reading of the questions provides *context*. For others, it's a total waste of time. When you're practicing on passages, try it each way and see what works best for you. Then, stick to that strategy. What you'll want to do is read each question and only the question. Don't read the answer choices. Don't try to memorize the questions. Just get a sense of what they're asking you about—questions about literary devices or a certain character, for example. This can provide clues that will make your reading more active.

2a. Skim the Passage

There are two stances on active reading; one is to identify the main idea of each paragraph before moving on. The other expands upon the idea of previewing questions and suggests that you skim only the first and last sentences of the paragraphs to get an overall sense of what the passage is about. When you go back, either guided by questions or, time permitting, to read the passage (as outlined in the next step), you'll be less likely to trip up on context. The trade-off is the time you spend doing this.

2b. Read the Passage

Just read, without fixating on details, without getting stuck or going blank. When you hit a sentence you don't understand in a book, you don't panic, do you? You don't assume: "I might as well throw this book away...without that sentence it's just a useless collection of incomplete alphabetical symbols." When you read normally, you read for the *main idea*. You read to understand what's going on. When you hit a tricky sentence, you figure that you'll be able to make sense of it from what comes later, or that one missing piece of the puzzle isn't going to keep you from getting the outline of the overall picture. This is exactly how you want to read an AP English Literature and Composition Exam passage.

What Is the Main Idea?

For the AP English Literature and Composition Exam, main idea means the general point. It is the ten-words-or-fewer summary of the passage. The main idea is the gist, or the big picture. For example, suppose there's a passage about all the different ways a man is stingy, how he cheats his best friend out of an inheritance, and scrimps on food around the house so badly that his kids go to bed crying from hunger every night. The passage goes on for 50 or 60 lines describing this guy. The main idea is that this guy is an evil, greedy miser. If the passage gives a reason for the miser's obsession with money, you might include that in your mental picture of the main idea: This guy is an evil, greedy miser because he grew up poor. No doubt the passage tells you exactly how he grew up and where (in an orphanage, let's say), and exactly what kind of leftover beans he eats (lima) and exactly how many cold leftover lima beans he serves to his starving kids each night (three apiece), but those are details, not the big picture. Use the details to build up to the big picture.

The Magic Topic Sentence Has Vanished

We don't want you to think that the main idea can be found in some magic "topic sentence." The writers on the AP Exam are sophisticated; they often don't use any obvious clues like topic sentences. With poetry analysis passages especially, looking for topic sentences is a waste of time; however, use context clues to make inferences regarding theme and main idea.

Don't Be Afraid to Skim!
The idea of "skimming" might inspire panic in some students who want to read every single word. But when done correctly, skimming is a great way to get a sense of the passage before diving into the questions.

Summary—How Do You Read an AP Multiple-Choice Prose Fiction Passage?

- Preview the questions (optional).
- Skim.
- Read for the main idea.

Reading Poetry Analysis Passages

Ideally, you read a poem several times, ponder, scratch your head, and read some more. Then again, ideally you have your favorite poem by your favorite poet, and all afternoon to read—not 15 minutes with some poem you couldn't care less about and 15 multiple-choice questions staring you in the face.

It's a test, so you've got to read the poem efficiently, and the key to the process is keeping your mind open, especially the first time through.

It might help to be clear about the difference between a narrative and the kind of poetry you'll see on the AP Exam. A narrative unfolds and builds on itself. Although one's understanding of what came earlier in the narrative is deepened and changed by later developments, by and large the work makes sense as it flows; it is meant to be understood "on the run."

Verse is different. Yes, the way it unfolds is important, but one often doesn't even grasp that unfolding until the second or third (or ninetieth) read. A poem is like a sculpture; it is meant to be wandered around, looked at from all sides, and finally taken in as a whole. You wouldn't try to understand a sculpture until you'd seen the whole thing. In the same way, think of your first reading of a poem as a walk around an interesting sculpture. You aren't trying to interpret. You are just trying to look at the whole thing. Once you've seen it, and taken in its dimensions, then you can go back and puzzle it out.

What we've just said applies to poetry in general. But how can you apply that to the AP Exam? Here's the answer: *When you approach a poem on the AP Exam, always read it at least twice before you go to the questions.*

Poem Preview
Leave analysis out of your first read of a poem. Instead, look at it as a whole and get a general feel for it.

Skim

The first read is to get all the words in your head. Go from top to bottom. Don't stop at individual lines to figure them out. If everything makes sense, great. If it doesn't, no problem. The main thing you want is a basic sense of what's going on. The main thing to avoid is getting a fixed impression of the poem before you've even finished it.

Focus and Chunking

The second read should be phrase by phrase. Focus on understanding what you read in the simplest way possible. This is when you should look for the main idea.

Don't worry about symbols. Don't worry about deeper meanings. The questions will direct you toward those aspects of the poem. You will need to go back and read parts of it, perhaps the entire thing, several more times, but only as is necessary to answer individual questions. To prepare yourself for the questions, all you need is a general sense of what the poem says and to get that understanding you need only the literal sense of the lines. We can't emphasize this point enough: *Keep it simple.*

Panic and Obsession

Don't panic if you can't seem to grasp an understanding of the poem. Many people are probably struggling and completely baffled by the same poem. Don't skip the passage. Look for questions that take you to specific line item details (In lines 56–60...") and attempt to answer those questions using the specific lines of poetry. POE is your friend here! Don't obsess over the poem or the answers. Do your best to provide an answer using POE, but if you really get stuck, don't dwell. Choose an answer (maybe your LOTD) and move on.

The Difficulties of Poetry Analysis

Good poetry makes conscious use of all language's resources. By pushing the limits of language, poetry creates a heightened awareness in the reader. Poets sometimes use uncommon vocabulary, odd figures of speech, and unusual combinations of words in strange orders; they play with time and stretch the connections we see between ideas. All of these essential resources can make poetry analysis seem difficult, but it's not impossible. One important thing to remember is that many poems are open to a myriad of valid interpretations. It's not your job to have a meaningful experience when reading poetry on a test; it's your job to read for language resources and main ideas that will help you to answers the questions correctly.

Reading Poetry Resourcefully

You can connect to a poem in many ways, but you aren't reading for a nice, meditative experience on the AP Exam: you're reading to answer the questions correctly. The following things are what you're looking to identify and analyze as you read:

- Punctuation use
- Diction (word choice)
- Imagery
- Theme/main idea
- Figurative language (metaphors, similes, synecdoche)
- Character
- Setting
- Structure
- Narrator

A Word By Any Other Name Would Still Smell As Neat
You won't necessarily have to define words like "synecdoche" or use them in a sentence, but you should be aware of the different varieties of figurative language, the better to be on the lookout for them. Be sure to read through the Glossary beginning on page 277.

The Pros Read Poetry for Prose

The secret to understanding AP poetry analysis passages quickly and fully is to simply ignore the "poetry parts." Ignore the rhythm, ignore the music of the language, and above all, ignore the form. This means you should do the following:

- Ignore line breaks.
- Read in sentences, not in lines. Emphasize punctuation.
- Ignore rhyme and rhyme scheme.
- Be prepared for "long" thoughts—ideas that develop over several lines.

When approaching poetry, many students tend to do the opposite of what we suggest here: they emphasize lines and line breaks and totally ignore sentence punctuation.

True, sometimes there's no problem: When lines break at natural pauses and each line has a packet of meaning complete in itself (these are termed *end-stopped* lines), the poem becomes easier to read.

Challenging Poetry

Consider the next selection. It's the first 13 or so lines of "My Last Duchess" by Robert Browning. This is the kind of poetry you can expect to find on the AP Exam, but it is unlikely that you would see a poem that is this well known.

The poem is a monologue spoken by a nobleman, the Duke of Ferrara, to a representative of the Count of Tyrol. Ferrara seeks to take the wealthy count's daughter for his bride and is in the midst of discussing the arrangement with the count's representative. When Ferrara speaks of his "last duchess," he refers to his first wife, who has quite recently died at the age of 17 under mysterious circumstances. The implication is that Ferrara has had his first wife murdered, an implication the poem brings home with understated menace.

You won't be given this kind of information on the test, but with practice, you should be able to figure out many of the aspects of the poem by yourself. For example, the first two lines of the poem (which is printed below in sections) give a careful reader some important information. The speaker of the poem is a duke, as he is talking about his "last duchess." He is standing in front of a painting of this woman who is no longer alive. All of this information, if assimilated readily and with an eye toward tone and the big picture, will help you answer questions, even if the questions don't ask specifically who the speaker is or whether the duchess is alive.

My Last Duchess
Ferrara

That's my last duchess painted on the wall,
Looking as if she were alive. I call
That piece a wonder, now: Frà Pandolf's hands
Line Worked busily a day, and there she stands.
(5) Will't please you sit and look at her? I said
"Frà Pandolf" by design, for never read
Strangers like you that pictured countenance,
The depth and passion of its earnest glance,
But to myself they turned (since none puts by
(10) The curtain I have drawn for you, but I)
And seemed as they would ask me, if they durst,
how such a glance came there; so, not the first
Are you to turn and ask thus…

This poem is challenging, but it's not impossible with the right reading strategies. Remember: you're supposed to come into the test with a plan! The first few lines are relatively straightforward: The Duke points to the painting, remarks on its lifelike quality, mentions the artist (Frà Pandolf), and invites his listener to sit and contemplate the portrait for a moment. Although lines 3–4, "Frà Pandolf's hands/ Worked busily a day" consist of distinctly unmodern speech and might give some folks a moment's pause, there are signposts to help guide readers. Even if you don't know that "Frà" is used as a title of address to an Italian monk (and who does?), you can still figure out the big picture of this poem.

Then comes the remainder of the passage, beginning from line 5, "I said/'Frà Pandolf' by design, for never read," and the trouble begins. Now, the truth is that what is written there is easy enough that if you can break the habit of placing too much emphasis on line breaks, you can read it as prose. Browning has deliberately written his verse so that the lines break against the flow of the punctuation. If you expect little parcels of complete meaning at every break, you'll end up lost. Let's consider the troubling part written as prose:

"I said 'Frà Pandolf' by design, for never read strangers like you that pictured countenance, the depth and passion of its earnest glance, but to myself they turned (since none puts by the curtain I have drawn for you, but I) and seemed as they would ask me, if they durst, how such a glance came there."

Poem Woes
If the way lines break in a poem is completely confusing for you, read the poem as if it were prose. This strategy will help you crack even notoriously challenging poems by poets such as Robert Browning.

This is just one long sentence, broken by parenthetical asides, in which the duke says, "I said 'Frà Pandolf' on purpose because strangers never see that portrait (or its expression of depth and passion) without turning to me (because nobody sees the portrait unless I'm here to pull aside the curtain) and looking at me as though they want to ask, if they dare, 'How did that expression get there?'"

Read the poem as prose and you'll see it's pretty easy. If you have trouble doing this, try putting brackets around each sentence.

Now if you're really alert, you'll notice that the Duke still hasn't exactly explained why he mentioned Frà Pandolf on purpose. He eventually does (in his sideways fashion), but if you read poetry without being ready for long thoughts that develop over several lines, you're going to read "I said, 'Frà Pandolf' by design, for never…" and expect the explanation—pronto. When it doesn't come you think you're lost, and once you think you're lost, you are. How is "that pictured countenance" an explanation of why he said "Frà Pandolf?" It isn't, and it never will be, but you can spend hours trying to come up with reasons why it is.

Don't get the wrong impression. Browning isn't easy reading. But you'll find that if you follow our suggestions for reading poetry, you can cut to the heart of what Browning and poets like him are saying. Ignore line breaks and instead pay close attention to punctuation and sentence structure. Be ready for "long" thoughts that develop over several lines or even stanzas. You'll still find the poems on the AP Exam challenging for a variety of reasons: because of their vocabulary, because of their compression of a great deal of information into just a few lines, and because of their often complicated and unusual sentence structure.

If you read poetry the way we suggest, however, you'll find that you can still use the context of what you do understand to answer questions.

Here's Browning's "My Last Duchess" in complete form. Read it according to our advice and see what you can get from it. (Many discussions of this famous poem exist online, and you can read a few in order to compare what you've figured out with what others have said about it.)

Prose Pros

Taken together, these pieces of advice boil down to one simple concept: before you read a poem as poetry, read it as prose.

FERRARA

That's my last duchess painted on the wall,
Looking as if she were alive. I call
That piece a wonder, now: Frà Pandolf's hands
Line Worked busily a day, and there she stands.
(5) Will't please you sit and look at her? I said
"Frà Pandolf" by design, for never read
Strangers like you that pictured countenance,
The depth and passion of its earnest glance,
But to myself they turned (since none puts by
(10) The curtain I have drawn for you, but I)
And seemed as they would ask me, if they durst,
how such a glance came there; so, not the first

Are you to turn and ask thus. Sir, 'twas not
Line Her husband's presence only, called that spot
(15) Of joy into the Duchess' cheek: perhaps
  Frà Pandolf chanced to say, "Her mantle laps
  "Over my lady's wrist too much," or "Paint
  "Must never hope to reproduce the faint
  "Half-flush that dies along her throat": such stuff
(20) Was courtesy, she thought, and cause enough
  For calling up that spot of joy. She had
  A heart—how shall I say?—too soon made glad,
  Too easily impressed; she liked whate'er
  She looked on, and her looks went everywhere.
(25) Sir, 'twas all one! My favor at her breast,
  The dropping of the daylight in the West,
  The bough of cherries some officious fool
  Broke in the orchard for her, the white mule
  She rode with round the terrace—all and each
(30) Would draw from her alike the approving speech,
  Or blush, at least. She thanked men—good! but thanked
  Somehow—I know not how—as if she ranked
  My gift of a nine-hundred-years-old name
  With anybody's gift. Who'd stoop to blame
(35) This sort of trifling? Even had you skill
  In speech—which I have not—to make your will
  Quite clear to such an one, and say, "Just this
  "Or that in you disgusts me; here you miss,
  "Or there exceed the mark"—and if she let
(40) Herself be lessoned so, nor plainly set
  Her wits to yours, forsooth, and made excuse,
  —E'en then would be some stooping; and I choose
  Never to stoop. Oh sir, she smiled, no doubt,
  Whene'er I passed her; but who passed without
(45) Much the same smile? This grew; I gave commands;
  Then all smiles stopped together. There she stands
  As if alive. Will't please you rise? We'll meet
  The company below, then. I repeat,
  The Count your master's known munificence
(50) Is ample warrant that no just pretense
  Of mine for dowry will be disallowed;
  Though his fair daughter's self, as I avowed
  At starting, is my object. Nay, we'll go
  Together down, sir. Notice Neptune, though,
(55) Taming a sea-horse, thought a rarity,
  Which Claus of Innsbrück cast in bronze for me!

Easier Poetry

Look at these lines from Thomas Gray's "Elegy Written in a Country Churchyard":

> Now fades the glimmering landscape on the sight,
> And all the air a solemn stillness holds,
> Save where the beetle wheels his droning flight,
> And drowsy tinklings lull the distant folds.

Read this passage aloud, and you can't help but stop on the line endings even if there were no commas. The lines build, one upon the next, shaping a picture as they combine to form a mildly complex sentence. The ease with which these lines can be read stems from the fact that each line contains only complete thoughts; there are no loose ends trailing from line to line. This is "nice" poetry; that is, it's nice to you. Each line ends on a natural pause that lets you gather your thoughts. Each line holds something like a complete thought with very little run-over into the next line. Although the stanza is written in one sentence, it easily could have been written in four separate sentences:

> The landscape fades.
> The air is still.
> The beetle wheels and drones.
> The tinklings [of bells worn by livestock] lull the folds.*

*Folds are enclosures where sheep graze, or the flocks of sheep themselves.

This paraphrase is lousy poetry, but it gets the main idea across. If the poetry you see on the AP Exam reads like the example above, great. But if you think every poem should be like that stanza or if you try to make every poem read like that one, you're headed for trouble. The poetry on the AP Exam is likely to be more challenging.

Summary

Basics of Reading Passages

o   You are reading in order to answer the questions—that's the whole point.

o   Reading for a test is different from normal reading. You have limited time, and you have to approach the passages in a way that takes that restriction into account.

o   You can reread the passage (or parts of it) anytime you want, and you should go back to the passage in order to answer the questions.

Reading Prose Fiction Passages

o   Preview the questions if it helps you.

o   Skim the passage.

o   Skimming should never take more than a minute.

o   Read for the main idea.

Reading Poetry Analysis Passages

o   Preview the questions if it helps you.

o   On the exam, read the poem twice before you answer the questions.

o   The first read is to get all the words in your head.
   • The main thing you want is a basic sense of what's going on.
   • Try not to get a fixed impression of the poem before you've even finished it.

o   The second read should be done phrase by phrase. Focus on understanding what you read in the simplest way possible. Don't worry about symbols. Don't worry about deeper meanings. Try to visualize what you're reading as you follow the narration of the poem. Also try reading the poem as you would read prose. (See "Poetry into Prose" below.)

o   You will need to go back and read parts of the poem—perhaps the entire poem—several more times, but only as necessary for your work on individual questions.

Poetry into Prose

o   Find the spine—the prose meaning—of the poem.
   • Ignore line breaks.
   • Emphasize punctuation. Read in sentences, not in lines.
   • Be prepared for "long" thoughts: ideas that develop over several lines.

o   Before you read a poem as poetry, read it as prose.

Chapter 4
Cracking the System: Multiple-Choice Questions

QUESTION TYPES AND FORMATS

Once you've finished working a passage using active reading techniques, you need to answer the questions. If you've paid attention so far, you already know you're going to answer *all* of the questions, using your Letter of the Day to guess when you aren't sure of the answer. You should also know by now that you must approach the test efficiently, making the most of your time in order to get the best possible score.

In order to answer the questions efficiently, you'll need to be able to recognize two main types of questions:

- general comprehension questions that concern the prose fiction selection or poem as a whole
- detail questions that focus on one part of the passage

and three question formats:

- Standard
- EXCEPT/LEAST/NOT
- Roman numeral

Answer all of the questions. Use your Letter of the Day to guess if you don't know the answer.

General Comprehension Questions

General comprehension questions ask about the overall passage. These questions don't send you back to any specific line(s) or paragraph(s) in the passage.

Here are some examples of general comprehension questions.

- The passage is primarily concerned with…
- Which one of the following choices best describes the tone of the passage?
- Which one of the following choices best describes the narrator's relationship to her mother?
- How does the author's use of irony contribute to the effect of the poem?
- To whom does the speaker of the poem address his speech?
- It is evident in the passage that the author feels her home town is…

As these examples show, a general comprehension question can target either the passage as a whole, as the first question about theme (main point) does, or it can focus on one aspect of the entire passage, as the second question about tone does. In either case, the scope of the question covers the whole passage from beginning to end. If (in the third question) the narrator's relationship to her mother sounds harmonious in the first couple of lines but is revealed as adversarial throughout the rest of the passage, then "adversarial" is the answer that "best describes" the relationship. You need to consider the overall impression given by the whole passage.

General comprehension questions will often ask about the following:

- **The theme (main point) or author's purpose.** What is the author writing about? Why? What does the author intend for readers to think or feel or believe or do after they finish reading?

- **The tone.** What is the author's (or the narrator's) overall attitude toward the subject of the passage? Is he or she critical? Approving? Neutral? Is the author being humorous, satirical, ironic or deadly serious? Is he or she skeptical or a believer? And—very important—how do you know what the author's attitude is?

- **The style.** Here you're looking for diction (word choice), syntax (sentence choice) and literary devices—in other words, how the author conveys the theme and purpose. Is the vocabulary sophisticated or something that almost all readers could understand? Are the sentence structures varied (a mix of simple and complex, loose and periodic)? Does the author rely on literary devices (such as allusions, repetition, and symbols) to convey the theme, or is the delivery straightforward?

- **The structure.** How does the narrative progress? Do events occur in chronological order? Is the progression interrupted by flashbacks or flashforwards or dream sequences? When are the main characters introduced? When do major points in the plot occur? Are two similar plots being developed in parallel? Is there a sudden change (perhaps in emphasis or tone) part of the way through? Why? How are the different pieces connected and—very important—why did the author choose to connect them in this way?

- **The narrator's point of view.** Does the author use a first-person narrator ("I") whose personality, background, and biases act as a filter through which events are described? Or is the narrator an objective, camera-type recorder of events? What impact does the type of narrator have on the passage? Is there more than one narrator?

- **The development.** How does the plot develop? What techniques does the author use in order to develop a character? How does the author develop the main point?

- **The character(s).** Who are the characters? How are they described? What qualities or attributes do they have? What do they indicate about the author's values, beliefs, or assumptions? Do they reveal any biases or assumptions of a time or place? Do the characters change? Stay the same?

- **The setting.** What, if anything, are you told about the setting? Where are the characters physically? What time period are they in? What do aspects of the setting reveal about the theme, the plot, or the characters? What effect do aspects of the setting have on the passage?

DETAIL QUESTIONS

Detail questions almost always send you back to specific places in the passage. They tell you where to look and ask something about a particular segment or even a specific word.

> Always read at least one sentence or line before and after the place indicated in the question, so you'll have the correct context.

Here are some examples of detail questions.

- What significant change occurs in the speaker's attitude toward the countryside in lines 5–9?
- How do the final words of the third paragraph, "but then, I should have known better than to trust him," alter the remainder of the passage?
- In lines 1–5, the phrase "This loaf's big" is used as a metaphor for
- The poet's use of the word "sublime" (line 21) suggests that
- What does the pond in the first paragraph symbolize?
- Which of the following is the best paraphrase for the sentence that begins at line 9?

If you're having trouble grasping the overall theme of a passage or the author's purpose, the specific questions are a good place to start. You'll learn more about the passage with each one you answer, and the whole passage just might fall into place.

QUESTION FORMATS

Standard

The most common question format on the exam, standard format questions have a straightforward question stem, followed by five answer choices. Here are some examples of standard format question stems:

> The metaphor "fountain of delight" in paragraph 2 has the effect of
> The dream described in lines 30–32 suggests that
> The author's attitude towards his subject could be characterized as

EXCEPT/LEAST/NOT

Even though the test writers put EXCEPT, LEAST or NOT in capital letters, you could still miss those crucial words if you're just racing through the question stems instead of reading them carefully, word for word. In essence, these three qualifiers invert the answer you'd normally be looking for in a standard format question. Consider these examples:

> Ludwig seems to value all of the following characteristics in a business partner EXCEPT
> Which of the following characteristics does Ludwig consider the LEAST important in a business partner?
> Ludwig is NOT looking for which of these characteristics in a business partner?

Which four characteristics does the passage say Ludwig wants to see in a business partner? Those four will be in the answer choices. But those aren't what you're looking for. You want the one characteristic he does NOT consider important, or considers the LEAST important, or is the EXCEPTion to what he thinks is important.

To tackle these tricky questions, disregard the EXCEPT, LEAST or NOT; cross them out. You'll be left with a standard format question:

> Ludwig seems to value [which of] the following characteristics in a business partner ~~EXCEPT~~
> Which of the following characteristics does Ludwig consider ~~the~~ ~~LEAST~~ important in a business partner?
> Ludwig is ~~NOT~~ looking for which of these characteristics in a business partner?

Now eliminate any choice that would be a correct answer for your new, Standard format question. The remaining choice will be the correct answer for the EXCEPT/LEAST/NOT version of the question.

Roman Numeral

These are two-part questions, but they're not as time-consuming as they seem if you approach them correctly.

Think of a Roman numeral question as a standard format question with only three answer choices: I, II and III. However, unlike standard format questions, Roman numeral questions can have more than one correct choice among the three offered. Deciding which one(s) is or are correct will automatically give you the answer to the five lettered choices that follow.

Let's work through an example.

> The description of the farm in lines 13–21 implies that the speaker
>
>   I. had a happy childhood there
>   II. regrets returning to the place where he grew up
> III. hates his present life in the city
>
> (A) I only
> (B) I and II only
> (C) I and III only
> (D) II and III only
> (E) I, II, and III

Assume the description of the farm is positive and nostalgic. That would eliminate choice II: the speaker is probably glad to return to a place of happy memories. So right away you can eliminate any lettered choice that includes II: (B), (D) and (E). Now you're left with (A) and (C). If the speaker had a happy childhood on the farm (I), you could infer that he might well hate his present life in the very different city environment (III). Which lettered choice includes both I and III? That's (C) and the correct answer.

How Much Grammar Do You Need to Know for the AP English Lit Exam?

There are usually three or four questions on basic grammar. That's one grammar question or fewer per passage, so grammar is not a big deal on the multiple-choice section. The samples we provide in Chapters 7 and 8 should give you a good idea of what the grammar questions are like. Because there are so few grammar questions, we don't recommend you spend a lot of time studying grammar. You'd be far better off working on writing timed essays or reading poetry.

Master Sentence I

Here's a great simple sentence to memorize for basic grammatical relations:

Sam threw the orange to Irene.

It isn't poetry, but this sentence clearly shows the basic grammatical relationships you need to concern yourself with on the AP Exam.

- *Sam* is the subject.
- *The orange* is the direct object.
- *Irene* is the indirect object.

Notice that in this sentence, the direct object is in fact an object (an orange). The orange is thrown to Irene, the indirect object. In other words, the indirect object receives the direct object. The concept is pretty simple.

Master Sentence II

There are two more sentence elements you should understand: the phrase and the clause. Here's a model sentence that should help you keep clear on their definitions.

Feeling generous, Sam threw the orange to Irene, who tried to catch it.

The heart of the sentence is still *Sam threw the orange to Irene*, as subject, verb, direct object, and indirect object all remain the same. But we've added a phrase to the beginning of the sentence and a dependent (also called *subordinate*) clause to the end. Both phrases and dependent clauses function as modifiers. *Feeling generous* (a phrase) modifies *Sam*; and *who tried to catch it* (a clause) modifies *Irene*.

The difference between clauses and phrases is simple:

> A **clause** has both a subject and a verb.
>
> A **phrase** does not have both a subject and a verb.

Because a clause has both a subject and verb, a clause is always close to being a sentence of its own. The dependent clause, *who tried to catch it*, could be turned into a complete sentence by replacing *who* with *Irene* or *she,* or adding a question mark at the end.

The hallmark of a phrase is its lack of a subject or verb (or both). Phrases obviously cannot stand alone. *Feeling generous* needs the addition of both a subject (*Sam*) and a verb (*was*) in order to become the sentence *Sam was feeling generous*.

Our model sentence contains another clause besides the dependent clause we've already mentioned. The other clause is *Sam threw the orange to Irene.* Because it has both a subject and a verb, it must be a clause. Notice that it doesn't need any changes in order to stand alone as a complete sentence: that makes it an *independent* clause.

Terms of Disservice

Grammar is one of those things that helps with just about everything else, from comprehension of a tricky sentence to linking up parallel ideas and identifying structure. But specific questions about grammar basically boil down to things like whether you know what an antecedent is. Because there are so few grammar questions on this test, it's better to focus on the active reading and POE skills that will help you get through the other questions.

ORDERING THE QUESTIONS

You can complete the questions in any order you like, but that doesn't mean you should jump around and do them in any old order. After you finish reading a passage, but before you begin answering the questions, ask yourself, "Do I feel confident about this passage? Would I be able to explain this to a friend? Could I explain its main idea?"

The answer to this question determines the order in which you should tackle the test questions.

- If you feel confident about your comprehension of the passage, complete the questions in the order they are given to you. Don't worry about the order of the questions; you're in good shape.
- If you don't feel confident about the main idea, do the detail questions first.

The reasoning behind this ordering method is simple. The main idea is the crucial thing to get from a reading passage, whether prose fiction or poetry. When you have the main idea nailed down, you aren't likely to miss more than a few questions on the passage. Knowing the main idea will help you answer all of the other general questions and many of the specific questions as well.

When you don't feel confident about the main idea (which usually means the passage is pretty confusing), you want to start with the specific questions because they tell you exactly where to go and also give you something on which to focus.

As you reread the lines toward which the specific questions point you, you should become more and more familiar with the passage. Often after doing a specific question or two, the meaning of the passage "clicks" for you, and you will get what's going on. Don't answer the general questions until you have a firm sense of the main idea. If, after answering all the specific questions, you still don't really know what the point of the passage is, give the general questions your best shot and move on.

CONSISTENCY OF ANSWERS #1

The main idea should be your guiding rule for most of the questions on any passage. We call this principle *Consistency of Answers*. As you work on a passage you will find that the best answer on several of the questions has to do with the main idea. The rule: **When in doubt, pick an answer that agrees with the main idea.**

CONSISTENCY OF ANSWERS #2

Pick answers that agree with each other. You'll also find that correct answers tend to be consistent. It's a simple idea that comes in very handy. For example, if you're sure the correct answer to question 9 is (B), and (B) says that Mr. Buffalo is extremely hairy, you can be sure that question 10's Mr. Buffalo isn't bald. Correct answers agree with each other.

Consistency Is Key
When in doubt, choose an answer that agrees with the main idea of the passage.

The best way to understand how to use this very effective technique is to see it at work. You'll see plenty of examples in the following chapters; we'll discuss this technique in detail when we work on actual questions.

Guessing Aggressively with POE

First things first: Don't leave any questions blank! There is no guessing penalty: Worst-case scenario, guess blindly. But guessing smartly is much better! POE is an acronym for Process of Elimination. You are probably already acquainted with POE in its simplest form: cross out the answers that you know are wrong. The Cracking the System approach to POE isn't really different, just more intense.

There are always two ways to answer a multiple-choice question correctly. The first is to have the answer in mind right from the moment you read the question. If you understand the passage and the question, you'll often see the best answer among the choices. Far more often, however, you'll be slightly (or not-so-slightly) unsure. The test writers are pretty good at spotting places in a text where students are likely to have trouble, and they tend to write questions about these spots. The test writers are also pretty good at writing wrong answers that are quite appealing. Before you doubt yourself, however, make sure you have read the question carefully. It's possible to understand the passage but misread a question. The extra second or two you devote to reading the question may increase the number of questions you answer correctly. Still, no matter how strong a reader you are, some questions will cause you to have doubts about the answer. That's when you use The Princeton Review—style POE. What does that mean? It means: *Stop looking for the right answer—look for wrong answers and eliminate them.* Let's look at the same example we used on page 62, from Zadie Smith's *White Teeth:*

> Early in the morning, late in the century,
> Cricklewood Broadway. At 0627 hours on January
> 1, 1975, Alfred Archibald Jones was dressed in
> *Line* corduroy and sat in a fume-filled Cavalier Muske-
> (5) teer Estate facedown on the steering wheel, hoping
> the judgment would not be too heavy upon him.
> He lay in a prostrate cross, jaw slack, arms splayed
> on either side like some fallen angel; scrunched up
> in each fist he held his army service medals (left)
> (10) and his marriage license (right), for he had decided
> to take his mistakes with him. A little green light
> flashed in his eye, signaling a right turn he had
> resolved never to make. He was resigned to it. He
> was prepared for it. He had flipped a coin and stood
> (15) staunchly by the results. This was a decided-upon
> suicide. In fact, it was a New Year's resolution.
>
> ....
>
> While he slipped in and out of consciousness, the
> position of the planets, the music of the spheres, the
> flap of a tiger moth's diaphanous wings in Central
> (20) Africa, and a whole bunch of other stuff that Makes
> Shit Happen had decided it was second-chance time
> for Archie. Somewhere, somehow, by somebody, it
> had been decided that he would live.

1. Lines 3–16 of the passage best describe the author's portrayal of Alfred Archibald Jones as

    (A) A harshly condemnatory treatment of a coward
    (B) A sympathetic portrayal of a man who regrets his life
    (C) A farcical portrayal of an attempted suicide
    (D) A mock heroic portrait of a vintage car enthusiast
    (E) A darkly ironic treatment of an overly sensitive man

This is a typical AP English Lit question. It asks for an evaluation of a passage for comprehension. The majority of the questions take this form. In the example above, you've been asked, essentially, "What's going on in lines 3–16?" The actual passage would have been longer (usually around 55 lines), and the rest of the passage would certainly help you understand this section by puttingt it in context, but nevertheless, there is enough here to answer the question.

If you don't immediately spot the best answer, use POE. Go to each choice and say, "Why is this wrong?" You can look back at the explanations on pages 62–63 to check your thinking.

Summary

o Recognize the basic categories of questions.
- General Comprehension
- Detail

o Don't worry about grammar for the AP English Literature and Composition Exam. It isn't worth enough points to cause perspiration.

o Do it your way.
- If you know the main idea, answer the questions in order.
- If you're uncomfortable with the main idea, answer detail and factual questions first.

o Use Consistency of Answers.
- When in doubt, pick an answer that agrees with the main idea.
- Pick answers that agree with each other.

o Guess aggressively as needed using POE.

Chapter 5
Basic Principles of
the Essay Section

FORMAT AND CONTENT OF THE ESSAY SECTION

Section II of the AP English Literature and Composition Exam is the Free-Response, or essay, section. While the College Board officially refers to this section of the exam as "Free Response," in this book we will often be referring to it as the "essay" section, and your responses as "essays," for the sake of brevity. The format of this section has been consistent for years. Here's what to expect.

- You will be asked to write a response, in essay form, to each of the following subjects:
  1. A passage of poetry or a comparison of two thematically related poems
  2. A passage of prose fiction
  3. A literary argument: an essay on a literary concept or idea supported by evidence from your own reading or a provided list
- You'll be given all the paper you need (including scratch paper), and you'll be instructed to write in pen (blue or black ink only).
- You'll have two hours to complete this section, which works out to be 40 minutes per essay.

> **Remember the Big Six!**
> The AP exam expects you to make use of the Big Six during the essay section. Remember, that's **character**, **setting**, **structure**, **narration**, **figurative language** like metaphor and personification, plus using the skills of **literary argumentation** (developing a thesis supported by textual evidence). In fact, the essays are all exercises in literary argumentation! So while you may be reading a twentieth-century novelist or an English Renaissance poet, don't forget the Bix Six. As you read each passage for the essay, think about how character, setting, structure, and narration can help you develop what you want to say, and how any figurative language you see in the passage works.

What Will You Be Writing About?

When ETS considers the mix of literary periods and styles on the test, they include the essay section in that mix. If you see two passages on eighteenth-century poetry in the multiple-choice section, you won't see any eighteenth-century poetry in the essay section. ETS also tries to give male and female authors (roughly) equal representation and aims to include at least one author who identifies as African American, Native American, Latino, or Asian.

Pacing

On each individual essay, you can take as much or as little time as you like as long as you don't go over the two-hour limit for all three essays. Each essay is worth the same number of points, so it's a good idea to pace yourself and allot 40 minutes for each, give or take a few minutes. If you spend an hour and a half on your first essay, you're not going to finish the other two. Remember to bring a watch so that you don't lose track of time.

The Importance of the Essay Section to Your Score

The essay section of the AP English Literature and Composition Exam counts for 55 percent of your total score. It is only slightly more important than the multiple-choice section of the test. It's obvious, but let's say it anyway: Both sections are important to your score.

Which section *feels* more important is another issue. For most students, the essay section feels like the whole test. The multiple-choice section seems like a bunch of hoops you have to jump through before getting to the part that matters. Students tend to look at the essay section with quite a bit of anxiety. However, we're going to take the anxiety out of this process and replace it with knowledge and confidence.

Here's the interesting part: While it is true that the multiple-choice and essay sections are nearly equal in respect to determining your score, there is a world of difference between the two sections when it comes to score improvement.

When It Comes to Improving Your Score, the Essays Are King

If you're the kind of student who gets A's in class and then bombs on standardized tests, using our multiple-choice techniques will make a huge difference. If you are already a natural test-taker, that's great—our techniques will help you take your skills to the next level. You probably fall somewhere in between (the vast majority of students do) and so using our techniques for the multiple-choice section squeezes out a half-dozen or so extra points to ensure that you get your best possible score. Why settle for anything less? But when you work on improving your score (and your skills), the essays are different.

These Essays Are Different

Essay points add up fast. If we can show you a way to improve your essays by just one point—*bam*—then that means three extra essay points just like that, one for each essay. And there are only 27 total essay points available. One more point on each essay works out to better than a 10 percent improvement on your essay score. If you can improve your essays just two notches, from, say, a 5 to a 7, you're in a whole new scoring bracket. Study this section and you will improve at least one point, and probably more.

Think about this: unlike the old, familiar multiple-choice questions, the essays are completely new. You've never done anything like them before, so you may as well learn to do them in a way that will get you the most points. "What!?" you're thinking, "It's the multiple-choice that's weird; I write essays *all the time* in school."

Sorry, but you're mistaken. You write essays, true–but not AP Exam essays.

More Great Titles from The Princeton Review
Are you a master of composition? Are you also taking the AP English Language and Composition course? Check out *Cracking the AP English Language and Composition Exam*, our comprehensive prep guide for the test.

Your Teacher Knows You

You usually write essays for teachers who know you and (we hope) care about you. They know what your writing looked like at the beginning of the semester, they know whether you do your homework, they know whether you spend most of class daydreaming, they know you occasionally make brilliant comments in class, and they know your real passion is for track or violin or painting or science or maybe even writing.

When your teachers see your name at the top of the page they already know a thousand things about you, and all of it goes into their reading of what you write. The AP Reader, on the other hand, doesn't know you at all.

You Know Your Teacher

Second, and just as important, you don't know anything about the Reader of your AP essays. Who is she or he? In school, you know your teachers. You probably know what they want to hear. You may know that they detest misspellings, or that they love it when you use humor, or that they give extra credit for artistic originality. The AP essays are written to someone who is completely anonymous. When was the last time you wrote an essay to a total stranger for a grade?

Read It—Write It—Go!

AP essays are written under intense time restraints. You've probably never seen the excerpt or the prompt, but that's ok. You have the reading and writing strategies to tackle anything at this point. Your teachers have probably told you that good writing is rewriting; however, you don't have time to write and revise on the AP Exam. In a test setting, your draft is your final submission, and that means you have to be extra attentive to structural and content quality of your writing. The type of writing you'll complete for the AP Exam is kind of the opposite of how you should approach a writing task. In short, the "ready, set, write" approach of the AP Exam feels a little unnatural, but you can do it.

Your AP teacher should be drilling you with this style of essay for the duration of the course because it is the closest thing to writing for the AP Exam that you'll experience before test day. Most in-class tests are administered over materials you've studied and know well, but AP Exam prompts are most likely unfamiliar to you and the rest of the test takers. We call this a cold reading and writing—that just means this is a passage you're seeing and writing on for the first time. You will be graded on quality of writing and content, but remember that comprehension and originality are also important. Address the prompts directly; don't talk around the questions, and be sure to stay on top of ...be sure to stay on top of the Conventions of Standard English (CSE). If you write clearly and on topic, you should be just fine.

It may be a little nerve wracking to write this way, but remember that everyone else is in the same boat. This chapter is designed to give you the tools you need to understand how the essays are scored so that you can tailor your writing to fit the rubrics. We aren't necessarily teaching you how to write well: We're trying to teach you how to write a high-scoring AP essay. AP essays are different beasts, but they can be tackled!

ALL ABOUT AP ESSAY SCORING

The 0 to 9 Scale

Each of your essays will be graded according to a 9-point scale. Zero is the worst score you can get and 9 is the best. Students' scores are *not* spread out evenly over that range; the number of 9's does not equal the number of 5's. In fact, the numbers aren't even close. (On the literary argument, the curve is a little flatter and the average score a little lower, for reasons we'll discuss later.)

About 65 percent of all essays are scored in the middle range: 4, 5, and 6. The extreme scores taper away quickly. ETS doesn't tell its essay Readers to bunch up the scores this way, and they don't fudge the scores around later in order to produce this tidy bell curve. It works out this way because of the nature of student writing and the nature of essay scoring in general.

"Holistic" Scoring

The essays are scored "holistically." What this means is that the Reader goes through your essay and gets an overall impression. That impression is translated into a single number, 0 to 9, which is your essay's score. There is no checklist of points such as two points for style, two points for grammar, one point for vocabulary, and one point for writing about, say, the metaphor in paragraph one. Nothing like that. The rubric, such as it is, is a vague one.

Instead, about a week before the actual grading session, ETS goes through several essays to get a feel for the students' writing. Next, the ETS staff combs through the students' writing looking for the perfect representative 9 essay, the perfect 5, the perfect 3, and so on. These representative essays are the "sample essays." The Readers are given the samples and are trained for a day, during which they read student essays, compare them with the samples, and discuss the grades they would assign. The next day, the Readers start giving out the real grades. An ETS consultant checks graded essays at random to make sure the scoring is consistent. ETS tries hard to keep things standard and fair—for example, each Reader only grades one type of essay. But there's no way around the facts: The Readers are individual people making subjective judgments.

Any Changes? Go Online
At the time of the printing of this book, the College Board did NOT indicate that the essay scoring would be changing from what we describe here BUT you can always visit the College Board's website to check if any plans have been updated or changed.

THE READER WANTS AN ESSAY THAT'S EASY TO SCORE

Readers are dedicated high school and university instructors who take a week out of their year to come to one site and grade essays. Of course, they are compensated for their time, but at times the grading can become monotonous. You need to make sure that your essay stands out from the hundreds of essays that each Reader scores.

Your job is to write an essay that's obviously better than average. You have to let the Reader feel confident about giving you at least a seven. Usually, the essays are generic and have no distinctive style to them. Often the essays are plot summaries that barely address the question. In many cases, the question is rewritten and the essay does not explore the topic adequately or with skill. Slogging through these mediocre essays, the Reader gives a score and turns to the next essay hoping for that outstanding paper. Readers want to reward the writers for what they do well, but the topic must be addressed. If an essay starts out dull and poorly written but makes one completely original point right at the very end, the writer can be rewarded. Sometimes, however, there are too many grammar and spelling errors that distract the Reader and the one important statement that the writer makes is lost among the myriad errors on the paper. If you merely summarize the plot of the passage or do not adequately address the question, the Reader may have to decide on a score of 4 or 5. You want to make it as easy as possible for the scorer to think your essay is good. Before we get to the basic tips for making it easy for the Reader to give you a high score, let's look at a scoring guide AP Readers use.

Help Them Help You
Remember that your Reader wants to be persuaded and to read an essay that possesses stylistic flair. Stand out!

Here's a Tip!

It doesn't hurt to think like a reader as you practice the essays. In the free-response essays, you're going to see these verbs. Be sure to understand what they mean to the people who will be scoring you.

Analyze: Examine methodically and in detail the structure of the topic of the question in order to interpret and explain the passage.

Choose: Select a literary work from among provided choices.

Read: Look at or view printed directions and provided passages.

A Typical Scoring Guide

Every Reader gets a scoring guide for the essay he or she is grading. The scoring guides for AP essays are always very similar. We've taken a few scoring guides and combined them, taking out the details that are particular to a passage or a poem such as the author's name and the names of characters and places in the story or poem. Notice as you look over the scoring guide how little specific guidance ETS actually provides; the Readers are given a lot of leeway.

8 to 9

These are well-organized and well-written essays that clearly analyze the work and how the author dramatizes the situation. These essays use apt, specific references to the passage in order to discuss the author's use of elements such as diction, imagery, pace, and point of view. While not flawless, these papers demonstrate an understanding of the text and of the techniques of composition. These writers express their ideas skillfully and clearly.

9 (Excellent—has all the qualities of an 8 but isn't perfect)

8 (Excellent—better than a 7 but not quite a 9)

6 to 7

The content of these papers resembles that of higher scoring essays, but is less precise and less aptly supported. These essays deal with literary elements such as diction, imagery, and pace, but are less effective than the upper-range essays. Essays scored at 7 will generally exhibit fewer mechanical errors and draw from the passage more incisively than those scored at 6.

7 (Above Average—has all the qualities of a 6 but analysis is still surface-level in places and language isn't necessarily advanced)

5

These essays are superficial. Although not seriously in error about the content or literary technique of the passage, they miss the complexity of the piece and offer only a perfunctory analysis of how the subject has been dramatized. The treatment of elements such as diction and imagery is overly generalized or mechanical. The writing adequately conveys the writer's thoughts but the essays themselves are commonplace, poorly conceived, poorly organized, and simplistic.

6 (Slightly Above Average but Surface-y—there's an attempt at analysis, but it's more a Captain Obvious attempt than one that exposes original thought or information)

5 (Average/Adequate—there's an attempt at analysis but mostly the facts are just listed and no real connections are made)

3 to 4

These essays reflect an incomplete understanding of the passage and do not completely respond to the question. The discussion is unclear or simply misses the point. The treatment of literary elements is scanty or unconvincing, with little support drawn from the passage. Typically, these essays reveal a marked weakness in a writer's ability to handle the mechanics of written English.

4 (Below Average—analysis isn't evident and essay is mostly a laundry list of evidence)

3 (Inadequate—essay is incoherent in places, has lapses in CSE and exhibits no analysis)

1 to 2

These essays contain the errors found in essays receiving a score of 3 or 4, but to an even more pronounced degree. One- to two-point scoring essays either completely misunderstand the passage or fail to address the question. Typically, these essays are incoherent, too short, or both. The writing demonstrates little or no control of written English, either grammatically or organizationally.

2 (Off-topic—although it may be well-written and cohesive, the essay is off topic or makes no reference to the text at hand)

0 (Zero)

This is a response that fails to address the question. There may only be a reference to the task.

1 (Absent—you almost have to drool on paper to receive this score. Show up and complete the essay for a 2 or higher!)

Blank

This indicates that the response is completely off topic or that a response has not been made.

ANALYSIS OF THE SCORING GUIDE

Look carefully over this guide. What do you see? There are two major points we want stamped into your mind.

First, the high-scoring essays are clear. They aren't perfect, they aren't moving and profound—they're just clear. Practically every point made in the "8 to 9" description is just another way of saying *clear*. Well-organized means *clearly organized*. *Apt examples drawn from the passages* is another way of saying the writer has used *clear* examples. Clarity is the goal.

Second, notice the jump that happens at the 5 score. Notice how the whole tone of the guide changes. Suddenly the guide isn't talking about the fine points of answering the question; it's talking about the life-choking drabness of it all. You can imagine the Reader perusing such an essay and thinking, "Another one that's just like the last twenty essays." Five-point essays are just a trap—a trap that is easy to fall into if you aren't ready for the AP essays. Many 5-point essays are written by good students, many of them A-students, and half of those students *think they wrote a pretty good essay*. But they didn't; they just wrote a generic essay. These are the kinds of adjectives that show up in the 5 category of AP scoring guides: *mechanical, perfunctory, pedestrian, commonplace, adequate*. In other words, the same dull essay most students write (or try to write until they get totally lost, leading to an even lower score). After grading her fifty-fifth essay, the Reader writes down the score and turns to the next essay, praying, "Please, not another boring one."

If you understand what you read and can write in grammatical English, a 5 is your absolute low-end score. You will almost certainly do better than that with our help.

The Adequate Essay Formula

Almost every adequate essay is written by a student who doesn't know how to craft a real essay idea based on the question and thinks that the "essay formula" can somehow save him. Here's the thought process that invariably leads to a middle score: "Let's see…they want me to write about the language…well, what *else* would I write about? The whole *thing* is language. This is crazy. And 'how the author dramatized the story'—well, with *language* of course—great, that's about one sentence worth of essay. What am I going to say? I don't know what they want! Oh God. I can't sit here forever; *I've got to write something*. I know! I'll restate the question as a statement and then come up with three examples: one for diction, one for imagery, and one for point of view. Then I'll summarize it all for a conclusion. *That's the essay formula, right?* Okay, here goes."

Panic + No Idea of What Is Wanted = The Adequate Essay

This student is perfectly intelligent. The "formula" isn't crazy; in fact, it's taught all over the place. Restate the question as a statement. Support the statement with three examples from the passage. Summarize it for a conclusion.

It sounds good, but when a student tries to use it, he'll realize he still doesn't have one interesting thing to say. From beginning to end he'll feel lost, and writing the essay will feel like one big, meaningless exercise. He'll struggle and pick out bits of the passage that catch his eye and try to discuss them. He won't be exactly sure why they catch his eye, but he'll make up something. The discussion will be vague, overly generalized, and mechanical. (That's the description of adequate essays in the AP scoring guide, remember.) The adequate essay has to be vague, because if it were precise the student would reveal that he has no precise understanding of what he's supposed to be writing about. The formula results in a weak, boring essay.

The formula, however, is actually a heroic effort on the student's part, because you're not used to writing this way. When you're writing this way, a 5 is a success.

HOW TO MAKE IT EASY FOR THE READER TO GIVE YOU A HIGH SCORE

The most important part of your essay is the content. Your goal is to write meaty, content-filled essays that just blow the Reader away. But the Reader has to get to that content. There are a few vital things you must do to let your excellence come shining through with full impact. These basics have to do with the surface of your writing. That might seem cheap, but it's not. If the surface of your essay is clean and clear, the Reader can see through to the depths.

Neatness Counts

Studies have shown that neatly written essays earn higher scores on holistically graded tests. It's not fair, but it's a fact of life. Do everything in your power to make your essays readable. Write slowly. Write large. Write dark. Your writing doesn't have to be pretty, but it must be legible.

Take pains to be as neat as you possibly can. When a neatly written essay shows up, the wave of relief, of *love*, flooding the Reader is difficult to describe. A clearly written essay makes the Reader think, "Ah, now I can do my job!" A messy essay, however, will probably annoy Readers; they generally will try not to let poor handwriting affect the score, but if your essay is messy and difficult to read, they'll likely lose patience quickly.

If your penmanship isn't great and you've been writing essays on a computer for years, seriously consider printing or writing in italics, which is a sort of hybrid of cursive and printing. Trust us here. You may think this advice is ridiculous and that your handwriting shouldn't matter. The fact is, it does. As persecuted as you feel writing these essays, the Reader feels twice as persecuted reading them. Script is harder to read than print. If it weren't, this book would be written in a nice cursive typeface. If your normal handwriting looks like that on a wedding invitation or you're president of the Calligraphy Club at school, then you can use cursive. Otherwise, you should probably print (neatly!).

Keep It Clean

Don't underestimate the power of a tidy-looking essay. Write neatly, and write in paragraphs. No one wants to read a single paragraph that goes on for pages!

Indent

Your Reader's first impressions are crucial. Think about that character at the job interview with gum in his hair. If his battle isn't already lost, it's definitely an uphill fight the rest of the way. The overall look of your essay is a first impression. It's the smile on your face as you walk in the door. Your essay should look neat, organized, and clear. Make your paragraphs obvious. Indent twice as far as you normally would. When in doubt, make a paragraph. Ever look at a book, flip it open, and see nothing but one long paragraph? Your next thought is usually, "Oh please, don't make me have to read this!" That's exactly what the Reader thinks when she sees an essay without paragraphs. Make sure the Reader can see the paragraphs right away. Neat presentation, clear handwriting, paragraphs just screaming out, "I'm so organized, it's scary!" will have the Reader thinking, "Now here's a high-scoring student" before even reading a word.

Write Perfectly...for the First Paragraph

Your "second first impression" (in case you were wondering, that's an **oxymoron**—see the glossary) is the first paragraph of the essay. Take extra care with your first paragraph. If you're unsure about the spelling of a word, don't use it. If you're unsure how to punctuate the sentence, rewrite it in a way that makes you feel confident. Don't make any mistakes in the first paragraph. Don't fret as much about the rest of the essay; the Readers expect mistakes. But the first paragraph needs to be strong because it sets the tone. If you try to write the whole essay perfectly you'll write so slowly, or fill up your brain with so much worry, that you'll probably run out of time.

All you need is a few sentences to convince the Reader that you can write a good sentence when you want to. The glow of a good beginning carries over the whole essay. Mistakes later on look like minor errors not even worth bothering with. After all, the Reader's already seen that you can write. Mistakes at the very beginning do just the opposite—they look like telling signs of inability and a weak grasp of fundamental English mechanics. Take extra care at the beginning of your essay, then relax and just write (*neatly*).

Show Off Your Literary Vocabulary

Readers do not give great grades to students who merely parrot the prompt. A good way to show that you understand what the question is asking is by paraphrasing the prompt in your response. If the prompt asks about diction, knowing that diction means "word choice" is great. Articulating how the author uses a particular form of diction is even better. Be sure that you know the meaning of key literary terms that frequently appear on the exam (remember that glossary on page 277), and have some good synonyms at hand so you can display varied word choice. For poetry analysis, the big ones are **diction**, **imagery**, **metaphor**, **rhyme**, and **form**. For prose fiction, substitute **point of view** and **characterization** for rhyme and form. Using the word "speaker" to refer to the poetry narrator and "narrator" when dealing with prose fiction are conventions worth employing because they will show that you are comfortable with the modes of writing that Readers will recognize from teaching students about literature.

Use Snappy Verbs and Tasty Nouns

Spice up your writing. Try to write with some pizzazz. Don't let the test environment, the tension, or the anxiety caused by writing for a stranger take over your brain. Take risks: You may fall flat every so often, but the Reader will appreciate your effort and reward it. When you've gotten our essay techniques down, you'll understand that 90 percent of dull student writing on AP essays comes from confusion about what to write, which leads to inhibition. Don't be inhibited. Jazz it up a little. Show some stylistic flair.

Obviously, it's possible to go overboard here and if the Reader gets the impression you're just being silly, it won't help your score. It is important write about the task at hand, not just your musings on life. But a dash of glitter is much better than none at all. By the way, big, important-sounding phrases are not your ticket to a high score. They're an obvious sign that you're full of it. So please don't try to write this kind of gibberish: "When Judy initially perceived Roger's rapid ambulatory movement along the pedestrian walkway bordering the automotive thoroughfare, she experienced tachycardia."

The Questions

Each passage will be preceded by instructions to "Read the passage below carefully and then write a well-organized essay about…." These instructions may also contain some additional material orienting you to the passage, telling you things like who wrote it, the novel it was drawn from, and any other special information the test writers feel you need to know in order to understand the passage. Be sure to give the instructions a complete look in case there's any useful information there.

Vital Vocab

Key words to use in your essays include *diction, imagery, metaphor, rhyme, form, point of view,* and *characterization.*

Impressing Your Readers

If you write like someone who enjoys writing, the Readers will be impressed. For example, a student might write, "When Judy first sees Roger going down the street, she thinks he seems interesting." That's probably true, but what a bore! There are a thousand ways to liven up that sentence. It all depends on your personality and what is really happening in the story. How about, "When Judy first glimpses Roger dashing through the shadows of Sullivan Street, her heart flutters; she's already in love, she just doesn't know it yet." Or, "When Judy spots Roger flying down the sidewalk with the Sullivan Street gang nipping at his heels, she's dumbstruck by the wild vitality of his whirling limbs and blazing eyes." Cheesy? Over the top? Who cares? Nobody expects you to write like Marcel Proust. Actually, the Readers expect you to write like someone who's suffering through a tedious, nerve-wracking exercise, because that's exactly how most of the essays are written.

We aren't saying you have to write tangled, complex sentences either; in fact, you should try to avoid them. Great, long, looping sentences usually just wander off into error and confusion. All you need to do is pay attention to your word choice. When you find yourself using a generic verb like *look*, *see*, *says*, *walk*, *go*, *take*, or *give*, or a generic noun like *street*, *house*, *car*, or *man*, ask yourself whether there isn't a more precise, more colorful word you can use. Why write *house* when you're referring to a *mansion*, or *car* when you're really writing about a *jalopy*? Just a little bit of this goes a long way. It shows you're not scared and it might even look like you're having fun, which is very good.

Answer the Question

If you write a great essay that the Reader doesn't think addresses the question, you'll get a lousy score. All three essays, even the literary argument, will be directed, and the questions will tell you exactly what the test writers want—that's the theory, anyway. In reality, the questions can be infuriatingly vague but at the same time, not answering the question is the ultimate sin. Understanding and answering the question are crucial to writing a high-scoring essay.

Timing

Just like the passages in the multiple-choice section, the essay prompts should be answered in the order that works best for you. The one that appears easiest should be your first feat. Get your writing juices flowing, and soak up some of your confidence as you write. You want to write all three essays; therefore, you have to keep a handle on your time. Completing the easiest essay topic (for you) first will help you to save time for the harder responses. You're handed an essay booklet and given 120 minutes (2 hours) to complete all three essays. Ideally, you'll use only 40 minutes for each essay; however, how you choose to delegate your time between essays may mean more time for one writing task and less for another. Again, keep a watch close. Set it to 12:00. It's easy to see how much time has progressed and how much is left if you keep up with your time in this manner.

Certain members of the Big Six are your friends when answering questions like "what is the meaning?" and "how do I know it?" Do the character, settings, structure, and narration inform your answers? They certainly can; give them a whirl.

The Two Most Important Things to Ask Yourself When Tackling an AP Essay

1. What is the meaning?

2. How do I know it?

When you sit down to write an essay, you really can't write word one until you've deciphered what the prompt is asking you to do. Find the actual command and underline it, highlight it or put a star by it. Remind yourself as you write exactly what you're working to accomplish with your essay.

Summary

General Essay Information

o There are three essays: one essay on a prose fiction passage, one essay on one or two poetry analysis passages, and one essay on a work that you select (the literary argument).

o You have two hours to complete all three essays. Time yourself. Spend 40 minutes on each essay.

o The essays are a great place to improve your score.

Essay Scoring

o Each essay is scored by a Reader who grades only that particular type of essay.

o Each essay is given a score from 0 to 9.

o The essays are scored "holistically." There is no checklist of available points or conventional rubric.

o The Reader wants to read an essay that's easy to score.

o When in doubt, the Reader will push your score toward the middle range of scores.

o High-scoring essays are interesting, clear essays. Middle-scoring essays are generic and boring. Low-scoring essays are plain old bad.

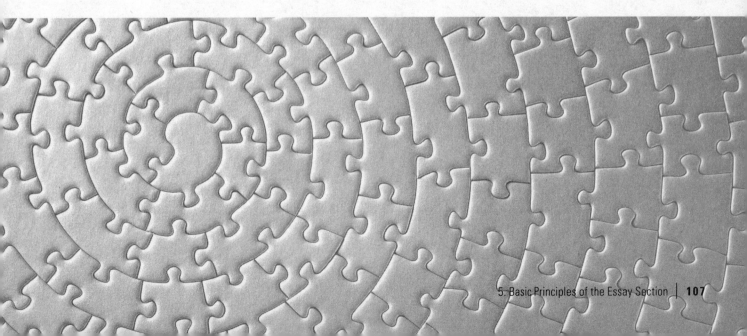

Presentation

o   Do everything in your power to make your essays readable.

o   Write carefully in large, dark handwriting. Your writing doesn't have to be pretty, but it must be clear.

o   Make your paragraph indentations easy to spot.

o   When in doubt, create a new paragraph.

o   Your first paragraph should be grammatically perfect. Your Reader will make a very quick judgment about your ability to write. Once the Reader has decided you can write a sentence, you'll get some slack later on (as long as you write neatly).

o   Have a solid literary vocabulary. You'll express yourself with greater clarity.

o   Try to use interesting, snappy verbs and nouns. It will impress the Reader and make her or him think you're comfortable, confident, and smart. Don't stress too much about overdoing the jazzy language, but don't go bananas.

o   Don't confuse interesting, snappy verbs and nouns with ten-dollar vocabulary words. Use the best, most precise word you can think of, not the one with the most syllables.

o   Understand the question. (Don't worry, there's much more on this subject in the next section.)

o   If you write a great essay that doesn't address the question, you won't get a great score.

o   Order the section. Do the essay you like best first, and save the worst one for last.

o   Manage your time—try to complete each essay in about 40 minutes.

Part V
Content Review and Practice for the AP English Literature and Composition Exam

Chapter 6
An Overview
of Literary
Movements

USING THIS OVERVIEW

If you have allotted yourself enough time, this section gives you the opportunity to familiarize yourself with the potential content of the exam. If you are reading this book months before you are to take the test, you can use this section in a methodical, poem-by-poem manner. By reading the 200 representative poems listed here, you will gain a thorough sense of the kinds of poems that the College Board chooses from when writing their tests. If you are using this book during crunch time and the test is a few weeks away, our suggestion is to read a poem or two from each movement and to familiarize yourself more broadly with the ideas associated with each movement. If you are picking up this book for the first time when you have only a few days left to study for the exam, then skip this section and go straight to Part III and Part IV of this book, which address cracking the test.

You may notice that this chapter is almost exclusively poetry-based. We have done it this way for two main reasons. First, students typically have more difficulty with poetry analysis than with prose friction. Reviewing this chapter will allow you to freshen up your knowledge on poets and poems, as well as the ideas associated with specific movements.

Second, if you are short on time, you can read more poems in a shorter amount of time than you can read full-length novels, plays, and short stories. Even reading a few poems from each movement will give you a sense of the notable characteristics of a specific period or genre.

Before getting into the overview, let's answer some questions you may have.

Check It Out

For a complete list of the authors and poets suggested by the College Board, download the AP English Literature and Composition course description at the College Board's website, **https://apstudent.collegeboard. org/apcourse/ap-english-literature-and-composition**. These authors and poems are also listed on pages 50–52 of this book. However, even though the College Board lists these poets as representative, that does not necessarily mean that these are the poets you will find on the exam. Getting to know the work of these poets, however, will give you a solid background with which to approach the poems that the test makers *do* choose.

Does the AP English Exam Require Certain Readings?

The test will choose texts from a variety of time periods and literary movements. While we have given you a historical survey you should learn, the College Board will be including a greater number of twentieth-century and contemporary works than those published before the twentieth century.

Though the Advanced Placement English curriculum avoids requiring any specific list of authors or texts to be taught, it does offer a *suggested* authors list. These authors tend to show up on the representative author list for the English literature exam and in this chapter:

W. H. Auden

Elizabeth Bishop

William Blake

Anne Bradstreet

Edward Kamau Brathwaite

Gwendolyn Brooks

Samuel Taylor Coleridge

H. D. (Hilda Doolittle)

Emily Dickinson

John Donne

T. S. Eliot

Robert Frost

Seamus Heaney

George Herbert

Langston Hughes

John Keats

Robert Lowell

Andrew Marvel

Marianne Moore

Sylvia Plath

Alexander Pope

Adrienne Rich

Anne Sexton

Percy Bysshe Shelley

Walt Whitman

William Carlos Williams

William Wordsworth

W. B. Yeats

For a more complete list, see pages 50–52.

How Can a List of Representative Authors Help Me Prepare for the Exam?

By itself, a list of authors or poets will not help you. To someone who doesn't know much about poetry, it will be more daunting than illustrative. However, when the list is reformatted to grouping writers by literary movement rather than listing them alphabetically, you may find that the once intimidating list has become much more understandable and helpful. You will still need to do a good deal of reading in order to apply the concepts of each literary movement to this exam, as no shortcut exists for becoming well-read. This chapter, however, will give you an efficient and organized method to follow, and a good overview of each movement.

What Is a Literary Movement?

A literary movement (or school of literature or poetry) is a grouping of writers who share similar aims, similar years of publication, and a similar base of operations. Some writers acknowledge or even encourage the idea of being seen as members of a single group, such as William Wordsworth and Samuel Taylor Coleridge, who consciously published some of their earlier poems in a volume that also included essays about their shared aesthetic ideals. Other writers actively reject the notion of being grouped, such as John Ashbery, who often maintains a bemused wariness when the term "New York School of poetry" is applied to his work.

How Can Knowing the Literary Movement of a Poem Help Me?

Regardless of whether or not the poets acknowledge their participation in a movement, you can put the following information to good use. For example, if you recognize that a poem is in the metaphysical tradition, you will have some immediate, ready-made ideas about form, structure, narration, content, figurative language and overall meaning. You will know to look for witty, surprising pairings of concrete and abstract ideas. You will expect irony and paradox to percolate beneath even the most religious content. And you will pay special attention to the ornate quality of the conceits. The moment you recognize that a poem is from the romantic tradition, you will be able to call up the phrases "sublime transcendence," "redemptive nature," and "imaginative power." If you have practiced using these phrases, you can use them appropriately for part of a meaningful and attentive analysis of the concrete particulars of a poem. Studying these poems within the framework of literary movements may also help you on the multiple-choice section, because knowing these bodies of work will help you recognize the kinds of questions and answers typically related to specific kinds of poems.

LITERARY MOVEMENT OVERVIEW

In the following overview, you will find some of the most important poets and poems of each movement as well as a list of what to look for in these poems. The best way to use these lists to help you crack the exam is to read some of the suggested poems and note where specific features of each movement show up in the poems. Practice writing an analytical essay on one poem from each movement, using at least two of the features from the list somewhere in your essay, and you'll be off to a great start. Or draft outlines of possible essays using different poems to familiarize yourself with the poems and relevant themes. The more familiar you are with some key phrases, the more likely you'll be to smoothly incorporate them into your analytical prose. Be warned: if you only adopt them without actually considering what they mean or without practicing using them, they are likely to seem artificial and may even hurt your score.

The following list concentrates on the schools of literature that are most commonly included on AP English Literature exams, and ignores other important movements that the College Board is less likely to emphasize. An excellent website for further study of the whole idea of literary movements is **www.poets.org**. It includes many links to brief poet biographies and sample poems from the movements listed in our overview. In fact, many of the representative poems in our overview were chosen because they are easily accessible through links from this website. Another great online resource is **www.poetryfoundation.org**.

Poetry Online
There are a bunch of great websites you can use to brush up on your knowledge of poems and poets. Check out **www.poets.org** and **www.poetryfoundation.org**.

Metaphysical Poetry

Representative Metaphysical Poets and Poems
- John Donne (1572–1631)—"A Valediction: Forbidding Mourning"; "The Sun Rising"; "Death Be Not Proud—Holy Sonnet X"; "Woman's Constancy"; "Love's Alchemy"
- George Herbert (1593–1633)—"Easter Wings"; "The Collar"; "Jordan (I)"; "Love (III)"; "The Windows"
- Andrew Marvell (1621–1678)—"The Mower's Song"; "The Mower to the Glow-Worms"; "The Mower Against Gardens"; "The Garden"; "To His Coy Mistress"

A Quick Definition
Metaphysical poetry is a mostly seventeenth-century English poetic mode that breaks with earlier Renaissance ideas about romantic poetry. Instead of following in the footsteps of the troubadours, Petrarch and Shakespeare, who often wrote love poetry that placed the object of their poems on a pedestal, metaphysical poems often exhibit introspective meditations on love, death, God, and human frailty. The poems of John Donne, for example, are much more realistic about sexual relationships. Metaphysical poetry is famous for its obscurity (and therefore a favorite choice of the College Board).

Get It Donne
If metaphysical poetry comes up on the test (and it probably will), think John Donne. Review some of the poems listed here before test day if you need a refresher.

What to Look for in Metaphysical Poetry
- Wit, irony, and paradox are paramount—wit is often seen in the pairing of dissimilar objects into the service of a clever, ironic analogy or paradoxical conceit. For example, see how Donne's speaker in "A Valediction: Forbidding Mourning" uses astronomy and math to illustrate his deep abiding love for his wife.
- Elaborate stylistic maneuvers (ornamental conceits, dazzling rhymes) are pulled off with aplomb. For example, look at how Herbert uses relative line length, stanza shape, rhyme, and repetition in "Easter Wings" to underscore the importance of human humility.
- Huge shifts in scale proliferate (for example, ants to planets). Consider how Marvell's speaker in "The Mower to the Glow-Worms" conflates glow-worms and comets, for example.
- These formal tendencies are used by metaphysical poets to talk about deep philosophical issues: the passage of time; the difficulty of ever being sure of any one thing; the uneasy relationship of human beings to one another and to God; the fearful, obsessive qualities that death often inspires in human consciousness. Sometimes, after all of the elaborate style is reduced and its content summarized, the truism that is left can seem clichéd. Most of the beauty of metaphysical poetry is in the dramatic unfolding of that truth through techniques like irony, conceits, and scale shifts.

Augustans

Representative English Augustan Poets and Poems

- John Dryden (1631–1700)—"Mac Flecknoe"; "Marriage a-la-mode"; "Absalom and Achitophel"
- Alexander Pope (1688–1744)—"The Rape of the Lock"; "Windsor Forest"; "Epitaph on Sir Isaac Newton"

Related Prose Fiction and Plays

- *Gulliver's Travels* and "A Modest Proposal" by Jonathan Swift (1667–1745)
- *A Beggar's Opera* by John Gay (1685–1732)

A Quick Definition

Augustan poetry is best known for its rhymed, heroic-couplet satire. These pairs of lines in iambic pentameter often produce great forward propulsion, and most students report that reading them aloud helps with comprehension. Coming between the baroque metaphysical poets and the enthusiastically sincere romantic poets, the wickedly funny Augustan poets went back to antiquity for their inspiration. They translated Greek and Roman epics into English using heroic couplets and wrote their own original work based on classical forms.

What to Look for in Augustan Poetry

- Wit, irony, and paradox are still as important here as they were for the metaphysical poets, but one must also add brevity to the list when discussing the Augustans. Their poems can be quite long but because they employ the heroic couplet so pointedly, their observations are often quite pithy. As Pope put it in his poem "Essay on Criticism," "True wit is nature to advantage dress'd,/What oft was thought, but ne'er so well express'd."
- The ongoing subject of Augustan poetry is human frailty. Even when these poets used biblical subjects and allusions for their plots, as Dryden does in "Absalom and Achitophel," the tone taken often mocks human behavior: "What cannot praise effect in mighty minds, When flattery soothes, and when ambition blinds!"
- These poets were also likely to dress absurdly mundane plots (such as the secret cutting of a noble maiden's hair in "Rape of the Lock") in the outward appearance of heroic epic poetry for comic effect.
- Current events figure in these poems, either allegorically or directly. In his famous epitaph for Sir Isaac Newton, Pope wrote: "Nature and nature's laws lay hid in night; God said 'Let Newton be' and all was light," which addresses the ongoing controversies between the forces of religion and science in Europe's eighteenth century. John Dryden's poem "Mac Flecknoe" satirizes another prominent poet of his day and takes sides in contemporary political debates, similar to how a present-day poet with Democratic leanings might make fun of Republican leaders.

Romantic Poetry

Representative English Romantic Poets and Poems
- William Wordsworth (1770–1850)—"I Wandered Lonely as a Cloud"; "Composed Upon Westminster Bridge Sept. 3, 1802"; "Lines Composed a Few Miles Above Tintern Abbey"; "My Heart Leaps Up When I Behold"; "Lucy"
- Percy Shelley (1792–1822)—"Ozymandias"; "Ode to the West Wind"; "Adonais—An Elegy on the Death of John Keats"; "The Cloud"; "Hymn to Intellectual Beauty"
- John Keats (1795–1821)—"Ode on a Grecian Urn"; "When I Have Fears that I May Cease to Be"; "To Autumn"; "La Belle Dame Sans Merci"; "Ode to a Nightingale"
- William Blake (1757–1827)—"The Tiger"; "The Lamb"; "A Poison Tree"; "The Sick Rose"

Representative American Transcendental Poets and Poems
- Ralph Waldo Emerson (1803–1882)—"Ode to Beauty"; "The World-Soul"; "Song of Nature"
- Walt Whitman (1819–1892)—"When I Heard the Learn'd Astronomer"; "A Noiseless Patient Spider"; "Crossing Brooklyn Ferry"; "There Was a Child Went Forth"; "Song of the Open Road"

Related European Prose Fiction
- *Ivanhoe* by Sir Walter Scott (1771–1832)
- *Les Miserables* by Victor Hugo (1802–1885)

Related American Prose Fiction
- *The Scarlet Letter* by Nathaniel Hawthorne (1804–1864)
- "The Poet," an essay by Ralph Waldo Emerson that inspired Whitman to become a poet;
- "Walking," an essay by Henry David Thoreau (1817–1862)

A Quick Definition
Romantic poetry written in English is a (mostly) nineteenth-century English and American poetic mode that breaks with earlier neoclassical ideas about poetry by specifically emphasizing that these poems were written in, as Wordsworth calls it, "the real language of men" and were about "common life." This poetry is emotional and often enthusiastic in its embracing of the large, impressive forces of nature and the infinite resources of the human imagination. Famous for having given us the image of tormented poets idly strolling over moors, looking through their wind-whipped hair at a tulip, these poems are often used on AP Exams because of their strong thematic content.

What to Look for in Romantic Poetry

- Natural imagery redeems the imagination of the individual stuck in the crowded, industrial torment of the city. See Wordsworth's "I Wandered Lonely as a Cloud," where the speaker, on a couch, imagines himself floating above a "host of golden daffodils."

In a Nutshell
Romanticism summed up: nature imagery, imagination, and transcendence.

- The human imagination empowers the individual to escape from society's strictures, established authority, and even from fear of death. Think about how Whitman's speaker in "When I Heard the Learn'd Astronomer" needs to leave the room where the lecture is happening in order to better understand the perfect silence of the stars.
- The sublime (impressively big, obscure, or scary) is the main descriptive mode rather than the "merely beautiful." Look at how the speaker in Shelley's "Ozymandias" relies on words such as "vast," "colossal," and "boundless" to create a sense of how intimidating the statue must have been, and actually is.
- Transcendence is the ultimate goal of all the romantic poets. Wordsworth turns a city into a beating heart in "Composed Upon Westminster Bridge Sept. 3, 1802"; in "Ode to the West Wind," Shelley turns the west wind into poetic inspiration; Keats turns an old urn into a meditation on life and death in his "Ode on a Grecian Urn"; Whitman in his "Noiseless Patient Spider" turns a spider into a human soul surrounded by a vacant, vast expanse, yearning to be connected. What do all these poems have in common? Each finds transcendence in the ordinary.

The Symbolists

Representative French Symbolist Poets and Poems

- Charles Baudelaire (1821–1867)—"Spleen"; "*Harmonie du soir* (Harmonies of Evening)"; "*Correspondances* (Correspondences)"
- Stéphane Mallarmé (1842–1898)—"*L'Apres-midi d'un faune* (The Afternoon of a Faun)"; "*Soupir* (Sigh)"; "*Salut* (Salutation)"
- Paul Verlaine (1844–1896)—"*Il pleure dans mon couer* (It Rains in My Heart)"; "*Chanson d'automne* (Autumn Song)"; "*Langueur* (Languor)"
- Arthur Rimbaud (1854–1891)—"*Le bateau ivre* (The Drunken Boat)"; "*Voyelles* (Vowels)"

Symbolist-Influenced Poets Who Wrote in English

- Oscar Wilde (1854–1900)—"Chanson"; "Impression du Matin"; "Harmony"
- W. B. Yeats (1865–1939)—"The Lake Isle of Innisfree"; "Towards Break of Day"; "Broken Dreams"; "Leda and the Swan"; "Sailing to Byzantium"

- Arthur Symons (1865–1945)—"White Heliotrope"; "Colour Studies"; "Perfume"
- T. S. Eliot (1888–1965)—"The Love Song of J. Alfred Prufrock"; "Ash Wednesday"

Related Symbolist Prose Fiction
- *A Rebours* (Against the Grain) by Joris-Karl Huysmans (1848–1907)
- *The Picture of Dorian Gray* by Oscar Wilde (1854–1900)

A Quick Definition
The symbolists are often considered the link between the schools of romanticism and modernism. Full of the yearning for transcendence, which they inherited from the romantic poets, the symbolists took this yearning in a more decadent and sensual direction, foreshadowing the kind of sexual frankness one often finds in modernist work. Many of their poems will seem obscure on the first few readings, and College Board test makers are probably not going to use any of the French symbolists on the exam, but if you take the time to analyze the deep symbols and intuitive associations found in their work, you will be in a better place when you are asked to interpret a poem by Yeats or Eliot, whose work often does show up on the exam.

What to Look for in Symbolist Poetry
- Many symbolist poems deal with the crepuscular (dusk and dawn), and with the time between waking and sleep. Consider Wilde's "*Impression du Matin*." Dreams or dream states figure prominently in many symbolist works of art, as dream experiences afford human beings one of the best opportunities to explore the relationship between states.
- *Synaesthesia*, the using of one sense to describe another, proved to be a favorite mode of the symbolists. For example, Rimbaud attributes colors and sounds to the different vowels in his poem "*Voyelles*."
- The French symbolists proved particularly adept at using words with three or four simultaneous meanings, creating a resonance among groups of these words. For example, Mallarmé in "*Salut*" toasts younger poets gathered around a white tablecloth that can simultaneously be seen as a white sail for a boat and a white, blank page upon which these poets will eventually write. By carefully choosing his words, the speaker of this poem keeps all three meanings viable throughout this beautifully dense poem.
- Often associated with the "art for art's sake" movement that placed aesthetics and form above political relevance or reducible message, symbolist poetry finds its artistic counterparts in these kinds of paintings: Whistler's *Nocturne Blue and Gold—Old Battersea Bridge*, Turner's *Moonlight*, and Monet's *Waterloo Bridge in Grey Weather*.

Symbolists and Music
As you can tell from the items in this list, symbolists were drawn to the properties of music and attempted to create some of the same effects in their poetry by concentrating on simultaneous effects (similar to harmony) and by choosing mellifluous words meant to inspire a kind of languor in the reader.

Modernism

Representative Modernist Poets and Poems

- Wallace Stevens (1879–1955)—"Thirteen Ways of Looking at a Blackbird"; "The Snow Man"; "Peter Quince at the Clavier"; "Anecdote of the Jar"
- William Carlos Williams (1883–1963)—"Red Wheelbarrow"; "This is Just To Say"; "Danse Russe"; "Spring and All"; "The Great Figure"; "The Yachts"; "Desert Music"; "The Descent"
- H. D. (Hilda Doolittle) (1886–1961)—"Star Wheels in Purple"; "Helen"; "Heat"
- Marianne Moore (1887–1972)—"Poetry"; "Baseball and Writing"; "To a Snail"
- T. S. Eliot (1888–1965)—"Love Song of J. Alfred Prufrock"; "Ash Wednesday"
- e. e. cummings (1894–1962)—"anyone lived in a pretty how town"; "next to of course god america i"; "spring is like a perhaps hand"; "i sing of Olaf glad and big"
- Ezra Pound (1885–1972)—"In Durance"; "In a Station of the Metro"; "Hugh Selwyn Mauberley"; "The Cantos"

Related Modernist Prose Fiction

- *A Portrait of the Artist as a Young Man* by James Joyce (1882–1941)
- *Mrs. Dalloway* by Virginia Woolf (1882–1941)
- *As I Lay Dying* by William Faulkner (1897–1962)
- *Heart of Darkness* by Joseph Conrad (1857–1924)
- *The Awakening* by Kate Chopin (1851–1904)

A Quick Definition

Modernism is often characterized as a revolutionary force. In the field of science, Einstein was reassessing time, space, and our relationship to these concepts. In global politics, two calamitous world wars bracketed decades of intense technological advances in the mass killing of soldiers and civilians. In the field of visual arts, surrealism, futurism, abstraction, and cubism overthrew most accepted traditional ideas about pictorial representation. Not surprisingly, literature in the twentieth century also saw a thorough questioning of what had come before and a willingness to experiment with new forms, a goal shared with the symbolists but one with which the modernists were much more daring. Modern poets valued the idea of "make it new." Ezra Pound coined the phrase and encouraged writers to take old topics and revamp them with a modern twist. Modernists believed that poetry should be valuable and understandable. Some, like Marianne Moore, even argued that a poet who writes convoluted and frustrating verse just for the purpose of complexity is no poet at all. Modern poets and writers were often expatriates disillusioned with American life.

What to Look for in Modernist Poetry

- Chock full of allusions, these poems reduce human experience to fragments. For example, e.e. cummings breaks language down into its component parts, using pieces of overheard conversation alongside more grandiose pronouncements. In Hilda Doolittle's 18-line poem entitled "Helen," she assumes the reader has a working knowledge of the incident that prompts the Trojan War (chronicled in *The Iliad* by Homer) to make sense of why "All Greece hates/the still eyes in the white face."

- Some of these poems are influenced by cubism, and they try to see the world from as many points of view as possible at the same time. Wallace Stevens's "Thirteen Ways of Looking at a Blackbird" comes in thirteen sections, each of which refers explicitly or implicitly to a blackbird, and can be seen as a kind of analogue to Picasso's cubist presentation of a still life in *Guitar, Bottle, Bowl of Fruit and Glass on Table*.

- Romantic notions of the importance of individuality were overtaken by systematic representations of human consciousness in the emerging fields of psychology and sociology, so poems from this time are often concerned with how an individual relates to his environment (see Eliot's "The Love Song of J. Alfred Prufrock") or how the environment and setting help to create the individual (see Stevens's "The Snow Man").

- Romantic yearning for freedom (the bloody excesses of the French Revolution are an extreme example) was usurped by proponents of political systems, such as socialism or fascism, that saw human beings not as individuals but as servants of the state (see the Russian Revolution and the rise of the Third Reich). Modernist poems sometimes efface individuality, choosing to focus on machines or other inanimate objects rather than nature or human beings. For example, William Carlos Williams's "The Yachts" contains brutal imagery: "Arms with hands grasping seek to clutch at the prows/ Bodies thrown recklessly in the way are cut aside./It is a sea of faces about them in agony, in despair/until the horror of the race dawns staggering the mind." But this use of imagery does not ever really feel personal; it feels more like a representation of mass death.

The Harlem Renaissance

Representative Poets and Poems of the Harlem Renaissance

- Paul Laurence Dunbar (1872–1906)—"Frederick Douglass"; "Sympathy"; "We Wear the Mask"
- Claude McKay (1889–1948)—"If We Must Die"; "The White House"; "The Tropics in New York"
- Langston Hughes (1902–1967)—"I, Too, Sing America"; "The Negro Speaks of Rivers"; "Theme for English B"; "Montage of a Dream Deferred"
- Countee Cullen (1903–1946)—"Incident"; "For A Lady I Know"; "Yet Do I Marvel"

Related Prose Fiction from the Harlem Renaissance

Their Eyes Were Watching God by Zora Neale Hurston (1891–1960), *Passing* by Nella Larsen (1891–1964), *Black Boy* and *Native Son* by Richard Wright (1908–1960), and *Invisible Man* by Ralph Ellison (1913–1994)

A Quick Definition

Art associated with the Harlem Renaissance was mostly created in the first half of the twentieth century, after World War I, during the movement of African Americans to northern industrial cities (called the Great Migration). Harlem in New York City was one of the most famous African American neighborhoods during this time. Jazz, poetry, painting, novels, dance, electrified blues, and the study of folklore thrived in these neighborhoods and took on many of the same concerns as the modernists.

What to Look for in Harlem Renaissance Poetry

- Content is often directly related to African American concerns and issues of the time. Consider Dunbar's "Frederick Douglass," which elegizes the famous abolitionist in such a way as to draw attention to his continuing positive influence on the culture: "Oh, Douglass, thou hast passed beyond the shore,/But still thy voice is ringing o'er the gale!"
- Many Harlem Renaissance poems rely on repetitive structure similar to blues lyrics (see Dunbar's "Sympathy") or on fragmented structure similar to jazz improvisation (see Hughes's "Montage of a Dream Deferred").
- Several of these poets, especially Langston Hughes, consciously sought a new American idiom alongside other African American artists such as blues singer Bessie Smith. Other poets combined European forms like the sonnet with a content and a tone more related to African American concerns, such as McKay's "If We Must Die."

Postmodernism

A Quick Definition

Academic controversy continues as to whether works labeled postmodern are merely a later version of the modernist tendencies developed in the twentieth century or whether they are actually part of a new and separate movement. Usually the most that academics can agree on regarding the postmodern is that the term is insufficient. Most postmodern works were created in the second half of the twentieth century, and though they share some of the concerns and motivations of modernists, they often take these principles to a much different end. If Einstein's theory of relativity represents the modern era, Heisenberg's uncertainty principle is the emblem of the postmodern. In reductive terms, the uncertainty principle holds that one cannot know both the speed and the location of an object simultaneously, which introduces a note of chance or chaos into scientific inquiry.

Even more so than other literary labels, "postmodern" is a label that is rejected by the majority of artists who are labeled as such. Instead, smaller contingents of writers exist, often in conflict with other postmodern groups. These smaller groups include the **Beats**, the **confessional** poets, **the Black Arts movement, the Black Mountain school,** and **the New York School of poets**. Each of these groups is dealt with separately below because each had such a different aesthetic program. A few statements can be applied to postmodern art in general, however, and will be discussed before going into the specific sub-movements.

What to Look for in Postmodern Poetry

- Parody, irony, and narrative instability often inform the tone.
- Allusions are just as likely to be made to popular culture as they are to classical learning.
- Strictly binary concepts (hot and cold; black and white) often collapse. Here, the predominant ideas are ones that spread across a spectrum rather than fit strictly into one box or the other.
- There is no real center. The Internet is a perfect example of a postmodern invention.
- The surface is often more interesting to postmodern artists than any ideas of depth. The following quote is attributed to Andy Warhol, a kind of patron saint of postmodernism and a notorious wig wearer: "Wear a wig and people notice the wig. Wear a silver wig and people notice the silver."

The Beats

Representative Beat Poets and Poems

- Lawrence Ferlinghetti (b. 1919)—"A Coney Island of the Mind"; "The Changing Light"; "Vast Confusion"; "Wild Dreams of a New Beginning"
- Allen Ginsberg (1926–1997)—"Howl"; "America"; "A Supermarket in California"; "Kaddish"
- Gregory Corso (1930–2001)—"Marriage"; "Bomb"; "The Mad Yak"
- Gary Snyder (b. 1930)—"Four Poems for Robin"; "For All"; "Hay for the Horses"

Related Beat Prose Fiction

Naked Lunch by William S. Burroughs (1914–1997) and *On the Road* by Jack Kerouac (1922–1969)

A Quick Definition

A post-World War II phenomenon, the Beats used different settings over the years to practice their brand of hallucinogenic, visionary, and anti-establishment art: New York City (many of the original group were Columbia University students or dropouts), San Francisco, Tangiers, Prague, and Mexico City witnessed Beat events, as did many places in between.

Beat poets were quite good at mythologizing themselves, sharing a sense of personal frankness with the confessional poets and a sense of interdisciplinary energy (especially in its overlap with music) with the New York School. Buddhism was important to many members (especially Gary Snyder) as were many of the tenets of William Blake's version of romanticism, such as the importance of the individual, the imagination freed from society's constraints, and the yearning for transcendence. In Ferlinghetti's "The Changing Light," a reader can feel the deep connection Beats often felt to nature even as the speaker of this poem is describing a city scene. In Corso's "Marriage," the oppositional stance the Beats took toward the suburban bourgeoisie is in bold relief. Ginsberg's "America" shares much of the same satirical tone, but Ginsberg was also capable of writing angry, ranting, Whitmanesque masterpieces like "Howl" and a tender, meditative elegy for his mother in "Kaddish."

"First thought, best thought" describes the aesthetic ideal of the Beat poet. Moved by jazz improvisation and Buddhist ideas of impermanence, these poets considered themselves the chroniclers of their age. Politics directly informs many of their poems, either through specific references to members of the government or specific references to issues important to them, such as Gary Snyder's commitment to the environment.

Confessional Poets

Representative Confessional Poets and Poems
- John Berryman (1914–1972)—"Dream Song 1"; "Dream Song 4"; "Dream Song 29"
- Robert Lowell (1917–1977)—"Skunk Hour"; "For the Union Dead"; "Memories of West Street and Lepke"; "Home After Three Months Away"
- Anne Sexton (1928–1967)—"Wanting to Die"; "The Truth the Dead Know"; "For My Lover, Returning to his Wife"
- Sylvia Plath (1932–1963)—"Daddy"; "Lady Lazarus"; "Balloons"; "Ariel"

Related Confessional Prose Fiction
The Bell Jar by Sylvia Plath

A Quick Definition
As the name suggests, confessional poets took the personal pronouns (I, me, my) seriously and explored intimate content in their poetry. Love affairs, suicidal thoughts, fears of failure, ambivalent or downright violent opinions about family members, and other autobiographically sensitive material moved front and center in these poets' works. As Berryman wrote, using his alter ego "Henry" as a mask for his own feelings of distress in "Dream Song 1," "I don't see how Henry, pried/ open for all the world to see, survived." These poets "pried open" their innermost thoughts and opened them for all the world to see, even if it meant sharing one's troubled feelings about one's father, as Plath did in a poem full of Holocaust imagery entitled *Daddy*, writing "Daddy, I have had to kill you./You died before I had time…"

In a cultural milieu much more discreet than that of the current era, these poets ripped the façade off an outwardly comfortable suburban life to reveal the doubts and anxieties that kept the occupants awake at night behind white picket fences. For example, Robert Lowell wrote in "Home After Three Months Away" how he felt when faced with the details of his life such as the recent birth of his child: "I keep no rank nor station./Cured, I am frizzled, stale and small." And Anne Sexton wrote with existential dread, "Since you ask, most days I cannot remember./I walk in my clothing, unmarked by that voyage./Then the almost unnameable lust returns." The "unnameable lust" is the speaker's desire for death, and she writes eloquently about it at a time when mental illness was much less understood or accommodated by law than it is today.

More than just poets who shared personal stories with their readers, these poets also invested a good deal of time and effort in their craft, constructing verse that paid careful attention to rewritten prosody.

Poetry and Art
Many of the New York School poets wrote art criticism, while Frank O'Hara even rose to the rank of assistant curator for the Museum of Modern Art.

New York School of Poets

Representative New York School Poets

- Barbara Guest (1920–2006)—"The Blue Stairs"; "Wild Gardens Overlooked by Night Lights"; "Sound and Structure"; "Echoes"
- Kenneth Koch (1925–2002)—"One Train May Hide Another"; "Talking to Petrizia"; "To Various Persons Talked to All at Once;" "Variations on a Theme by William Carlos Williams"
- Frank O'Hara (1926–1966)—"In Memory of My Feelings"; "The Day Lady Died"; "A Step Away from Them"; "Lines to a Depressed Friend"
- John Ashbery (b. 1927–2017)—"The Painter"; "The Instruction Manual"; "Daffy Duck in Hollywood"; "The New Higher"

A Quick Definition

New York School poets saw themselves as fellow travelers of the abstract expressionist school of painters. Their aesthetic mode overlapped with Beat spontaneity and confessional-poet frankness, but was much more ironic and more interested in the surreal combination of high art and popular art allusions. Many of their poems, especially those called "Lunch Poems" by Frank O'Hara, seem to be catalogs of what one might see on a walk in midtown Manhattan. The urban environment, of course, allows for many spontaneous intersections. A taxi goes by a construction site. A billboard advertising tourism to a natural paradise hovers over a traffic jam, providing ironic contrast.

These poets often see themselves as helping the reader see the world in new and different ways. For example, Guest writes "The Blue Stairs" in an ekphrastic mode (or a mode based on putting visual art into words), "Now I shall tell you/why it is beautiful/Design: extraordinary/color: cobalt blue" while O'Hara writes in "The Day Lady Died," an elegy for Billie Holiday, "and I am sweating a lot by now and thinking of/leaning on the john door in the 5 SPOT/while she whispered a song along the keyboard/to Mal Waldron and everyone and I stopped breathing." Guest's speaker describes looking at a painting while O'Hara's speaker describes hearing a song at a jazz club, but both speakers are interested in inspiring us to look or listen again.

Surrealists wanted to jar their audience's senses by juxtaposing uncommon objects. John Ashbery mixes "Rumford's Baking Powder, a celluloid earring, Speedy Gonzales, the latest from Helen Topping Miller's fertile Escritoire" in his poem "Daffy Duck in Hollywood," and Kenneth Koch consciously mixes tones in his poem "To Various Persons Talked to All at Once," writing, "I suppose I wanted to impress you./It's snowing./The Revlon Man has come from across the sea./This racket is annoying./We didn't want the baby to come here because of the hawk./What are you reading?/In what style would you like the humidity to explain?" These poets reveled in the combination of the serious and the silly, the profound and the absurd, the highly formal and the casual.

Black Arts Movement

Representative Black Arts Movement Poets and Poems
- Gwendolyn Brooks (1917–2000)—"The Bean Eaters"; "We Real Cool"; "The Lovers of the Poor"; "The Mother"
- Amiri Baraka (also known as LeRoi Jones) (b. 1934–2014)— "Preface to a Twenty Volume Suicide Note"; "Black Art"; "Ka'Ba"; "In the Funk World"
- Sonia Sanchez (b. 1934)—"Ballad"; "Malcolm"; "I Have Walked a Long Time"; "For Sweet Honey in the Rock"
- Ntozake Shange (b. 1948–2018)—"My Father Is a Retired Magician"; "For Colored Girls Who Have Considered Suicide When the Rainbow Is Enuf"

A Quick Definition
These poets were often associated with members of the Black Power movement who grew frustrated with the pace of the changes enacted by the civil rights movement of the 1950s and 1960s. These poems are often politically charged, unrepentant challenges to the white establishment.

Black Mountain Poets

Representative Black Mountain Poets and Poems
- Charles Olson (1910–1970)—Excerpts from *The Maximus Poems*
- Denise Levertov (1923–1997)—"The Mutes"; "In California During the Gulf War"; "When We Look Up"
- Robert Creeley (1926–2005)—"Age"; "For Love"; "A Wicker Basket"; "America"

A Quick Definition
Besides teaching in the same place (Black Mountain College in Black Mountain, North Carolina) for some time and sharing an abiding interest in process over product, these poets seem quite different. Olson's poems spill across the page while Creeley's lines compress into tight corners. Levertov tackled political issues head-on, but Olson delved deeply into the archeology and history of Gloucester, Massachusetts.

Other Important Representative Poets and Poems

Along with the 176 poems listed in the previous section, there are 25 more poems listed in the following section. The poets and poems listed below are important but do not fit easily into the structure of literary movements.

Emily Dickinson (1830–1886). Writing in near absolute isolation during the transcendental period, this astonishingly prolific and powerful poet does not easily fit into the transcendental rubric, and shares many more attributes with the compressed wit and irony of the metaphysical poets. Poems: "Because I could not stop for death"; "I heard a fly buzz when I died"; "Tell all the truth but tell it slant"; "I measure every grief I meet."

Robert Frost (1874–1963). Frost was active during modernism's heyday, concerning himself with more traditionally minded verse forms and a locally colored content that cloaked a profound philosophical vein. Poems: "Out, Out"; "Birches"; "The Death of the Hired Man"; "Mending Wall"; "Design"; "Stopping by Woods on a Snowy Evening."

W. H. Auden (1907–1973). Auden, one of the giants of twentieth-century literature, wrote the first half of his poems as an English citizen before World War II, and the second half of his poems as an American citizen after World War II. His work is more similar to the modernists than to any other school, but he really transcends labels. Poems: "As I Walked Out One Evening"; "In Memory of W. B. Yeats"; "The Unknown Citizen"; "Musée des Beaux Arts."

Elizabeth Bishop (1911–1979). Sometimes placed with the confessional poets because of her friendship with Robert Lowell, Bishop is more reticent than the confessional poets. Poems: "In the Waiting Room"; "Filling Station"; "At the Fishhouses"; "One Art"; "The Moose."

Adrienne Rich (1929–2012). An important feminist and political poet, Rich shares some background with the confessional poets, but takes the role of the poet in society so seriously that she transcended the personal and became a kind of icon. Poems: "Diving into the Wreck"; "North American Time"; "Aunt Jennifer's Tigers"; "Miracle Ice Cream."

Seamus Heaney (1939–2013). Heaney uses rural imagery to take on issues of identity, from the post-colonial confusion of what it means to be Irish to the late twentieth-century confusion of what it means to be a poet. Poems: "Digging"; "The Harvest Bow."

REFLECT

Respond to the following questions:

- For which content topics discussed in this chapter do you feel you have achieved sufficient mastery to answer multiple-choice questions correctly?

- For which content topics discussed in this chapter do you feel you have achieved sufficient mastery to discuss them effectively in an essay?

- For which content topics discussed in this chapter do you feel you need more work before you can answer multiple-choice questions correctly?

- For which content topics discussed in this chapter do you feel you need more work before you can discuss them effectively in an essay?

- What parts of this chapter are you going to re-review?

- Will you seek further help, outside of this book (such as from a teacher, tutor, or AP students), on any of the content in this chapter—and, if so, on what content?

Chapter 7
Poetry Analysis
Questions

READING POETRY LIKE A PRO

Answering multiple-choice questions about poetry analysis passages involves many of the same principles as does answering questions about prose fiction. There are some differences, however.

First, the poetry analysis passages tend to contain more questions that rely on knowledge than the prose fiction passages. You will certainly see a question or two on the literary devices (for example, personification or metaphor) in the poem. You might see a question about the way a line scans or what the rhyme scheme is called, but these are nothing to worry about: Recent tests have not included a single question on scansion or the names of classical poetic forms. The test writers do, however, like to use poetry for questions about grammar, because poets use the kind of tangled syntax that makes for challenging grammar questions.

Second, the poetry you'll see on the AP Exam tends to make for harder reading than the prose fiction passages. Hard, but not impossible. There's a certain style of poetry that tends to appear on the AP English Lit Exam. In order to write questions properly, the test writers are limited in the kind of material they can use. As a result, you won't see poems that stretch language and meaning to its limits, or poems that are open to such a variety of interpretations that asking meaningful multiple-choice questions about them is too difficult. Nor will you see beautiful and elegant but direct and simple poems. Also, you won't see any especially "out there" or experimental postmodern poetry on the exam. The AP Exam generally features poems of 30 to 70 lines that use difficult language to make a precise point. The poem below and the questions that follow should give you a good idea of what to expect on the test. This is an excellent place to practice what you've learned in previous chapters. For even more practice, work through the two poetry analysis drills and the bonus questions at the end of this chapter.

Use all of the techniques we've taught you.

- Read the poem as prose.
- Focus on the main idea.
- When answering the questions, use POE and Consistency of Answers.
- Be sure to read before and after line references.

SAMPLE POETRY ANALYSIS PASSAGE AND QUESTIONS

Andrew Marvell's "On a Drop of Dew"

Read the following poem carefully and choose answers to the questions that follow.

       See how the orient[1] dew,
       Shed from the bosom of the morn
          Into the blowing[2] roses,
Line   Yet careless of its mansion new,
(5)   For the clear region where 'twas born
          Round in itself incloses:
       And in its little globe's extent,
       Frames as it can its native element.
         How it the purple flow'r does slight,
(10)   Scarce touching where it lies,
       But gazing back upon the skies,
         Shines with a mournful light,
           Like its own tear,
       Because so long divided from the sphere.
(15)   Restless it rolls and unsecure,
         Trembling lest it grow impure,
       Till the warm sun pity its pain,
       And to the skies exhale it back again.
         So the soul, that drop, that ray
(20)   Of the clear fountain of eternal day,
       Could it within the human flow'r be seen,
         Remembering still its former height,
         Shuns the sweet leaves and blossoms
      green,
(25)   And recollecting its own light,
       Does, in its pure and circling thoughts,
       express
       The greater heaven in an heaven less.
         In how coy[3] a figure wound,
(30)   Every way it turns away:
       So the world excluding round,
       Yet receiving in the day,
       Dark beneath, but bright above,
       Here disdaining, there in love.

(35)   How loose and easy hence to go,
       How girt and ready to ascend,
       Moving but on a point below,
       It all about does upwards bend.
       Such did the manna's sacred dew distill,
(40)   White and entire, though congealed and chill,
       Congealed on earth: but does, dissolving, run
       Into the glories of th' almighty sun.

1. The overall content of the poem can best be described by which statement?
   (A) The characteristics of a drop of dew are related to those of the human soul.
   (B) The life cycle of a drop of dew is contemplated.
   (C) The human soul is shown to be a drop of dew.
   (D) The physical characteristics of a drop of dew are analyzed.
   (E) The poet offers a mystical vision of a drop of dew as a spiritual entity that has all the qualities of the human soul.

2. The poem contains
   I.   a biblical allusion
   II. an extended metaphor
   III. an evocation of spiritual longing

   (A) I only
   (B) II only
   (C) III only
   (D) I and II only
   (E) I, II, and III

3. In context, "careless of its mansion new" (line 4) most nearly means
   (A) the dew drop does not understand the value of its beautiful surroundings
   (B) the dew drop does not assist the flower in any way
   (C) the dew drop is unconcerned with its beautiful surroundings
   (D) the human soul does not value the body
   (E) the human soul does not take part in the care of the body

---

[1] pearly, sparkling
[2] blooming
[3] modest

4. The speaker's metaphor for the human body is

   (A) "the orient dew" (line 1)
   (B) "the sphere" (line 14)
   (C) "the clear fountain" (line 20)
   (D) "the sweet leaves and blossoms green"
       (lines 23–24)
   (E) "th' almighty sun" (line 42)

5. Which of the following is the antecedent of "its" in
   "Does, in its pure and circling thoughts, express"
   (lines 26–27)?

   (A) "soul" (line 19)
   (B) "day" (line 20)
   (C) "flow'r" (line 21)
   (D) "height" (line 22)
   (E) "leaves" (line 23)

6. All of the following aspects of the dew drop are
   emphasized in the poem EXCEPT

   (A) its disregard for the physical world
   (B) its desire to regain the heavens
   (C) its purity
   (D) its will to live
   (E) its roundness

7. Lines 9–14 suggest the drop of dew is

   (A) frightened of death
   (B) full of unhappy longing
   (C) envious of the rose's vitality
   (D) part of a larger body of water in the sky
   (E) uncertain of the future

8. Lines 19–28 make explicit

   (A) the analogy between the drop of dew and the soul
   (B) the actual differences between the drop of dew and
       the soul
   (C) the true nature of the drop of dew
   (D) the soul's need for the body
   (E) the soul's thoughts

9. Each of the following pairs of phrases refers to the same
   action, object, or concept EXCEPT

   (A) "mansion new" (line 4)…"purple flow'r" (line 9)
   (B) "globe's extent" (line 7)…"the sphere" (line 14)
   (C) "that drop" (line 19)…"that ray" (line 19)
   (D) "exhale" (line 18)…"dissolving" (line 41)
   (E) "Every way it turns away" (line 30)…"It all about
       does upwards bend" (line 38)

10. Which of the following best paraphrases the meaning in
    context of "So the world excluding round,/yet receiving
    in the day" (lines 31–32)?

    (A) Although the dew drop evaporates in the sun, it
        arrives anew each day.
    (B) The world evaporates the drop of dew when it
        receives the light of the sun.
    (C) The dew drop is impervious to everything but
        time.
    (D) Although the dew drop and the soul shut out the
        material world, they let in the light of heaven.
    (E) The only thing that matters to the dew drop is
        light.

11. In line 42, the sun is symbolic of

    (A) fire
    (B) rebirth
    (C) the soul
    (D) God
    (E) time

12. Which of the following sets of adjectives is best suited to
    describing the poem's tone?

    (A) Mysterious, moody, and spiritual
    (B) Pious, proper, and academic
    (C) Intricate, delicate, and worshipful
    (D) Witty, clever, and ironic
    (E) Straightforward, impassioned, and sincere

13. In the final four lines of the poem, the poet suggests that

    (A) the dew drop will ultimately be destroyed by the
        sun
    (B) the cycle of life and death is continual
    (C) the dew drop will return to earth in the form of
        "manna"
    (D) souls as pure as a drop of dew will ascend to
        heaven
    (E) death brings spiritual unity with God

14. Which of the following adjectives is LEAST important to
    the poem's theme?

    (A) "blowing" (line 3)
    (B) "clear" (line 20)
    (C) "pure" (line 26)
    (D) "bright" (line 33)
    (E) "loose" (line 35)

About Andrew Marvell's "On a Drop of Dew"

This poem is challenging but absolutely typical of what you will find on the AP Exam. Marvell (1621–1678) was one of the metaphysical poets (check your overview of literary movements), and the previous poem is an excellent example of this school of poetry's verse. The metaphysical poets were a loosely connected group of seventeenth-century poets who fashioned a type of elaborately clever, often witty verse that has a decidedly intellectual twist to it. The metaphysical poets are noted for taking a comparison—for example, "a drop of dew is like the soul"—and developing it over dozens of lines. Lots of metaphysical poetry appears on the multiple-choice section, not because metaphysical poetry is necessarily great but because unlike most poetry, it lends itself well to multiple-choice questions. So, reading any of the metaphysicals' poetry is great practice for the AP Exam.

Let's Get Metaphysical
Others from the metaphysical school include John Donne, George Herbert, Thomas Carew, Abraham Cowley, and Richard Crashaw.

Answers and Explanations to the Questions

1. The overall content of the poem can best be described by which statement?

   (A) The characteristics of a drop of dew are related to those of the human soul.
   (B) The life cycle of a drop of dew is contemplated.
   (C) The human soul is shown to be a drop of dew.
   (D) The physical characteristics of a drop of dew are analyzed.
   (E) The poet offers a mystical vision of a drop of dew as a spiritual entity that has all the qualities of the human soul.

Here's How to Crack It

This is a main-idea question. Remember, you could have left it alone and come back to it if you hadn't found the main idea yet, but chances are you didn't have too much trouble. If you had any trouble eliminating choices, it was probably with (C). Does the poet really show that the human soul is a drop of dew? No. Marvell uses a drop of dew to speak about the human soul, but he isn't suggesting that a person's inner spirit is actually composed of condensed water. In fact, in the poem the drop of dew isn't so much a water droplet as it is a receptacle for light. This point becomes important in later questions. You should have eliminated (B) on the premise that it is much too literal to be correct; you're looking for the deeper main idea of the poem. If (D) threw you, then you weren't paying attention to the word *physical*. You should have asked yourself, "Wait a minute, this dew drop trembles with fear at the thought of becoming impure: Can I call that a physical analysis?" Marvell's drop of dew is a being with a personality and desires; all of these things are studied, not just its physical characteristics. Although (E) looks good at first glance, there's no way to prove that the author is offering a "mystical" vision. Choice (A) is similar in concept but without any added stuff to throw you off, so it's the best answer.

2. The poem contains

    I. a biblical allusion
    II. an extended metaphor
    III. an evocation of spiritual longing

    (A) I only
    (B) II only
    (C) III only
    (D) I and II only
    (E) I, II, and III

Here's How to Crack It

Question 2 is one of the notorious Roman numeral questions. Remember to use POE and work from the easiest point to the most difficult. You should see that (II) is found in the passage: The dew drop is an extended metaphor for the human soul. An extended metaphor is also known as a **conceit**, appearing frequently in metaphysical poems. You can eliminate (A) and (C); they don't include (II).

Item (III) might send you back to the poem, where lines 11–13 ("But gazing back upon the skies,/Shines with a mournful light,/Like its own tear") should convince you that (III) is a keeper. Eliminate (B) and (D). You're finished.

Only (E) is left. If you're curious about (I), the biblical allusion is the word *manna*, which refers to a kind of bread that came to the starving Israelites from out of heaven. If you had any doubts about (I) or (III) you might have reasoned that both points are consistent with the main idea and should be kept. The correct answer is (E).

3. In context, "careless of its mansion new" (line 4) most nearly means

    (A) the dew drop does not understand the value of its beautiful surroundings
    (B) the dew drop does not assist the flower in any way
    (C) the dew drop is unconcerned with its beautiful surroundings
    (D) the human soul does not value the body
    (E) the human soul does not take part in the care of the body

Here's How to Crack It

Question 3 is a straightforward line-reference question. After reading around the line reference, you can easily eliminate (D) and (E). The line in question discusses only the dew drop upon a rose petal. It does not refer to the human soul. Of the remaining choices, (A) and (B) both imply that in context, "careless" means that the dew drop does not take care of the rose, which is simply a misreading. Chances are you didn't have much trouble on this question. The correct answer is (C).

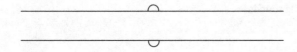

4. The speaker's metaphor for the human body is

   (A) "the orient dew" (line 1)
   (B) "the sphere" (line 14)
   (C) "the clear fountain" (line 20)
   (D) "the sweet leaves and blossoms green" (lines 23–24)
   (E) "th' almighty sun" (line 42)

Here's How to Crack It

To answer this question you must either trace Marvell's involved metaphor, noting that in lines 19–21 he describes the soul as being housed within the "human flow'r," or use POE. All four incorrect answers refer to either a spiritual entity (the dew) or its source (the sphere, fountain, and sun) and so can be eliminated. The correct answer is (D).

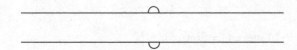

5. Which of the following is the antecedent of "its" in "Does, in its pure and circling thoughts, express" (lines 26–27)?

   (A) "soul" (line 19)
   (B) "day" (line 20)
   (C) "flow'r" (line 21)
   (D) "height" (line 22)
   (E) "leaves" (line 23)

Here's How to Crack It

Question 5 is a typical grammar question and hinges on your knowing the term **antecedent**. That term, and other grammatical terms you need for the test, can be found in the glossary. By asking for the antecedent, the question is simply asking what the word *its* stands for in the given phrase. Analyzed grammatically, the only correct usage (and you'll only be asked about correct usage) is the soul. You might also have reasoned, "For which of the choices would it make sense to have 'pure and circling thoughts'?" Only (A) makes sense.

6. All of the following aspects of the dew drop are emphasized in the poem EXCEPT

(A) its disregard for the physical world
(B) its desire to regain the heavens
(C) its purity
(D) its will to live
(E) its roundness

Here's How to Crack It

Question 6 is an EXCEPT question. An excellent way to proceed is to disregard the EXCEPT; cross EXCEPT out.

Eliminate any choice that fits the remaining question, which now reads: All [Which] of the following aspects of the drop of dew are emphasized in the poem.

To do this you *must* refer back to the passage. Remember: Never work from memory! "Careless of its mansion new" lets you eliminate (A). "Like its own tear/ Because so long divided from the sphere" takes care of (B). "Trembling lest it grows impure" lets you eliminate (C). The dew drop's roundness is emphasized in several places; (E) was easy to eliminate. This leaves only (D), which is the correct answer.

7. Lines 9–14 suggest the drop of dew is

(A) frightened of death
(B) full of unhappy longing
(C) envious of the rose's vitality
(D) part of a larger body of water in the sky
(E) uncertain of the future

Here's How to Crack It

Question 7 is a line-reference question that tests your comprehension of a set of lines. If you had trouble with this question you should practice reading poetry for comprehension. You can eliminate (C) and (E) easily as they have nothing to do with the poem. The other choices can almost be justified from the poem, but *almost* means *wrong*. Choice (A) could be eliminated because of the word *frightened*. The drop of dew is perhaps frightened of earthly life (remember, it "trembles" at the thought of becoming "impure") but as a metaphor for the soul, it is not afraid of death. Certainly no such statement can be found in the poem. Choice (D) is incorrect because Marvell treats the dew drop not only as water, but as a container of light and as a metaphor for the soul. For Marvell the drop comes from the sky, not a body of water in the sky. The correct answer is (B).

8. Lines 19–28 make explicit

    (A) the analogy between the drop of dew and the soul
    (B) the actual differences between the drop of dew and the soul
    (C) the true nature of the drop of dew
    (D) the soul's need for the body
    (E) the soul's thoughts

Here's How to Crack It

The key here is to understand the question. When something is made explicit, it is stated or spelled out. *Explicit* is the opposite of *implicit*. Your task is to see what lines 19–28 show clearly. Using POE, you should eliminate (D) immediately; it only talks about the drop of dew whereas the lines in question refer primarily to the human soul. Choice (E) is a trap answer. The lines in question do refer to the soul's thoughts, but they do not spell them out; the thoughts are not made explicit. Choice (C) is similarly wrong: The drop of dew's "true nature" is not the subject of these lines; only the similarity of the drop of dew and the soul is. Choice (B) talks about differences between the soul and the drop of dew. This answer choice is the exact opposite of the lines' intent. They discuss the similarities of the drop and the soul. In fact, they make the analogy between the drop of dew and the soul explicit—therefore, (A) is the correct answer.

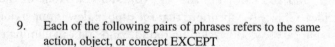

9. Each of the following pairs of phrases refers to the same action, object, or concept EXCEPT

    (A) "mansion new" (line 4)…"purple flow'r" (line 9)
    (B) "globe's extent" (line 7)…"the sphere" (line 14)
    (C) "that drop" (line 19)…"that ray" (line 19)
    (D) "exhale" (line 18)…"dissolving" (line 41)
    (E) "Every way it turns away" (line 30)…"It all about does upward bend" (line 38)

Here's How to Crack It

This is another EXCEPT question, which are common on the exam. Cross out EXCEPT and eliminate answers that satisfy the remaining statement: Each of the following pairs of phrases refers to the same action, object, or concept. Use POE. In (A), "mansion new" and "purple flow'r" both refer to the rose the drop of dew perches on. Eliminate it. In (C), "that drop" and "that ray" seem to refer to different things but both in fact refer to the soul—so eliminate (C). In (D), "exhale" and "dissolving" both refer to the process by which the drop of dew vanishes (evaporation, if you want to be scientific about it). In (B), "globe's extent" and "sphere" seem to both refer to the dew drop, but in fact, the sphere refers to the skies above—the "heavenly sphere." Thus, (B) is the correct answer.

Nitpicky? Maybe, but this question is an excellent example of the kind of careful reading you'll be called upon to do on the actual test.

10. Which of the following best paraphrases the meaning in context of "So the world excluding round,/yet receiving in the day" (lines 31–32)?

(A) Although the dew drop evaporates in the sun, it arrives anew each day.
(B) The world evaporates the drop of dew when it receives the light of the sun.
(C) The dew drop is impervious to everything but time.
(D) Although the dew drop and the soul shut out the material world, they let in the light of heaven.
(E) The only thing that matters to the dew drop is light.

Here's How to Crack It

This kind of comprehension question is probably the most common type of poetry analysis question on the AP Exam. In essence, you'll be given a line and asked to answer the question, "So, what does it mean?" As always, read around the line and then use POE. Paraphrase "the world excluding round" as "the drop that turns away from the world" and you can eliminate (A), (B), and (E). None of those choices include that idea. Choice (C) mentions that the drop of dew is impervious. That isn't a good paraphrase of "world excluding round," and you can eliminate it with confidence by reasoning that *time* is not mentioned in the lines in question at all. That leaves only the correct answer, (D).

11. In line 42, the sun is symbolic of

(A) fire
(B) rebirth
(C) the soul
(D) God
(E) time

Here's How to Crack It

On this question, we hope you saw that the sun symbolized God. The word *almighty* should have been a big clue. Additionally, metaphysical poets are often concerned with spiritual issues. If you've used your overview of literary movements to prepare for this exam, the answer may be even more obvious. The correct answer is (D).

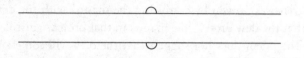

12. Which of the following sets of adjectives is best suited to describing the poem's tone?

    (A) Mysterious, moody, and spiritual
    (B) Pious, proper, and academic
    (C) Intricate, delicate, and worshipful
    (D) Witty, clever, and ironic
    (E) Straightforward, impassioned, and sincere

Here's How to Crack It

This is a tone question. On tone questions, always use POE, and remember that "half bad equals all bad." Every answer choice has something right in it but only the correct answer choice has *nothing* wrong in it. In (A), yes, the poem's tone is spiritual, but is it mysterious and moody? Not really. Eliminate it. Choice (B) has one promising word—*pious,* as the poem discusses God—but *proper* and *academic* do not fit. That isn't right. Eliminate it. In (D), well, it's true that the poem is witty and clever, but is it also ironic? Metaphysical poets typically are ironic—that is, hidden messages and contradictions often lurk below the surface of a metaphysical poem's text, but "On a Drop of Dew" is an exception. Marvell says what he means in a clever way, but not ironically. Choice (E) should just sound wrong. "On a Drop of Dew" is an intensely crafted work, but it is not impassioned nor straightforward. That leaves (C), which sums things up fairly well: intricate, delicate, and worshipful.

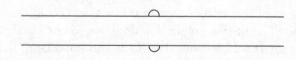

13. In the final four lines of the poem, the poet suggests that

    (A) the dew drop will ultimately be destroyed by the sun
    (B) the cycle of life and death is continual
    (C) the drop of dew will return to earth in the form of "manna"
    (D) souls as pure as a drop of dew will ascend to heaven
    (E) death brings spiritual unity with God

Here's How to Crack It

If you answered question 11 correctly, this one shouldn't be much tougher. If you understand that the sun symbolizes God then you should also understand that the dew's dissolving into the sun is a metaphor for the soul's ascent to heaven. The incorrect answer choices all add extraneous points or misconstrue the emphasis of this essentially simple idea. Choice (A) suggests that the dew would be destroyed. That misses the point. The dew's evaporation is not a destruction, but a reunion with the divine. Choice (B) is extraneous: The cycle of life is not a thematic point of the poem. Choice (C) tries to trap you by confusing the manna with the dew drop. The poem suggests that the dew drop is like manna in that both are distilled from the spiritual realm. The poem does not suggest that the dew will somehow become manna. Choice (D) should have been easy to eliminate: Nowhere does the poem talk about whether or not souls are as pure as a drop of dew. The correct answer is (E).

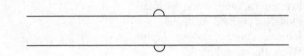

14. Which of the following adjectives is LEAST important to the poem's theme?

    (A) "blowing" (line 3)
    (B) "clear" (line 20)
    (C) "pure" (line 26)
    (D) "bright" (line 33)
    (E) "loose" (line 35)

Here's How to Crack It

The test writers are fond of asking questions about theme, despite the fact that pinning down the theme of many poems is problematic. When you're asked about the theme, don't try to come up with an exact definition of the theme. Just think about the main point, the important stuff. Again, POE is the way to work. Cross out LEAST and work with the remaining question, eliminating choices that are important to the theme. An important aspect of the poem is the metaphor of the dew drop and the soul. A good way to start would be to eliminate those choices that describe any aspect of that relationship. In this way you could eliminate (B), (C), and (D), because all are qualities of the dew drop that relate to qualities of the soul. A moment of study should tell you that (E) is also important. The dew drop is "loose," or ready to ascend; it grips this world only lightly. That is a thematic point. And (A)? Well, *blowing* means blooming. Is it important that the rose is in bloom? Does Marvell return to the fact of the rose being in bloom later in the poem? Does blooming somehow relate to the soul? No. (A) is least thematically important, and thus (A) is the correct answer.

Bonus Grammar Questions

Try these for strenuous, but excellent, practice. They're harder than real AP questions, but not by much. The following is an excerpt from Percy Bysshe Shelley's "Alastor; or, The Spirit of Solitude."

> Nature's most secret steps
> He like her shadow has pursued, wher'er
> The red volcano overcanopies
> Its fields of snow and pinnacles of ice
>
> *Line*
> (5) With burning smoke, or where bitumen lakes
> On black bare pointed islets ever beat
> With sluggish surge, or where the secret caves
> Rugged and dark, winding among the springs
>
> Of fire and poison, inaccessible
> (10) To avarice or pride, their starry domes
> Of diamond and of gold expand above
> Numberless and immeasurable halls,
>
> Frequent with crystal column, and clear shrines
> Of pearl, and thrones radiant with chrysolite.

1. The word "inaccessible" (line 9) modifies which of the following words?

    (A) "lakes" (line 5)
    (B) "caves" (line 7)
    (C) "springs" (line 8)
    (D) "poison" (line 9)
    (E) "avarice" (line 10)

You should recognize that *inaccessible* is an adjective (the ending *-ible* gives it away). That observation means that you need to decide which noun or pronoun it modifies. Unfortunately, all of the choices are nouns. If you look carefully, you will see that *or* (in line 7) introduces an independent clause. Because of the use of commas, the participial phrase *winding among the springs* modifies *caves*. *Of fire and poison* is a prepositional phrase modifying *springs*. *To avarice or pride* is another prepositional phrase that limits *inaccessible*. The correct answer, then, is (B), *caves*. Tough, isn't it?

Try this poem by Emily Dickinson.

> There's a certain Slant of light,
> Winter Afternoons—
> That oppresses, like the Heft
> Of Cathedral Tunes—
>
> *Line*
> (5) Heavenly Hurt, it gives us—
> We can find no scar,
> But internal difference,
> Where the meanings, are—
>
> None may teach it—Any—
> (10) 'Tis the Seal Despair—
> An imperial affliction
> Sent us of the Air—
>
> When it comes, the Landscape listens—
> Shadows—hold their breath—
> (15) When it goes, 'tis like the Distance
> On the look of Death—

2. In line 5, "it" refers to

(A) "Cathedral Tunes" (line 4)
(B) "Heavenly Hurt" (line 5)
(C) "Slant of light" (line 1)
(D) "look of Death" (line 16)
(E) "imperial affliction" (line 11)

Asking what a pronoun refers to is a favorite of the AP Exam writers. Do you see that this isn't so much a question of grammatical analysis as it is of comprehension? The correct answer is (C). The *slant of light* is the antecedent.

Poetry Analysis Passage Drill 1

Suggested time: 12–15 minutes

Questions 1–13. Choose your answers to questions 1–13 based on a careful reading of the following poem by Phillis Wheatley.

"On the Death of J.C. an Infant"

NO more the flow'ry scenes of pleasure rise,
Nor charming prospects greet the mental eyes,
No more with joy we view that lovely face
Smiling, disportive, flush'd with ev'ry grace.

Line
(5)   The tear of sorrow flows from ev'ry eye,
Groans answer groans, and signs to sighs reply;
When sudden pangs shot thro' each aching heart,
When, Death, thy messenger dispatch'd his dart?
Thy dread attendants, all-destroying Pow'r,
(10) Hurried the infant to his mortal hour.
Could'st thou unpitying close those radiant eyes?
Or fail'd his artless beauties to surprize?
Could not his innocence thy stroke controul,
Thy purpose shake, and soften all thy soul?

(15) The blooming babe, with shades of Death o'er-spread,
No more shall smile, no more shall raise its head,
But, like a branch that from the tree is torn,
Falls prostrate, wither'd, languid, and forlorn.
"Where flies my James?" 'tis thus I seem to hear
(20) The parent ask, "Some angel tell me where
"He wings his passage thro' the yielding air?"
Methinks a cherub bending from the skies
Observes the question, and serene replies,
In heav'ns high palaces your babe appears:
(25) Prepare to meet him, and dismiss your tears."
Shall not th' intelligence your grief restrain,
And turn the mournful to the chearful strain?
Cease your complaints, suspend each rising sigh,
Cease to accuse the Ruler of the sky.
(30) Parents, no more indulge the falling tear:
Let Faith to heav'n's refulgent domes repair,
There see your infant, like a seraph glow:
What charms celestial in his numbers flow
Melodious, while the foul-enchanting strain
(35) Dwells on his tongue, and fills th' ethereal plain?

Enough—for ever cease your murm'ring breath;
Not as a foe, but friend converse with Death,
Since to the port of happiness unknown
He brought that treasure which you call your own.
(40) The gift of heav'n intrusted to your hand
Cheerful resign at the divine command:
Not at your bar must sov'reign Wisdom stand.

1. Taken as a whole, the poem is best understood to be

   (A) an epitaph
   (B) an elegy
   (C) a parable
   (D) a dirge
   (E) a sestina

2. All of the following are speakers in the poem EXCEPT

   I. Death
   II. James
   III. the parent
   IV. a cherub

   (A) I only
   (B) I and II only
   (C) II and III only
   (D) III and IV only
   (E) II, III, and IV only

3. The poet's use of syncope throughout poem serves

   (A) to save copying time, since this poet wrote
       in longhand
   (B) to form alliteration with the surrounding words
   (C) to make the line fit the poem's meter
   (D) to make it evident that a new subject is
       being addressed
   (E) to represent the dialect of the speaker

4. Line 29 contains an example of

   (A) an apostrophe
   (B) an allusion
   (C) free verse
   (D) a metaphor
   (E) a euphemism

5. The poet makes use of all of the following literary devices in lines 1–4 EXCEPT

   (A) metaphor
   (B) consonance
   (C) iambic pentameter
   (D) enjambment
   (E) parallelism

6. Grammatically, the word "wings" (line 21) is a

   (A) noun
   (B) direct object
   (C) adjective
   (D) adverb
   (E) verb

7. The tone in lines 1–21 is best characterized as

   (A) disdainful
   (B) nostalgic
   (C) reverential
   (D) woeful
   (E) earnest

8. Lines 30–31 can best be paraphrased as

   (A) "Dismiss your tears and return your faith
        to heaven"
   (B) "Your tears are important: know that heaven will
        heal you"
   (C) "The angels of heaven will mend the tears in
        your heart"
   (D) "Your faith, not your tears, will replace the repugnant
        structures of heaven"
   (E) "Parents, repair your faith so you too may see your
        infant in the vaults of heaven"

9. Each clause in lines 28–29 is best described as a

   (A) question
   (B) command
   (C) concession
   (D) invitation
   (E) declaration

10. The primary purpose of lines 22–25 is to

   (A) engage the listeners by offering a peaceful
        anecdote
   (B) remind the parents they will see their infant in
        heaven
   (C) recount the infant's words to those left on earth
   (D) console the grieving parents
   (E) speculate where the infant has gone

11. In lines 13–14, "thy" refers to

   (A) each aching heart
   (B) the poet
   (C) Death
   (D) the attendants
   (E) the infant

12. Lines 19–21 are notable for the use of which of the
    following?

    I. A rhyming triplet
    II. A change in the speaker
    III. A change in punctuation

   (A) I only
   (B) I and II only
   (C) I and III only
   (D) II and III only
   (E) I, II, and III

13. Which course of action would the speaker most wish the
    audience to take?

   (A) Be resigned to the harsh realities of life
   (B) Stop indulging in misery
   (C) Understand the gift that has been sacrificed
   (D) Accept that the loss of a child is inevitable
   (E) Entrust the infant to a higher power

POETRY ANALYSIS PASSAGE DRILL 1: ANSWERS AND EXPLANATIONS

Sold into slavery at age seven, Phillis Wheatley was educated by her Boston slave owner and in 1773 became the first published African American poet. Her preferred poetic form was the couplet, and elegies comprised more than one-third of her published works.

1. **B**   This is a definition question. An elegy is a poem that mourns the death of someone, which makes the correct answer (B). None of the remaining answers would work. An epitaph is the inscription on a tombstone, so eliminate (A). A parable is a story that instructs, so (C) is also incorrect. A dirge is a song lamenting the dead, so (D) can be eliminated. A sestina has a different rhyme scheme and is only 39 lines long, so eliminate (E).

2. **B**   The poem contains only three speakers: the poet, the parent (lines 19–21), and a cherub (lines 24–25). Pay close attention to the word EXCEPT, as this means you're looking for the characters who do not speak in the poem. Therefore, you can eliminate any answer choice that includes (III) or (IV): that's (C), (D), and (E). The only difference between (A) and (B) is James, (II), so you don't need to figure out if Death speaks. (For what it's worth, he doesn't respond to any question asked of him—nearly every question in this poem is rhetorical.) Because James (the infant—notice the poem's title) never speaks, the answer is (B)—both (I) and (II).

3. **C**   This question is tricky if you don't know the definition of syncope. *Syncope* involves the shortening of a word by removing internal letters and inserting an apostrophe. Poets often employ this technique, and Wheatley uses it frequently in this poem. By modifying the sound of certain words, the poet ensures that the line's metrical rhythm is kept intact. The correct answer is (C).

4. **B**   This is another definition question. The use of the word *Ruler* makes this line an example of an allusion, specifically a biblical allusion as "Ruler" refers to God. Wheatley often wrote about her Christian faith in her poems, so it would not be surprising to find such allusions in her poems. The correct answer is (B).

5. **A**   One example of consonance, (B), in lines 1–4 is the repetition of the s sound (scenes, rise, prospects, smiling, grace). The poem is written in iambic pentameter, (C). The end of line 3 contains an example of enjambment, (D). Lines 1 and 3 contain parallel structure, (E). The device not appearing in these four lines is metaphor. The correct answer is (A).

6. **E**   Make sure to read the entire sentence, not just line 21. Start in line 20 at the beginning of the quotation: "Some angel tell me where He wings his passage thro' the yielding air?" The word *wings* is not being used as a noun, as it is normally used. Eliminate (A) and (B). The parent is asking where the infant wings (or flies) through the air (i.e., where did he go?). Thus, the word *wings* is being used as a verb. The correct answer is (E).

7. **D**   Remember that this poem is an elegy. Elegies are written about someone who has died, so the tone is likely sorrowful. Lines 1–12, for example, confirm this. The poet expresses great sadness through the use of phrases like *no more joy, tear of sorrow, Death,* and *Hurried the infant to his mortal hour.* The tone is indeed sorrowful, which makes the best answer (D).

8. **A** The meaning of the word *repair* in this context is to return to or to go to a place, not to fix something. Knowing that, eliminate (B), (C), and (E). If you know what *repugnant* means (repulsive), then eliminate (D), since there is nothing in these lines that suggest the "heav'n's refulgent domes" are repulsive or offensive. (By the way, *refulgent* means "shining brightly.") This leaves the correct answer, which is (A).

9. **B** The three clauses begin with cease, suspend, and cease, which are all verbs in the imperative mood. The imperative mood is used when a speaker makes a command. In this poem, the speaker is requesting that the parents stop complaining about, sighing/crying for, and implicating God in the loss of their infant. There are no questions asked in these lines, so eliminate (A). The speaker doesn't ask them to give up something—the parents have already lost something—in order to reach an agreement, so (C) is also incorrect. The speaker is not inviting the parents to stop, so eliminate (D). A declaration would fall under the indicative mood, and declaratives usually express statements and contain a subject, which is not the case in these lines; (E) is incorrect. The speaker is clearly making requests, so the best answer is (B).

10. **D** With purpose questions, ask yourself why are these lines here, not what did the writer say. If you do the latter, you will likely pick (B) or (E), neither of which is the purpose of these lines. The speaker is offering the mourning parents solace and, to do so, offers them a peaceful thought: a cherub telling the parents their child is safe in heaven. Therefore, the speaker's purpose is to comfort them. The correct answer is (D). These lines are not an example of anecdote, (A), and the words are that of the cherub, not the infant, (C).

11. **C** The word *thy* is a possessive pronoun. When dealing with pronouns, you want to locate the antecedent. Whose stroke controlled? Whose purpose should be shaken? Whose soul should be softened? You will need to go back to line 8 to find the antecedent, which is Death. It is Death who hurried the infant to his mortal hour and with whom the speaker is pleading. The correct answer is (C).

12. **E** Examine each item separately. Item (I) could be tricky. Note that the first eighteen lines contain nine pairs of couplets. Then *hear* seems to be alone while the couplet pattern continues until line 40, where the poem concludes with a triplet. There are eighteen lines between 21 and 40—eighteen lines that contain nine pairs of couplets. Thus, it's likely that lines 19–21 form a triplet as well; in the spoken English of Wheatley's time hear could have rhymed with where and air. Item (I) is valid. (Note: Even if you didn't have time to notice that rhyme scheme, seeing that *hear* seems to break the couplet pattern should be enough to convince you to keep (I).) Eliminate (D). For (II), these lines indicate what the parent is asking, so there is a change in who is speaking. Eliminate (A) and (C). Finally, for (III), quotation marks are used for the first time, so there is also a change in punctuation—a change from anything used previously. Therefore, the correct answer is (E).

13. **E** The speaker expresses the idea of God and Heaven several times. In the Christian faith, when a baby dies, he or she will go to heaven if baptized. The speaker, in an effort to comfort the grieving parents, is reminding them of this and urging them to put their faith in God. Choices (A), (B), and (D) are all too negative and do not align with the message of the speaker. While the speaker does acknowledge the sacrifice, the takeaway message is more than their sacrifice—it is to hold fast to their faith in God.

Poetry Analysis Passage Drill 2

Suggested time: 12–15 minutes

<u>Questions 1–11.</u> Choose your answers to questions 1–11 based on a careful reading of the following poem by Carl Sandburg.

"Skyscraper"

Line

By day the skyscraper looms in the smoke and sun and has
  a soul.
Prairie and valley, streets of the city, pour people into
  it and they mingle among its twenty floors and are
(5) poured out again back to the streets, prairies and
  valleys.
It is the men and women, boys and girls so poured in and
  out all day that give the building a soul of dreams and
  thoughts and memories.
(10) (Dumped in the sea or fixed in a desert, who would care
  for the building or speak its name or ask a policeman
  the way to it?)

Elevators slide on their cables and tubes catch letters
  and parcels and iron pipes carry gas and water in and
(15) sewage out.
Wires climb with secrets, carry light and carry words,
  and tell terrors and profits and loves—curses of men
  grappling plans of business and questions of women in
  plots of love.

(20) Hour by hour the caissons reach down to the rock of the
  earth and hold the building to a turning planet.
Hour by hour the girders play as ribs and reach out and
  hold together the stone walls and floors.
Hour by hour the hand of the mason and the stuff of the
(25) mortar clinch the pieces and parts to the shape an
  architect voted.
Hour by hour the sun and the rain, the air and the rust, and
  the press of time running into centuries, play on the
  building inside and out and use it.

(30) Men who sunk the pilings and mixed the mortar are laid
  in graves where the wind whistles a wild song without
  words
And so are men who strung the wires and fixed the pipes
  and tubes and those who saw it rise floor by floor.
(35) Souls of them all are here, even the hod carrier begging at
  back doors hundreds of miles away and the bricklayer
  who went to state's prison for shooting another man
  while drunk.
(One man fell from a girder and broke his neck at the end
(40) of a straight plunge—he is here—his soul has gone
  into the stones of the building.)

On the office doors from tier to tier—hundreds of names
  and each name standing for a face written across with a
  dead child, a passionate lover, a driving ambition for a
(45) million dollar business or a lobster's ease of life.

Behind the signs on the doors they work and the walls tell
  nothing from room to room.
Ten-dollar-a-week stenographers take letters from corpora-
(50) tion officers, lawyers, efficiency engineers, and tons of
  letters go bundled from the building to all ends of the
  earth.
Smiles and tears of each office girl go into the soul of the
  building just the same as the master-men who rule the
(55) building.

Hands of clocks turn to noon hours and each floor empties
  its men and women who go away and eat and come
  back to work.
Toward the end of the afternoon all work slackens and all
(60) jobs go slower as the people feel day closing on them.
One by one the floors are emptied… The uniformed
  elevator men are gone. Pails clang… Scrubbers work,
  talking in foreign tongues. Broom and water and mop
  clean from the floors human dust and spit, and machine
(65) grime of the day.
Spelled in electric fire on the roof are words telling miles
  of houses and people where to buy a thing for money.
  The sign speaks till midnight.
Darkness on the hallways. Voices echo. Silence holds…
(70) Watchmen walk slow from floor to floor and try the
  doors. Revolvers bulge from their hip pockets… Steel
  safes stand in corners. Money is stacked in them.
A young watchman leans at a window and sees the lights
  of barges butting their way across a harbor, nets of
(75) red and white lanterns in a railroad yard, and a span
  of glooms splashed with lines of white and blurs of
  crosses and clusters over the sleeping city.
By night the skyscraper looms in the smoke and the stars
  and has a soul.

1. What is implied by lines 10–12 ("Dumped . . . to it")?

   (A) The building depends on people.
   (B) It would be just as easy to tear down the skyscraper and dump its bricks and mortar and steel girders as it is to let it stand.
   (C) The skyscraper is important only because of the city in which it is located.
   (D) There would be no point in having the building unless people used it.
   (E) The speaker doesn't think the building has any value.

2. It can be inferred that the poet

   (A) admires the workers who built the skyscraper
   (B) would prefer it if the skyscraper were gone
   (C) works in the skyscraper or in a building much like it
   (D) venerates the skyscraper
   (E) is critical of the contemporary social order

3. What is the significance of the description in lines 44–46 ("each . . . life")?

   I. It implies that each man is an individual, despite the sameness of their office doors with the names.
   II. It points to the ruthless nature of the senior men working in the skyscraper.
   III. It suggests that the executives in the offices are essentially all the same.

   (A) I only
   (B) II only
   (C) I and III
   (D) II and III
   (E) I, II and III

4. The image in line 28, "the press of time running into centuries," suggests

   (A) the speaker's attitude of awe for the building
   (B) one of the poem's themes
   (C) the central metaphor of the poem
   (D) an allusion to the city itself
   (E) the negative quality of the building

5. According to the poem, which of the following is NOT true of the skyscraper?

   (A) It has outlasted its original creators.
   (B) It carries advertising messages to surrounding residents.
   (C) It is permanent but not eternal.
   (D) It is empty at night.
   (E) It has systems that mirror those of a living being.

6. How do the first and last lines contribute to the structure of the poem?

   (A) They reinforce the fact that the skyscraper has a soul.
   (B) They give the poem a formal, "bookended" quality, stating and then restating an image.
   (C) They reinforce the theme of time passing while the skyscraper endures.
   (D) They present the skyscraper's connection to major objects in the universe.
   (E) They paint a vivid picture of the building's enduring nature.

7. What can you infer from the poet's diction?

   (A) His intended audience was ordinary people, like the blue-collar construction workers, the watchmen and the "Ten-dollar-a-week stenographers" (line 49) in the poem.
   (B) He was writing primarily for men.
   (C) He was accustomed to writing novels and short stories, not poetry.
   (D) He wanted his writing to appeal to the "the master-men who rule the building" (lines 54–55), the "corporation officers, lawyers, efficiency engineers" (lines 49–50).
   (E) He didn't have much formal education.

8. In line 22, the statement that "the girders play as ribs" is an example of which literary device?

   (A) An allusion
   (B) A double entendre
   (C) A simile
   (D) Pathos
   (E) Hyperbole

9. The narrator's most likely reason for mentioning "the bricklayer who went to state's prison for shooting another man while drunk" (lines 37–39) is

    I. to show that the workers who built the skyscraper have human vices and frailties.
    II. to emphasize the contrast between the construction workers who built the skyscraper and the white-collar executives who work there now.
    III. to give an individual identity to at least one of the faceless workers "laid in graves where the wind whistles a wild song without words" (lines 30–32).

    (A) II only
    (B) I and II
    (C) III only
    (D) II and III
    (E) I and III

10. The watchmen, the office girls, the night cleaners and the construction workers have all of the following characteristics in common EXCEPT

    (A) They are enablers.
    (B) They won't outlast the skyscraper.
    (C) They won't end up in an office with their name on the door.
    (D) They give the building its soul.
    (E) They are proud of their association with the building.

11. Which of the following best summarizes the significance to the poem of lines 16–19 ("Wires...love")?

    (A) Just as the skyscraper gives people a place to work, so the telephone lines give them a way to make plans to achieve what they want.
    (B) It reinforces the poet's assertion that it is the people using the skyscraper who give it life and soul.
    (C) The telephone wires in the skyscraper may be inanimate, but they carry dramatic conversations and plans for action.
    (D) Although the stenographers are faceless and the executives are behind identical doors on identical floors, these people are not bland and ordinary. Their lives are filled with secrets and intrigue and ambition.
    (E) It explains what is hinted at in lines 47–48: "Behind the signs on the doors they work and the walls tell nothing from room to room."

POETRY ANALYSIS PASSAGE DRILL 2: ANSWERS AND EXPLANATIONS

About "Skyscraper"

Skyscrapers—a solution to the shrinking amount of land in big city downtown areas—were still a relatively new phenomenon when American poet Carl Sandburg wrote this in 1916. The Wainwright Building in St. Louis, built only 25 years earlier, is often considered the first such building. They were called "skyscrapers" because, in comparison to the surrounding buildings, they were tall enough to scrape the sky.

1. **A** Remember, when a question stem sends you to a specific line in a poem, always read at least a line before and a line after in order to understand the context. If you looked only at lines 10–12, you might think the correct answer is (C). In this case, you only need to read one line before—"It is the men and women, boys and girls so poured in and out all day that give the building a soul of dreams and thoughts and memories"—to see that the correct answer is (A). The skyscraper has value and permanence and a sense of life by virtue of the people who work in it and maintain it and consider it important, not because of the city in which it stands. Choice (D) is too narrow—people do more than use the building. Choices (B) and (E) aren't implied: the speaker doesn't suggest that dumping the skyscraper in the sea would be easy, and doesn't give his own opinion of the building's value.

2. **E** This question calls for two things: an understanding of the poem as a whole, and an ability to distinguish the poet from the narrator. The first requirement eliminates (C)—there is much more to the descriptions in the poem than an obvious familiarity with the day-to-day routine of working in a downtown office building. Choice (A) is gone for the same reason—the original construction crew is only one of the groups of people the poet describes. In addition, there is no suggestion that he particularly admires them. The poet's tone is too neutral to suggest either hostility, (B), or veneration, (D), for the building, so eliminate those two choices. That leaves (E). He juxtaposes the "Ten-dollar-a-week stenographers" (line 49) and "the master-men who rule the building" (lines 54–55). He states that, at night, "Scrubbers work, talking in foreign tongues" (lines 62–63) and refers to the blue-collar workers who erected the building so white-collar "corporation officers, lawyers, efficiency engineers" (lines 49–50) could work there. The poet is suggesting a criticism of the class system and gender inequality of his time. Although the narrator's tone is relatively neutral when he refers to these groups, it is the author who chose to include them in the poem.

3. **E** Here's the Roman numeral format, so approach it first as a standard format question with only three choices. What about Statement (I)? That's true; each man has something unique in his personal life, whether it's a "dead child" or "a passionate lover." Statement (II) is also true; each man has a "driving ambition" for wealth. And Statement (III) is true; although the men's personal lives and ambitions are unique, they each have those things, in addition to their identical "office doors from tier to tier" (line 43). Each executive is one of "the master-men who rule the building" (lines 54–55).

    Now look at the lettered choices. Which one includes all three Roman numeral answers? That's (E).

4. **B** POE works well on this question. The quoted phrase is neither a metaphor nor an allusion, so (C) and (D) can be eliminated. When you read the line before and after, there is no mention of the speaker's opinion, which eliminates (A). The only negative word in line 27 is "rust"; otherwise the description is neutral, so (E) can also be eliminated. That leaves (B) and indeed, when you consider the poem as a whole, one of the themes running through it is time. For example, the builders ended their short lives long ago, but the skyscraper they constructed still stands. "Hands of clocks turn" (line 56); day turns into night turns into day. The skyscraper "has a soul" (lines 1–2), which is eternal.

5. **D** In this EXCEPT/LEAST/NOT format question, first eliminate the "NOT," leaving the standard format question, "which of the following is true of the skyscraper?" Then eliminate the four choices that would be correct answers to that question. Choices (A) (lines 30–32), (B) (lines 66–67), and (E) (lines 22–23) are all true of the building. So is (C)—the skyscraper may be anchored to the planet (lines 20–21), but time and weather are wearing it down (lines 27–29). It is "permanent" compared to the long-gone men who built it, but not "eternal" as the sun and stars are. That leaves (D) as the correct answer. Scrubbers (line 62) and watchmen (line 70) work in the building at night, so it is not empty. This is the only statement that is NOT true of the building.

6. **B** The key words in the question stem are "contribute to the *structure*." This is an example of how reading the question stem carefully, word for word, pays off. All of the answer choices are true of the first and last lines, but only one concerns the poem's structure. That's (B). The first line presents the skyscraper and its soul, looming "in the smoke and sun." The poem then goes on to develop the building's relationship to people, past and present, and its own life-like qualities. Then the last line returns to recap the first line; the building and its soul now loom "in the smoke and the stars."

7. **A** This question asks you to assess the poet's vocabulary and choice of words throughout the entire poem, then make an inference from your assessment. What do you see in the language he chooses? Is it dominated by sophisticated words that only well-educated people would understand? No, so you can eliminate (D). Is it filled with lyrical references to dewdrops and cherubs? Is it overflowing with symbols and imagery and obscure references to ancient Greek gods? No – Sandburg uses concrete, down-to-earth, everyday language. Even words that seem unusual now ("caissons," or foundations, and "hod carrier," or a low-level laborer who brought supplies to tradesmen) were common in 1916. That accessible vocabulary points to ordinary, everyday people as his intended audience (A). The poet doesn't describe many women (only the office girls in line 53 and possibly the stenographers in line 49 and the scrubbers in line 62). However, that's not surprising; in 1916 men held most of the jobs. Nothing in the choice of language seems particularly aimed at either men or women, eliminating (B). The unrhymed free verse in this poem might make (C) seem like an attractive choice. However, the question asks about diction, not about poetic form, so (C) is incorrect. Using plain, everyday language doesn't necessarily point to a lack of formal education, (E). In fact, Sandburg did attend college and West Point, although the progression of his education was erratic. Therefore, you can eliminate (E).

8. **C** A simile compares two unlike things (here, inanimate steel girders and living ribs of bone), using "as" or "like." This particular simile reinforces the concept of the skyscraper having life. None of the other choices would apply to the quote in the question stem. An allusion, (A), is a brief reference to a significant person, place or thing (such as a character in a Shakespearean play, or a place in a Greek myth). It depends on readers being familiar with the reference. A double entendre, (B), refers to a word or statement which can be interpreted in different ways. It is often used for humor or irony. Pathos, (D), is designed to trigger feelings of pity or sympathy in the reader. Hyperbole, (E), is an exaggeration intended to create emphasis.

9. **C** The question stem asks for the "most likely reason," singular, so unless two of the Roman numeral choices say virtually the same thing in different words (which they don't), you're looking for only one answer. That eliminates (B), (D) and (E). Statement (I) must be incorrect because it's not mentioned in the remaining choices, (A) and (C). Nothing in the description of the white-collar executives suggests that they wouldn't be equally capable of getting drunk and shooting someone, so you can eliminate (II). That leaves (III) and makes (C) the correct answer.

10. **E** This is a tricky question that requires careful reading of the question stem. It says these four groups "have" characteristics in common—not "likely have" or "probably have." This stem isn't asking for inference or interpretation; it allows for only what the poem directly and specifically says.

    Since this is an EXCEPT/LEAST/NOT format question, cross out the EXCEPT and find the four answer choices that would be correct for the resulting standard format question. Choice (A) is correct: the construction workers enabled the skyscraper to exist, the office girls enable to executives to send out their letters, the night cleaners enable workers to return the next day to an environment free of "human dust and spit, and machine grime" (lines 64–65), and the watchmen with their revolvers enable protection from intruders and from thieves who want the money in the steel safes. The construction workers didn't outlast the skyscraper they built; none of the other human groups will outlast it, either, so (B) is correct. Only the members of the privileged class—the "corporation officers, lawyers, efficiency engineers" (lines 49–50)—get an office with their name on the door. In the poet's 1916 class society, no one from the other four groups would have that chance, so (C) is correct. Choice (D) is correct; the building has a soul in virtue of the "[men and women]… poured in and out all day" (line 5) and the workers who built it (lines 30–32), while the scrubbers and watchmen who take over at night, after the "floors are emptied" (line 61), give the skyscraper its soul in the stars (lines 69–70). That leaves (E) as the correct EXCEPT answer. The narrator is neutral about the relationships between each of the four groups and the building. They may be proud of their association with it; they may not be. From what the poem says, we don't know, and the question stem doesn't allow inferences.

11. **B** Again, careful reading of the question stem is essential. You're asked about the *significance* of lines 16–19 to the poem, not about what the words mean (C) or what the poet might be implying (D). Those two choices are both incorrect. Choice (E) has some merit in presenting lines 47–48 as an expansion. However, it's too narrow. The question asks for the best summary of the significance to the poem as a whole, not just to part of it. Choice (A) is also too narrow; it misses the connection between the life of people and the soul of the skyscraper that runs throughout the poem. Only (B) makes that connection.

Summary

- Don't worry about scansion (you know: iambic pentameter, dactyls, spondees, and the like). You probably won't see even one question on it.

- Remember:
  - Read the poem as prose.
  - Focus on the main idea.
  - When answering the questions, use POE and Consistency of Answers.

- Be sure to read around line references.

- Metaphysical poetry is excellent practice for the kind of poetry you'll see on the AP Exam. John Donne, Andrew Marvell, George Herbert, Thomas Carew, Abraham Cowley, and Richard Crashaw are all poets whose work provides excellent AP practice. Also, the poetry of Emily Dickinson and Robert Frost is rich in intricate grammatical structures.

- On EXCEPT, NOT, and LEAST questions, cross out the negative word and eliminate any choice that fits the remaining question.

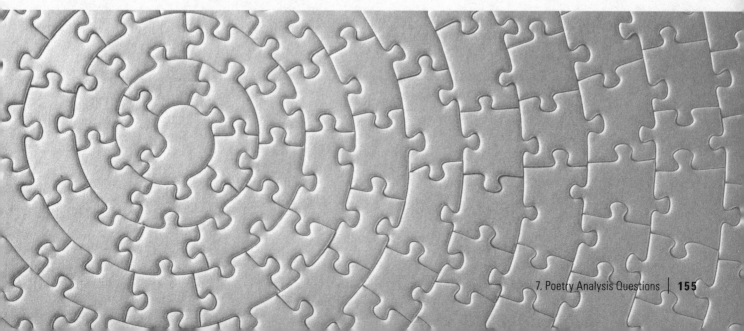

REFLECT

Respond to the following questions:

- Which types of multiple-choice questions discussed in this chapter do you feel you have achieved sufficient mastery to answer correctly?

- On which types of multiple-choice questions discussed in this chapter do you feel you need more work before you can answer correctly?

- What strategies discussed in this chapter do you feel you will be able to apply effectively when taking the exam?

- What parts of this chapter are you going to re-review?

- Will you seek further help, outside of this book (such as from a teacher, tutor, or AP students), on any of the content in this chapter—and, if so, on what content?

Chapter 8
Prose Fiction
Analysis Questions

USING THE SAMPLE PASSAGES AND QUESTIONS

There's no limit to the different kinds of questions that ETS can (and does) write for the AP English Literature Exam. As a result, we can't show you every type of question that may show up on the test. We can come pretty close, though, as questions are often reused from year to year. The best way to study these questions is by practicing on examples, but to understand and use the example questions, you need a passage.

In this chapter and the next, we provide passages with sample questions. This chapter has a prose fiction analysis passage. Chapter 8 has a poetry analysis passage. Read the passages carefully using our reading techniques, and then look over the questions.

There's no need to complete the questions immediately because we're going to take you through them one step at time, discussing the best approaches and specific techniques to use in answering them. Of course, if you want to see how you do on them before referring to our instructions, go right ahead.

After you've looked over the passages, read each question, try to answer it, and then follow our explanations. The correct answer to each question is given in the explanation, but don't just skim through the explanation looking for the answer to see whether you chose correctly. Read all of each explanation, regardless of whether you got the question right. Our explanations will point out details you overlooked and discuss how you might have approached the question differently.

At the end of this chapter and Chapter 8, you'll have the opportunity to try a full passage and set of questions so that you can practice using the techniques and approaches discussed in these chapters.

TAKING CONTROL OF PROSE FICTION ANALYSIS PASSAGES

Expect anything from mystery to humor to fantasy (and a host of other literary genres, or categories) in the exam's prose fiction analysis passages, representing periods ranging from the sixteenth century to modern times. Moreover, each prose fiction analysis passage is just a piece of a larger work, sometimes with bits truncated (cut out) in order to fit the exam's roughly 700–800 word average length. So, you may feel that you've been dropped into the middle of something when you first start reading, and that you've been left hanging when you reach the end. As disorienting as that may seem, each passage is a self-contained selection that holds the answers you need.

You'll find two or three prose fiction analysis passages (interspersed with poetry analysis) in the multiple-choice section, with about 10 to 12 minutes to answer 12 to 15 questions about each one. That's less than a minute per question, and you need time to read the passage, too. How can you accomplish that?

First, by *working* (instead of simply *reading*) the passage, using the active reading techniques described in Chapter 1. Your only objective is to answer the questions correctly, so use your active reading skills to take control and make the passage give you the information you need. Practice active reading until it becomes second nature.

Second, by using the time management and pacing techniques explained in Chapter 2. Work at a steady pace, and don't waste time on questions you can't answer. Guess (using your Letter of the Day) and move on, quickly noting the question number in case you have a chance to go back to it.

Third, learn to recognize the question types, question formats and the best way to approach each one. Review the information in Chapter 4, and practice with the passages in this book. That way, when you see a particular type of question on the exam, you'll be well prepared with a plan of attack.

A Passage in 12–15 Minutes

1. Work—don't just read—the passage. Read actively.
2. Manage your time; pace yourself.
3. Learn the question types.

GETTING TO KNOW THE QUESTIONS

Typical prose fiction analysis passage questions are designed to test your critical reading skills. They give you an opportunity to show that you can grasp both the overall theme (the main point), and how various elements of the passage function to develop that theme. These questions assess your ability to analyze, interpret and make inferences—to "read between the lines" and dissect *how* the author conveys his or her meaning. It also checks that you can do all of that quickly and accurately.

Prose fiction analysis passage questions tend to focus on elements that are likely familiar to you from previous literature studies, such as

- characters (their significance and function in the passage, as well as the relationships among them)
- setting and its significance
- situation and its significance
- narration
- plot
- theme(s)
- structure (how the passage progresses)
- perspectives (the narrator's and the author's) and the relationships of part to whole and parts to each other

Sound Familiar?
This items listed right here (well, left here, heh), are the Big Six, plus some guest stars.

- style (vocabulary and syntax, devices the author uses to convey his or her meaning)
- tone (the author's or narrator's attitude) and the elements that reveal it
- literary devices (figurative language such as allusions, metaphors and symbols) and their functions in the passage

In the rest of this chapter, you can practice taking control of two prose fiction analysis passages and making them give you the correct answers. First is a sample passage. Try using active reading techniques and answering the questions. Then read the answer explanations that follow; they describe not only how to reach the correct answer, but also how to approach this type of question when you encounter it in other passages. At the end of this chapter is a prose fiction analysis passage drill with questions and answer explanations to give you more practice.

SAMPLE PROSE FICTION ANALYSIS PASSAGE AND QUESTIONS

Edgar Allan Poe's "The Duc De L'Omelette"

Keats fell by a criticism. But who ever died of inept poetry? Ignoble souls!—De L'Omelette perished of an ortolan[1]. The story then, in brief:

Line That night the Duke was to sup alone. In the
(5) privacy of his bureau he reclined languidly on that otto-man for which he sacrificed his loyalty in outbidding his king—the notorious ottoman of Cadet.

He buries his face in the pillow. The clock strikes! Un-able to restrain his feelings, his Grace swallows an olive.
(10) At this moment the door gently opens to the sound of soft music, and lo! the most delicate of birds is before the most enamored of men! But what inexpressible dismay now overshadows the countenance of the Duke? *Horreur! Dog! Protestant! —the bird! Ah Good God! This modest*
(15) *bird you've quite unclothed and served without paper!"* It is superfluous to say more:—the Duke expired in a parox-ysm of disgust....

"Ha! ha! ha!" said his Grace on the third day after his decease.
(20) "He! he! he!" replied the Devil faintly, drawing himself up with an air of hauteur.

"Why surely you are not serious," retorted De L'Om-elette. "I have sinned—that's true—but, my good sir, consider!—you have no actual intention of putting such—
(25) such—barbarous threats into execution."

"No what?" said his Majesty—"come, sir, strip!"

"Strip, indeed! very pretty i' faith! no, sir, I shall not strip. Who are you, pray, that I, Duke De L'Omelette, Prince de Foie-Gras, just come of age, author of the
(30) 'Mazurkiad,' and member of the Academy, should divest myself at your bidding of the sweetest pantaloons ever made by Bourdon, the daintiest dressing gown ever put together by Rombert—take say nothing of undressing my hair—not to mention the trouble I should have in drawing
(35) off my gloves?"

"Who am I?—ah, true! I am Baal-Zebub, Prince of the Fly. I took thee, just now, from a rosewood coffin inlaid with ivory. Thou wast curiously scented, and labeled as per invoice. Belial sent thee—my Inspector of Ceme-
(40) teries. The pantaloons, which thou sayest were made by Bourdon, are an excellent pair of linen drawers, and thy dressing gown is a shroud of no scanty dimensions."

"Sir!" replied the Duke, "I am not to be insulted with impunity!—Sir! you shall hear from me! In the meantime
(45) au revoir!"—and the Duke was bowing himself out of the Satanic presence, when he was interrupted and brought back by a gentleman in waiting. Hereupon his Grace

rubbed his eyes, yawned, shrugged his shoulders, reflected. Having become satisfied of his identity, he took a bird's-
(50) eye view of his whereabouts.

The apartment was superb. Even De L'Omelette pro-nounced it "quite well done." It was not its length nor its breadth—but its height—ah, that was appalling!—there was no ceiling—certainly none—but a dense whirling
(55) mass of fiery-colored clouds. His Grace's brain reeled as he glanced upward. From above, hung a chain of an unknown blood-red metal—its upper end lost. From its nether extremity swung a large cresset. The Duke knew it to be a ruby; but from it there poured a light so intense, so
(60) still, so terrible. Persia never worshipped such, no great Sultan ever dreamed of such when, drugged with opium, he has tottered to a bed of poppies, his back to the flowers, and his face to the God Apollo. The Duke muttered a slight oath, decidedly approbatory.
(65) The corners of the room were rounded into niches, and these were filled statues of gigantic proportions. But the paintings! The paintings! O luxury! O love!—who gazing on those forbidden beauties shall have eyes for others.

The Duke's heart is fainting within him. He is not, how-
(70) ever, as you suppose, dizzy with magnificence, nor drunk with the ecstatic breath of the innumerable censers. (It's true that he thinks of these things to no small degree—but!) The Duke De L'Omelette is terror-stricken; for, through the lurid vista which a single uncurtained window
(75) is affording, lo! gleams the most ghastly of all fires!

The poor Duke! He could not help imagining that the glorious, the voluptuous, the never-dying melodies which pervaded that hall, as they passed filtered and transmuted through the alchemy of the enchanted window-panes,
(80) were the wailings and the howlings of the hopeless and the damned! And there, too!—there!—upon the ottoman!—who could he be?—he, the Deity—who sat as if carved in marble, and who smiled, with his pale countenance, bitterly?
(85) A Frenchman never faints outright. Besides, his Grace hated a scene—De L'Omelette is himself again. Hadn't he read somewhere? wasn't it said "that the devil can't refuse a card game?"

But the chances—the chances! True—desperate; but
(90) scarcely more desperate than the Duke. Besides wasn't he the slyest player in the craftiest card-club in Paris?—the legendary "21 club."

"Should I lose," said his Grace "I will lose twice—that is I shall be doubly damned—should I win, I return to my
(95) ortolan—let the cards be prepared."

His Grace was all care, all attention, his Majesty all confidence. His Grace thought of the game. His majesty did not think; he shuffled. The Duke cut.

The cards are dealt. The trump is turned—it is—it is—

---

[1] An ortolan is a small dove-like bird considered a supreme delicacy by nineteenth-century gourmets.

(100)   the king! No—it was the queen. His Majesty cursed her
masculine habiliments. De L'Omelette placed his hand
upon his heart.

They play. The Duke counts. The hand is out. His majesty counts heavily, smiles and is taking wine. The Duke
(105)   palms a card.

"It's your deal," said his Majesty, cutting. His Grace
bowed, dealt, and arose from the table—turning the King.
His Majesty looked chagrined.

Had Alexander not been Alexander, he would have been
(110)   Diogenes; and the Duke assured his antagonist in taking
his leave, "Were one not already the Duke De L'Omelette
one could have no objection to being the Devil."

1. The primary purpose of the passage is to portray

   (A) the characteristics of an exaggerated type through the
        figure of L'Omelette
   (B) a reassuringly humorous vision of hell through a
        narrative in which the Devil himself is bested
   (C) the evil consequences of excessive pride
   (D) the developing relationship between L'Omelette and
        the Devil
   (E) the pivotal change that occurs in L'Omelette through
        his encounter with the Devil

2. Which of the following best describes the Duke De
   L'Omelette?

   (A) He is a typical eighteenth-century nobleman.
   (B) He is a caricature of a snob.
   (C) He is a man more wicked than the Devil.
   (D) He is a man with perfect aesthetic judgment.
   (E) He is a man transformed by his encounter with a
        power greater than his own.

3. In context, lines 27–35 serve to reinforce the reader's
   impression of the Duke's

   (A) quick temper
   (B) exquisite taste
   (C) sense of self-importance
   (D) accomplishments and social position
   (E) misunderstanding of his situation

4. The author's portrayal of the Duke De L'Omelette is best
   described as

   (A) a sympathetic portrait of a man with overly delicate
        sensibilities
   (B) a comically ironic treatment of an effete snob
   (C) a harshly condemnatory portrait of a bon vivant
   (D) an admiring portrait of a great artist
   (E) a farcical treatment of the very rich

5. Which of the following descriptions is an example of the
   narrator's irony?

   (A) "Unable to restrain his feelings, his Grace swallows
        an olive." (lines 8–9)
   (B) "I took thee, just now, from a rosewood coffin inlaid
        with ivory." (lines 37–38)
   (C) "The Duke knew it to be a ruby; but from it there
        poured a light so intense, so still, so terrible."
        (lines 58–60)
   (D) "And there, too!—there!—upon the ottoman!—
        who could he be?—he, the Deity—who sat as if
        carved in marble, and who smiled, with his pale
        countenance, bitterly?" (lines 81–84)
   (E) "His Grace was all care, all attention, his Majesty all
        confidence." (lines 96–97)

6. In line 53, the word "appalling" suggests the Duke

   (A) has found the room's decor unacceptable
   (B) has approbation for clouds
   (C) suffers from insomnia
   (D) finds the apartment extraordinary
   (E) suffers from a paroxysm

7. Which of the following best implies the contextual
   meaning of the phrase "sacrificed his loyalty" (line 6)
   within the context of the story?

   (A) The Duke has fallen into disfavor with the King by
        outbidding him.
   (B) The Duke has betrayed his country.
   (C) The Duke has allowed his desire for the ottoman to
        override his deference to the King.
   (D) The Duke recognizes no one as more powerful than
        himself.
   (E) The Duke values the ottoman more greatly than his
        prestige.

8. In which of the following lines is the narrator most
   clearly articulating the Duke's thoughts?

   (A) "Ignoble souls!" (line 2)
   (B) "It is superfluous to say more:—"(lines 15–16)
   (C) "Having become satisfied of his identity, he took a
        bird's-eye view of his whereabouts." (lines
        49–50)
   (D) "But the chances—the chances! True—desperate;"
        (line 89)
   (E) "They play." (line 103)

9. Which of the following lines implies a speaker other than the narrator?

   (A) "But who ever died of inept poetry?" (lines 1–2)
   (B) "That night the Duke was to sup alone." (line 4)
   (C) "The apartment was superb." (line 51)
   (D) "His majesty did not think, he shuffled."
       (lines 97–98)
   (E) "Had Alexander not been Alexander, he would have
       been Diogenes." (lines 109–110)

10. Which of the following best describes the situation in lines 22–25 and the events that came immediately *before* it?

    (A) The Duke has just noticed the Devil and laughs
        at him. The Devil returns the laugh, but quietly
        because he feels insulted.
    (B) The Duke has just heard the Devil explain the
        tortures that lie in store for him. He believes the
        Devil is joking and laughs. The Devil mocks his
        laughter, implying that it is no joke.
    (C) The Duke and the Devil have been talking, but the
        exact topic has purposely been left vague.
    (D) The Duke has just heard the Devil's plans for him
        and laughs defiantly at the Devil. The Devil puns
        on the Duke's use of the word "Ha!" by saying
        "He!" By doing so, the devil indicates "He," that is
        the Duke, will be punished for his sins.
    (E) The Duke, believing he speaks with a lowly servant,
        laughs at the threats the Devil has made. The Devil
        plays along, laughing with the Duke in order to
        draw out the Duke's eventual humiliation.

11. Which of the following reinforces the effect of the passage most strongly?

    (A) Lighthearted situations narrated with deep
        seriousness
    (B) Humorous irony in the introduction, contrasted with
        serious reflection in the conclusion
    (C) Calculated objectivity offset by occasional
        interjections of subjective emotion
    (D) Underlying contempt partially concealed by
        objectivity
    (E) First-person outbursts of effusive emotion in an
        otherwise third-person narration

12. The narrator's attitude toward the Duke can be best described as

    (A) complete objectivity
    (B) ambiguous pity
    (C) slight distaste
    (D) bemused confusion
    (E) satiric glee

13. The passage contains

    I. abrupt shifts in tense
    II. an abrupt shift in place
    III. abrupt shifts in emotional state

    (A) I only
    (B) I and II only
    (C) I and III only
    (D) II and III only
    (E) I, II, and III

14. The phrase, "as if carved in marble" (lines 82–83), is an example of

    (A) an apostrophe
    (B) irony
    (C) lyricism
    (D) a metaphor
    (E) a simile

15. Grammatically, the phrase, "Were one not already the Duke De L'Omelette" (line 111), establishes the

    (A) simple past tense
    (B) past imperfect tense
    (C) present conditional tense
    (D) subjunctive mood
    (E) simple present tense

About Poe's "The Duc De L'Omelette"

This passage was adapted from a short story called "The Duc De L'Omelette." You'll sometimes see adapted passages on the AP English Literature Exam. All it means is the passage was edited to make it appropriate for all high school students and to meet the test's length requirements. The actual Poe story uses a great deal of French, but keeping the French parts would give an unfair advantage to those who studied French.

The passage demonstrates the kind of language and stylistic devices you'll see on prose fiction analysis passages on the AP English Literature Exam, but they aren't all this weird. If it seemed long, don't panic—it is about one-third longer than the usual AP passage. (We wanted to use a long passage in this example to give you plenty to work with and to provide abundant fodder for our sample questions. Keep in mind that with a total of 55 questions, some passages on the test will have fewer than 15 questions.) If you see a passage of this length on the test, there will then be a shorter passage somewhere to compensate.

Answers and Explanations to the Questions

We give detailed explanations to the 15 questions that followed the passage. Fifteen is the number of questions you should expect to see on a passage of this length. The passages and questions on our practice test are designed to imitate the actual exam. Here, we've chosen the questions with an eye toward teaching you our techniques, but even so, the mix of the types of questions is fairly representative of the questions you'll see on an AP passage.

We've broken the questions down into small groups in order to illustrate specific types of questions you're likely to see. We don't want you to memorize the names of these types or spend a lot of time practicing identifying these types. There are no points for doing that. If you do remember them, great, but all we want is for you to become familiar with the most common types of questions on the test and to see how the same techniques, applied in slightly different ways, work on question after question.

GENERAL COMPREHENSION QUESTIONS

The first question is a general question and as you know, general questions ask about the whole passage, not just some detail of the passage.

The question sets will often (but not always) start out with general questions. We've placed the questions on this passage in the order that lets us best explain them to you. Remember that when you actually take the test, you want to attempt the questions in the order given (if you felt comfortable with your comprehension of the passage). If you feel pretty lost, then you should put any general questions off until last, in the hope that working with the specific questions will give you more confidence about your comprehension of the passage and its main idea.

Primary Purpose

The classic general question is the primary purpose question:

---

1. The primary purpose of the passage is to portray

    (A) the characteristics of an exaggerated type through the
    figure of L'Omelette

    (B) a reassuringly humorous vision of hell through a
    narrative in which the Devil himself is bested

    (C) the evil consequences of excessive pride

    (D) the developing relationship between L'Omelette and the
    Devil

    (E) the pivotal change that occurs in L'Omelette through his
    encounter with the Devil

Here's How to Crack It

Understand the question by understanding the answer choices. What does "primary purpose" mean?

When you see a primary purpose question, it means you must look for an answer that covers the broad outline of the story. This advice goes for all general questions; it is what makes them general. Remember that you are looking for a choice that accurately describes some facet of the entire passage.

Now use the answer choices themselves to focus on exactly what primary purpose the test writers are looking for.

The question itself indicates that the primary purpose of the passage is to portray something. What is it portraying? Use POE.

Take (A). Does the whole passage deal with an exaggerated type? Well, the Duke is an exaggeration of something: This is a guy who takes time to approve of the decor in hell. Choice (A) seems to be a reasonable summation of the whole passage. Leave it. Now take each of the remaining choices in turn.

Now to (B). The whole passage is not all about a "reassuringly humorous vision of hell." Each paragraph does not point out how harmless hell is. The humorous part is the Duke's taking it all more or less in stride. Eliminate (B).

Choice (C) talks about "the evil consequences of excessive pride." The passage is all about the Duke's excessive pride, but what are the consequences? There are none. The end of the story finds the Duke returning to his ill-prepared ortolan, which is right where he started, so you have to wonder whether it's going to kill him all over again. Remember, *half bad equals all bad*. Eliminate (C).

POE In Action
Here's how you might approach a question using the POE strategy. Look for the *wrong* answers first.

And while you're at it, eliminate (D) unless you think that the whole passage is about the relationship between L'Omelette and the Devil. It isn't. The Devil doesn't have much personality in the story at all. He serves as a foil for the Duke, little else.

Eliminate (E) because the Duke doesn't change at all. When the point of a passage is to show a dramatic change, you'll know it. The whole passage will build to that change.

You're left with (A), the correct answer.

What phrase have we kept repeating? "The whole passage." General questions call for you to consider the whole passage, not one small piece of it.

Another thing we did was focus on key phrases in the answer choices. "What consequences?" we asked when we looked at (C). We didn't get taken in by the phrase "excessive pride." Learning how to focus on an answer choice is a skill that comes with practice. As you follow our explanations, your skill will improve. In fact, after that discussion, the next question should be a breeze.

Overall Character

AP passages tend to be focused on one thing. Here the focus is on the Duke. A passage might focus on the description of an event or a place, but the most common focus is on a character. Yes, here's where the first of the Big Six comes in handy.

2. Which of the following best describes the Duke De L'Omelette?
    (A) He is a typical eighteenth-century nobleman.
    (B) He is a caricature of a snob.
    (C) He is a man more wicked than the Devil.
    (D) He is a man with perfect aesthetic judgment.
    (E) He is a man transformed by his encounter with a power greater than his own.

Here's How to Crack It

The correct answer is (B) and finding it probably didn't cause you much trouble. About the only problem might have been the term *caricature*, which means "exaggerated portrait." It is a term you should know (it's in our glossary). Do you notice any similarities between the correct answer to question 1 and the correct answer here? You should. One speaks of an exaggerated portrayal of a type, and one speaks of a caricature of a snob. These are almost the same answer. The only difference is that the second question spells out what "type" is being caricatured: the snob. This is an example of Consistency of Answers. Both answers are consistent with the main idea, and when answers are consistent with the main idea, they are consistent with each other. In this case the answers are extremely similar. If you thought the Duke was an exaggerated portrayal in question 1, why would he suddenly become a "typical eighteenth-century nobleman" in question 2? That would be inconsistent, so eliminate (A). The Duke is either exaggerated or he's typical, but he can't be both. Choice (C) is for students who read into things too much. The Duke wins the card game at the end. Does that mean he's more wicked than the Devil? No. Choice (D) is too strong. "Perfect?" De L'Omelette thinks his tastes are perfect, but does the story suggest that his tastes are perfect? No, only that they are extremely, almost comically, particular. Choice (E) isn't supported by the passage. You'd think the Duke would be transformed by his encounter with the Devil, but he isn't. At the end of the story you should have gotten the feeling that L'Omelette is going to go right back to his old ways.

Consistency of Answers doesn't just apply to general questions. It is just as helpful with detail questions.

Try This Tip
When in doubt, make your answers agree with each other.

DETAIL QUESTIONS

Detail questions (aka specific questions) make up the majority of questions on the multiple-choice section of the test. These are questions (or answer choices) that direct you to a specific place in the passage and ask about your comprehension of the details.

Line-Reference Questions

Most of the time (but not always), the detail questions give you a line number or a range of lines with which to work. We call these questions line-reference questions. For line-reference questions there are just two things you need to keep in mind:

- Go back to the passage and reread the lines in question. Don't rely on your memory, particularly under the time pressure of the exam. Your memory will likely lead you astray. Also, read at least one full sentence before the line reference and one full sentence after the line reference. Keep in mind that a word or phrase you are being asked to define may not have the meaning you would infer from the wording of the question. It is important that you refer to the word in the context of the line.
- Keep the main idea in mind, and use Consistency of Answers whenever possible.

Try This One

3. In context, lines 27–35 serve to reinforce the reader's impression of the Duke's

    (A) quick temper
    (B) exquisite taste
    (C) sense of self-importance
    (D) accomplishments and social position
    (E) misunderstanding of his situation

Here's How to Crack It

This question calls for you to go back and read a fairly large range of lines—a whole paragraph. Go back and read it. Because the several lines referred to in this question make up a more or less self-contained paragraph, reading a full sentence before and after the reference doesn't make a big difference in getting the question right, but it doesn't hurt, either, and takes just an extra two or three seconds. Make it a habit to read a little above and below the lines referred to; it'll be worth a couple of points in the long run.

Essentially, the lines in question discuss the Duke's outrage at the Devil's command to disrobe.

If you misunderstand the question, you have a good chance of getting the answer wrong. The passage shows aspects of all the answer choices. The Duke shows a quick temper, mentions his tastes (which are not so much exquisite as they are ostentatious), mentions his accomplishments, and misunderstands his situation. But the correct answer is (C).

All the answer choices seem right, so what gives? The solution lies in understanding the question and how the question relates to the main idea. The question asks: What does the passage serve to reinforce? Nearly everything in this very compact story serves to reinforce the central impression of the story—the Duke's outrageous sense of self-importance. He isn't merely a snob; he's completely besotted with his own fabulous self. The Duke thinks he's the apex of human intellectual and social development. In fact, (A), (B), (D), and (E) are all facets of the Duke's vanity. His anger is angered vanity. His tastes are flawless; they must be, thinks the Duke, because they're his. When the Duke mentions his work, the "Mazurkiad," you can almost see him puff up with the greatness of it all. Even his misunderstanding is an aspect of his vanity. The Duke doesn't quite comprehend his surroundings because he can't imagine being in a position to take orders from anyone. All these things revolve like planets around the Duke's sense that he's the center of the universe.

If you had a solid grasp on the central theme of the story, the Duke's self-love, you might have found this question easy. Choices (A), (B), (D), and (E) are details. Choice (C) is the main thing. If you had trouble, all you had to do to get this question correct was muse, "Hmm, they all look possible, but which one is most consistent with the main idea?" Well, a snob thinks he's better than everyone and is very important. Choice (C), sense of self-importance, is most in agreement with that.

Question 3 is an example of using Consistency of Answers. Here's another:

4. The author's portrayal of the Duke De L'Omelette is best described as

(A) a sympathetic portrait of a man with overly delicate sensibilities
(B) a comically ironic treatment of an effete snob
(C) a harshly condemnatory portrait of a bon vivant
(D) an admiring portrait of a great artist
(E) a farcical treatment of the very rich

Here's How to Crack It

Take each answer a word at a time and remember, half bad equals all bad. If any part of the answer is wrong, don't hesitate to eliminate it. Yes, it's true that the portrait is of a man with delicate sensibilities (A), but is it sympathetic? Hardly. Get rid of it. You might not understand "effete" in (B), so hold on to it. However, "harshly condemnatory" in (C) should sound wrong to you. The Duke is harshly condemnatory of the servant who brings in his meal, but the passage itself does not disapprove of either of them. Half bad equals all bad, so eliminate it. Now look at (D): John Keats was a great artist, but the Duke? From these 12 lines you sure can't say that, so cross this one off too. On to (E). "Farcical?" Perhaps. But is this passage about the "very rich"? No, it's about the Duke De L'Omelette. Half bad equals all bad, so you're left with (B) even if you're not quite sure what it means. But here's a pop quiz: What technique tells you the answer must be (B)? Consistency of Answers.

Now we aren't saying every single question uses Consistency of Answers. It should be one of the first things you think about when you approach a question, but there are definitely questions that focus on a detail in such a way that Consistency of Answers doesn't come into play.

Here's an example:

_____○_____

5. Which of the following descriptions is an example of the narrator's irony?

(A) "Unable to restrain his feelings, his Grace swallows an olive." (lines 8–9)

(B) "I took thee, just now, from a rosewood coffin inlaid with ivory." (lines 37–38)

(C) "The Duke knew it to be a ruby; but from it there poured a light so intense, so still, so terrible." (lines 58–60)

(D) "And there, too!—there!—upon the ottoman!—who could he be?—he, the Deity—who sat as if carved in marble, and who smiled, with his pale countenance, bitterly?" (lines 81–84)

(E) "His Grace was all care, all attention, his Majesty all confidence." (lines 96–97)

Here's How to Crack It

Notice that in this question the line references come in the answer choices. That's not uncommon. Properly speaking, this isn't a specific question or a general question or a literary-term question. The answer choices send you back to the passage to find a specific example of something that occurs throughout the whole passage: irony, which is a literary term. But, you don't get points for putting questions in categories anyway; the important thing is to get the question right, efficiently.

Count on This
You can count on only a very few specific things showing up on the exam. One of them is irony.

The way to get this question right is to know what irony is. Learn to recognize its many forms. We discuss irony in our glossary of literary terms for the AP English Literature and Composition Exam. (Yep, we're going to say that every time we mention irony.)

The correct answer is (A). You should have noticed the entire tone of the piece is somewhat ironic. Most of the passage is written with a deliberate undercurrent of meaning that changes the effect of the literal meaning of the lines. This, above all, is the hallmark of irony; there's more than meets the eye. But let's get back to (A). Why is it ironic? Let's take the statement "Unable to restrain his feelings, his Grace swallows an olive." At face value, the Duke's feelings became so strong that he had to swallow an olive. Now, in no way can swallowing an olive be the outcome of unrestrained feelings unless one has pretty unusual feelings, which is precisely the point. The Duke's anticipation of dinner having reached a fevered pitch, he buries his face in a pillow. The clock bangs out the long-awaited hour and unable to restrain himself, the Duke swallows an olive. One thing this shows is how fanatically the Duke takes his meals. At the same time, the juxtaposition (to _juxtapose_ means to place things side by side) of the Duke's unrestrained feelings and his act of swallowing an olive show something else: the Duke's biggest feelings are actually puny; the Duke's crescendo of passion is capped by swallowing an olive. That's the ironic part. The author in effect says, "In the Duke's opinion this is something big, but we can all see that it's rather small." When the literal meaning of a word or phrase implies its opposite, you're dealing with irony.

Hey, didn't we say that the whole piece was ironic? If that's true, what makes the other choices wrong? Well, okay, the whole piece *is* ironic. In effect, the passage tells us that the Duke thinks he's absolutely first-rate but we can see that he's really quite laughable. However, for this question you must consider the answer choices in isolation. None of them alone carry the double meaning that is so crucial to irony. Choice (B) is a description of a coffin. Choice (C) describes the ruby that illuminates the Devil's chamber in hell. Choice (D) describes the moment the Duke realizes, at last, that the creature he's dealing with is truly the Devil himself. Choice (E) simply describes the Duke's and the Devil's attitude as they begin the card game.

———————————◯———————————

Okay, enough about irony, on to the next kind of question.

Single Phrase or Word Questions

AP questions will often ask you to look at a single word or phrase:

———————————◯———————————

6. In line 53, the word "appalling" suggests the Duke

    (A) has found the room's decor unacceptable
    (B) has approbation for clouds
    (C) suffers from insomnia
    (D) finds the apartment extraordinary
    (E) suffers from a paroxysm

Here's How to Crack It

It's true that for the AP English Literature and Composition Exam, a strong vocabulary helps a lot. If you did not know the meaning of *decor* in (A), *approbation* in (B), *insomnia* in (C), or *paroxysm* in (E), you may have been at a loss. You could eliminate (A) because you know that the Duke found the apartment "superb," and you could have guessed that the referenced line has nothing to do with the Duke's inability to sleep (that he suffers from insomnia). Then you would be left with (B), (D), and (E).

Keep in mind that you are only to answer the question being asked—to examine the contextual meaning of one word. You can safely eliminate (E) from the list because in the sentence that contains the word "appalling," a reference to the Duke's suffering or discomfort is not implied. Even if you don't know what *paroxysm* means (a convulsion), you can use POE to get rid of this answer choice. Now look carefully at (B). In line 53, "appalling" refers to the room, not the clouds. So you can eliminate this choice too, even if you don't know that *approbation* is approval. You're left with the correct answer, (D), in which the two words, which may seem very different, have a commonality in how they both describe something shocking.

———————————◯———————————

Questions 5 and 6 are two questions in a row that don't use Consistency of Answers. The streak's over. Here's a question that asks about a single phrase, yet you can still use Consistency of Answers to assist your POE.

7. Which of the following best implies the contextual meaning of the phrase "sacrificed his loyalty" (line 6) within the context of the story?

(A) The Duke has fallen into disfavor with the King by outbidding him.

(B) The Duke has betrayed his country.

(C) The Duke has allowed his desire for the ottoman to override his deference to the King.

(D) The Duke recognizes no one as more powerful than himself.

(E) The Duke values the ottoman more greatly than his prestige.

Here's How to Crack It

When approaching this question, you should first go back and read around the citation. Because the citation is a fragment of a sentence, you should read at least a full sentence before and after the reference. (If you want to read more, by all means, do. The full sentence before and after is just a guideline. If it takes you a little more reading to get your bearings in the passage, that's fine.)

Now, use POE to get rid of what is obviously wrong. If you stay focused with what the phrase in question means it should be easy to eliminate a few answers. Does "sacrificed his loyalty" mean the Duke has betrayed his country? That should sound a little too intense: We're talking about buying a couch here (an ottoman is a kind of couch). Eliminate (B). Does the Duke recognize no one as more powerful than himself? That may or may not be true, but how could you get that meaning from "sacrificed his loyalty?" Of course, if you try really hard you can talk yourself into anything. Don't talk yourself into answers. This is POE. Eliminate (D).

Can you eliminate two more answer choices? The best way is to ask yourself which answer choice is most in keeping with the Duke's character. Do you think the Duke cares about his prestige more than his couch? Of course he does. He would never sacrifice his prestige. L'Omelette thinks of appearances above all else. Eliminate (E). What about (A)? It is certainly reasonable that the Duke fell into disfavor with the King for outbidding him. But is this what "sacrificed his loyalty" means? No. And if you have any doubts, ask yourself what that interpretation has to do with the rest of the passage. Is the rest of the passage about the Duke's loss of favor with the King? No. That leaves (C), the correct answer. It is perfectly in keeping with the other answers and the rest of the passage: the Duke shows little deference to the Devil; why would he defer to the King?

The next two questions ask for your comprehension of a detail, but the questions center less around the meaning of the words than about what they indicate about the narrator.

Question-Comprehension Questions

Some questions are straightforward, some are vague, and a few are downright tricky. You need to pay close attention to the wording of questions and when you see an unusual phrase, it's a good idea to ask yourself why the phrase is worded that way. For many questions, just understanding what the question is asking is half the battle.

8. In which of the following lines is the narrator most clearly articulating the Duke's thoughts?

    (A) "Ignoble souls!" (line 2)
    (B) "It is superfluous to say more:—" (lines 15–16)
    (C) "Having become satisfied of his identity, he took a bird's-eye view of his whereabouts." (lines 49–50)
    (D) "But the chances—the chances! True—desperate." (line 89)
    (E) "They play." (line 103)

Here's How to Crack It

This question has little to do with the main idea. Your first task is to understand the question. What is meant by "articulating the Duke's thoughts"? Well, try to put it in your own words. The question could be rewritten as: "When is the narrator speaking for the Duke?" There's nothing wrong with putting a question in your own words so as to understand it better. In fact it's a good idea as long as you're careful and don't just drop off the parts of a question that confuse you. Reading the questions accurately is just as important as reading the passages. The passage isn't worth any points; the questions are.

Use POE. Eliminate what you can right away. When is the narrator clearly speaking as himself? Choices (B), (C), and (E) all seem like examples of straightforward narration, so eliminate them. That leaves just (A) and (D). In (A), the narrator responds to a question. He exclaims in a very Duke-like way, but the Duke hasn't even been introduced yet. How could the reader know it was the Duke speaking? The reader couldn't. All that's left is (D), the correct answer. In (D), the narrator steps into the Duke's mind for a moment to record his thoughts, and then just as quickly steps out with the words "but no more desperate than the Duke."

Question 9 picks up where question 8 left off; a variation on the same theme:

---

9. Which of the following lines implies a speaker other than the narrator?

   (A) "But who ever died of inept poetry?" (lines 1–2)
   (B) "That night the Duke was to sup alone." (line 4)
   (C) "The apartment was superb." (line 51)
   (D) "His majesty did not think, he shuffled." (lines 97–98)
   (E) "Had Alexander not been Alexander, he would have been Diogenes." (lines 109–110)

Here's How to Crack It

Read questions carefully. The difference between question 8 and question 9 is that question 8 asks which answer choice shows the Duke's speech (or thoughts), whereas question 9 wants to know which implies a speaker other than the narrator. Question 9 is tougher. If your approach to question 9 got stuck somewhere back on question 8 and you were still looking for the narrator to speak the Duke's thoughts (or perhaps the Devil's), you might have easily gotten this question wrong.

As always, use POE. Clearly, (B), (C), (D), and (E) are spoken by the narrator. What about (A)? Well, (A) is spoken by the narrator as well but *implies* another speaker, someone who asks the question, "Who ever died of poor poetry?" The narrator, speaking as himself, responds to that question: "Ignoble souls!" If the structure of this interchange wasn't clear to you, here's an explanation: "Who ever died of poor poetry?" is a rhetorical question (a question to which the answer is obvious—of course, most people would say, no one has ever been killed by a bad poem). That's where the narrator jumps in and says, "Oh ho, you think the answer to that question is so very obvious but that's because your souls have no finer qualities; it may seem unbelievable to you but some very delicate spirits have died of immaterial things like bad poetry. De L'Omelette, for example, died of a badly prepared meal." All that (and a little more) is contained in the first paragraph of the passage. This paragraph is a good example of how gifted writers make every word count.

Ready for one more detail question? It's a good example of how weird things can get on the AP Exam, as it asks about the meaning of a piece of the passage that isn't there.

Weirdness

10. Which of the following best describes the situation in lines 22–25 and the events that came immediately *before* it?

   (A) The Duke has just noticed the Devil and laughs at him. The Devil returns the laugh, but quietly because he feels insulted.

   (B) The Duke has just heard the Devil explain the tortures that lie in store for him. He believes the Devil is joking and laughs. The Devil mocks his laughter, implying that it is no joke.

   (C) The Duke and the Devil have been talking, but the exact topic has purposefully been left vague.

   (D) The Duke has heard the Devil's plans for him and laughs defiantly at the Devil. The Devil puns on the Duke's use of the word "Ha!" by saying "He!" By doing so, the devil indicates "He," that is the Duke, will be punished for his sins.

   (E) The Duke, believing he speaks with a lowly servant, laughs at the threats the Devil has made. The Devil laughs in order to play along with the Duke and draw out the Duke's eventual humiliation.

Here's How to Crack It

You may sometimes run across a weird or unexpected question on the test. In this case, you're being asked to make sense of an abrupt shift in the story, from the Duke's death to his meeting the Devil, and essentially to fill in the blanks.

Use POE and remember to read at least one sentence before and one sentence after, so as to piece things together. Choice (A) can be eliminated outright, as there is no indication in the text that the Devil feels insulted. (The "hauteur" hints that the opposite may be true.) Choice (C) is vague, but what the Duke and Devil have been discussing is not--the Duke refers to a specific topic, "barbarous threats," and elaborates in the next paragraph. Choice (D) suggests that "He!" is being used as a bizarre pun, but there's nothing to support that in the text. Finally, Choice (E) can also be eliminated, for although the Duke may not know that he speaks to the Devil, he also does not suggest that he speaks to a "lowly servant." Choice (B) is correct, and is the best (and simplest) explanation of the Devil's mocking reply.

Staying simple doesn't just apply to poetry analysis. Many students get into trouble when reading the answer choices and think about the wrong answers so much that they get led into outer space. This comes from looking at every answer choice as though it could be correct. Four out of the five answer choices are wrong. At least one answer choice is usually wildly wrong. If something looks nuts, don't spend five minutes trying to figure it out. If it looks nuts, it is.

11. Which of the following describes the effect of the passage most strongly?

(A) Lighthearted situations narrated with deep seriousness
(B) Humorous irony in the introduction, contrasted with serious reflection in the conclusion
(C) Calculated objectivity offset by occasional interjections of subjective emotion
(D) Underlying contempt partially concealed by objectivity
(E) First-person outbursts of effusive emotion in an otherwise third-person narration

Here's How to Crack It

Again, from the question alone you can't know exactly what the question asks. That's fine. Look over the answer choices. You can see that they refer to the tone, style, and structure of the passage. The test writers like to throw these mixtures at you. The way to work on this kind of question is to break the answer choices into bite-size parts, then check the passage to see whether you can find an example of that part. For example, are there lighthearted situations, (A)? Well, going to hell isn't exactly lighthearted. (So the choice is already wrong, but let's keep going.) Are the situations narrated with deep seriousness? No, not exactly. Narrated with a straight face perhaps, but not deeply serious. The idea is to break the choices into pieces you can use. Remember, half bad equals all bad.

The correct answer is (E). As always, use POE and look at the whole passage. Make your initial eliminations. Choice (A) is wrong because the situations are not so much lighthearted as absurd and the narrator is not deeply serious, but nearly as bizarre and out of control as the Duke. Choice (B) isn't worth a second look unless you really think cheating the Devil at cards is deadly serious. Choice (D) should be unappealing as well. What "contempt"? What "objectivity"? Eliminate it. Although the Duke shows contempt for his situation, this isn't the overall effect of the passage that the question asks for.

This leaves (E) and (C). Take each answer choice and go back to the passage. Do you see any "calculated objectivity"? Not really; almost every sentence is loaded with one of the Duke's preposterous emotions. Almost everything comes to us through a filter of the Duke's impressions, especially in the longer sentences. It isn't accurate to call the subjective (first-person element) "occasional." That is enough to eliminate (C), leaving you with just one remaining choice, (E). For safety's sake you should now examine it. "Outbursts of effusive emotion"? Well, there are all those exclamation points all over the place. As a matter of fact, half of the time the author seems to be shouting. The story is told in the third person, yet much of the time the Duke's persona, his voice, or the attitude behind his voice seems to be speaking. Choice (E) is correct.

The Complexity of the Test

It's unlikely that you'll see an AP question this complex and multi-layered, but it's better to expect the unexpected and over-prepare than to be caught off guard. Think of it this way: if you can parse a question like this, you're ready for the AP Exam.

Use the Glossary

If any of the terms we've used in this explanation—*first person, third person, subjectivity*—gave you trouble, you should refer to their definitions in the glossary, which is located at the end of this book.

Attitude questions are just like tone questions; they ask about the underlying emotional content of the passage:

12. The narrator's attitude toward the Duke can be best described as

    (A) complete objectivity
    (B) ambiguous pity
    (C) slight distaste
    (D) bemused confusion
    (E) satiric glee

Here's How to Crack It

The correct answer is (E). POE, as usual, helps a great deal. On tone questions, there are usually a couple of answer choices that you can dismiss without a second glance. There's no way you could call the passage an example of (A), complete objectivity; it's much too weird. Doesn't the whole passage feel high-strung, as though old Edgar A. Poe had a few too many cups of coffee on top of whatever else he was drinking that day? That feeling never goes with objectivity. Choice (B), pity, is just off the wall. Choice (C) might have been appealing because it didn't sound too extreme. In general, mild is better than extreme on tone questions but unfortunately, "slight distaste" is wrong; there's no evidence that the narrator feels a slight distaste for the Duke. Remember, you wanted to pick what the *narrator* feels. You might have felt slight distaste, but the question didn't ask how you felt. Speaking of how you felt, (D) is a type of answer choice that occasionally appears on the exam. When students are struggling, they're drawn to answers that suggest their own mental state, such as *confused*, *depressed*, *anxious*, and *fearful,* even when such words are plain wrong. The answer feels right, not because it's correct but because it's how the student feels taking a test. There's no evidence in the story that the narrator is confused or doesn't understand the Duke; in fact, he seems to understand the Duke a little too perfectly.

This brings up (E), the correct answer. "Glee" may seem a bit strong, but it fits. The narrator tells the story with energy, enthusiasm, and a completely unabashed use of exclamation points—that's a tip-off right there. Good writers don't overuse exclamation points. (The great Irish novelist James Joyce called them, derisively, "shriek marks.") Poe doesn't overuse them here, but it could easily seem like it. Poe uses exclamation points because, if for the Duke a badly prepared bird is upsetting enough to kill him, the Duke's life must be filled with exclamation points. This is one of the elements (and there are many) which make the passage satiric. *Satire* (see the glossary) is an important concept for the AP Exam. When a passage pokes fun at an exaggeratedly foolish type (in this case, the type of arrogant man who considers himself supreme in all things), you can be sure it's satire. The gleefulness stems from the evident enjoyment Poe takes in describing the Duke's peculiar foolishness. Of course, Poe has the Duke win in the end, which makes sense because Poe himself had a lot of the Duke in him.

Structure Questions

Question 13 tests whether you've noticed certain structural shifts in the passage. The question is in the Roman numeral format, so your first step is to identify the correct choice(s) from among the three Roman numeral alternatives.

---

13. The passage contains

    I. abrupt shifts in tense
    II. an abrupt shift in place
    III. abrupt shifts in emotional state

    (A) I only
    (B) I and II only
    (C) I and III only
    (D) II and III only
    (E) I, II, and III

Here's How to Crack It

Take each point one at a time, and look to the passage to see whether what you want is there. If you know where to look, this question is a snap.

Let's start with (II). Why (II)? It's the easiest of the three to see, and why not? You don't have to examine the (I), (II), and (III) points in order. When the Duke dies "in a paroxysm of disgust" (lines 17–18) there is an abrupt change of place—to hell. So eliminate any answer that doesn't contain (II)—(A) and (C).

Now to point (I). Did you also notice that there is an abrupt change of tense at that same line about "a paroxysm of disgust"? The change from the Duke's bedroom to hell is so striking that many students overlook the fact that the tense of the story changes. The second paragraph is in the present tense. It changes when the narrator says, "it *is* superfluous to say more—the Duke expir*ed* in a paroxysm of disgust." That's the simple past and the simple present in one sentence; your English teacher would hang you for it! (For just one example of the shifts, look at how the tense changes back to the present for one paragraph at the end when L'Omelette and the Devil play cards. It's easy to overlook.) Okay, so that means you can eliminate anything that doesn't contain item (I)—(D). You're already down to just two answer choices—(B) and (E).

All that's left is (III). Abrupt shifts in emotional state. You probably knew they happened. It felt like they happened, but where exactly? Was it really abrupt? Hey, don't overthink and worry yourself to death. There are abrupt shifts in emotional state. In the middle of the story the Duke goes from admiring the Devil's decor to being stricken with terror when he realizes that he is in fact dealing with Satan, to getting control of himself again and challenging the Devil to cards, all in the space of about 20 lines. That qualifies as abrupt. Items (I), (II), and (III) are all examples contained in the passage, so they must be in the answer choice. The correct answer is (E).

Literary Term Questions

14. The phrase, "as if carved in marble" (lines 82–83), is an example of

    (A) an apostrophe
    (B) irony
    (C) lyricism
    (D) a metaphor
    (E) a simile

Here's How to Crack It

This is an absolutely straightforward literary terms question. You are sure to see a few questions like it on the test. Of course you should use POE, but the best solution for literary term questions is to know the terms. That's why we've included our glossary. As we mentioned earlier, there are just a few things you can be sure will make an appearance somewhere on the test. Among those things are the terms *simile* and *metaphor*.

The correct answer here is (E). The phrase is a simile. A comparison that uses *like* or *as* is a simile. Even if these terms don't show up on your test as the best answers to a question (and chances are that's exactly how they will show up), at the very least they'll show up as answers you'll be able to eliminate. If you aren't aware that the phrase in question is a simile, eliminate what you can and take your best guess. Believe it or not, all the terms in the question are defined in our glossary.

Okay, one more question.

Grammar Questions

15. Grammatically, the phrase, "Were one not already the Duke De L'Omelette" (line 111), establishes the

    (A) simple past tense
    (B) past imperfect tense
    (C) present conditional tense
    (D) subjunctive mood
    (E) simple present tense

Here's How to Crack It

The correct answer is (D). When a sentence begins with *were*, it's subjunctive—count on it. What's a *mood*? Well, to those who make it their business to know (language scholars, mostly), *mood* refers to what a verb form indicates besides time. In the sentence "Go away!" *go* isn't just in the present tense. It expresses command. Thus, it is in the imperative mood. In "Jack laughs," *laughs* indicates a state of being. It is in the indicative mood. *Indicative*, *imperative*, and *subjunctive* are the principle moods of English. The use of the subjunctive and its forms have faded from our language, which is why starting a sentence with the word *were* might sound a little strange. It is grammatically correct English, however.

Unless you intend to teach Latin or go to graduate school for linguistics, mood isn't a term you'll need to know precisely; for your purposes on the test, and probably for the rest of your life, you can think of a mood as not exactly a verb tense, but close.

Brush Up on Grammar

If you're rusty on your grammatical terms, Chapter 4 contains definitions with examples of the basic terms you need to know, such as *direct object, indirect object, phrase,* and *clause.*

There may be a few grammar questions on the AP Exam. Use POE and take your best shot. In general, studying specific concepts in English grammar for the sake of a few points on the multiple-choice section is not worth the time. Studying grammar for other reasons is by no means a waste of time as a working command of English grammar is essential for effective writing. We'll have more to say about grammar in the next chapter, when we deal with a sample poetry analysis passage and questions.

A FEW FINAL WORDS

If you worked through the passage as we instructed, you just learned a great deal about how to take the multiple-choice questions on the AP English Literature and Composition Exam. It probably took close to five times longer here than working on a real passage would, but that's to be expected—you're learning. This does bring up an important point though: time. We've taken you through the passage and familiarized you with some typical questions so that when you're on your own you can work efficiently and accurately, answering all the questions in about 12–15 minutes.

But what if it doesn't work that way? Let's say you had reasoned that this passage was the most difficult on the test and decided to do it last. By the time you got to it, you had only seven minutes left. Seven minutes to do that passage! You would use up most of that time just reading it. Should you give up?—No! This is where all the study you've put into the questions can really pay off. Check out the Art of the Seven-Minute Passage—and enjoy!

The Art of the Seven-Minute Passage

When you hit the last passage on the test, check your time. If you have seven minutes or fewer left, you have to change your strategy. You don't have enough time to do the passage the normal way. It's time for emergency measures. What is the worst thing to do in an emergency? Panic. Don't. The best defense against panic is preparation. Know exactly what you're going to do. Here it is:

7 Minutes to Go!
If you find yourself in a situation in which you only have 7 minutes left but several questions still unanswered, don't panic. Instead, follow this simple six-step system.

- Don't read the passage. Just *don't* do it.

- Go straight to the questions.

- Answer the questions in the following order:

  1. **Answer any literary term or grammar questions.** You barely need the passage at all for these questions. If you know the point at issue you'll just snap up a point. Otherwise apply as much POE as you can and guess.

  2. **Go to any question that asks for the meaning of a single word or phrase.** These questions always include a line reference. Go to the passage and read a sentence before and after the reference. Answer the question.

  3. **Go to any other question that gives you a line reference in the question.** (Not line-reference answer choices, but questions.) Read the reference and answer the question.

  4. **Go to any question on tone or attitude.** By this time, you've read quite a bit of the passage just by answering questions. You've read enough to be able to make a good guess about where the author's coming from.

  5. **Go to any questions that have line references in the answer choices.** Answer them all.

  6. **Do whatever is left over**—character questions, primary purpose questions, weird questions, and so on. If you need to, read some of the passage to get them. Go ahead and read. Keep working until the proctor tells you to put down your pencil.

That's the Art of the Seven-Minute Passage. It works in six, five, four, three, two, or one minute too; with less time, you don't get as far down the list, that's all.

What If I Have Seven Minutes and Fifteen Seconds Left?

Seven minutes or fewer is a good rough guideline for when to use the Don't Read the Passage technique. Your pace on multiple-choice passages should be about 12–15 minutes a passage. If you have an awkward amount of time left for the last passage—that is, somewhere between seven and fifteen minutes—you'll have to decide which approach to use. You have two choices. The first is to just read and work faster, to step on the gas big-time. The other choice is to go straight to the questions, that is, to use the Art of the Seven-Minute Passage technique. It's your call. At the seven-minute mark (or 7 minutes and 3 seconds, whatever), you should go straight to the questions. With 10 minutes left you should probably try to read the passage fast but then attempt the questions in the seven-minute order. At, say, 14 minutes, you should just work normally, but keep in mind that you don't have any time to waste worrying about those silly things students worry about, like whether you've guessed too many (C)'s, or ponder the occult meaning of the pattern of dots you've made.

Prose Fiction Analysis Passage Drill

Suggested time: 12–15 minutes

Questions 1–14. Choose your answers to questions 1–14 based on a careful reading of the following passage. (The passage, an excerpt from a novel by Leo Tolstoy, describes one of the central characters and his dog.)

Getting on his boots and stockings, taking his gun, and carefully opening the creaking door of the barn, Levin went out into the road. It was still gray out-of-doors.
Line "Why are you up so early, my dear?" the old woman,
(5) their hostess, said, coming out of the hut and addressing him affectionately as an old friend.
"Going shooting, granny."
Laska ran eagerly forward along the little path. Levin followed her with a light, rapid step, continually looking
(10) at the sky. He hoped the sun would not be up before he reached the marsh. But the sun did not delay. In the trans-parent stillness of morning the smallest sounds were au-dible. A bee flew by Levin's ear with the whizzing sound of a bullet. He looked carefully, and saw a second and a
(15) third. The marsh could be recognized by the mist which rose from it, thicker in one place and thinner in another, so that the reeds and willow bushes swayed like islands in this mist. Laska walked beside her master, pressing a little forward and looking round. … Levin examined his pistols
(20) and let his dog off. Levin patted Laska, and whistled as a sign that she might begin.
Laska ran joyfully and anxiously through the slush that swayed under her.
Running into the marsh among the familiar scents, Las-
(25) ka detected at once a smell that pervaded the whole marsh, the scent of that strong-smelling bird that always excited her more than any other. Sniffing in the air with dilated nostrils, she felt at once that not their tracks only but they themselves were here before her, and not one, but many.
(30) They were here, but where precisely she could not yet de-termine. To find the very spot, she began to make a circle, when suddenly her master's voice drew her off. "Laska! here?" he asked, pointing her to a different direction. She stopped, asking him if she had better not go on doing as
(35) she had begun. But he repeated his command in an angry voice, pointing to a spot covered with water, where there could not be anything. She obeyed him, pretending she was looking, so as to please him, went round it, and went back to her former position, and was at once aware of
(40) the scent again. Now when he was not hindering her, she knew what to do, and without looking at what was under her feet, and to her vexation stumbling over a high stump into the water, but righting herself with her strong, supple legs, she began making the circle which was to make all
(45) clear to her. The scent of them reached her, stronger and stronger, and more and more defined, and all at once it became perfectly clear to her that one of them was here, behind this tuft of reeds, five paces in front of her; she

stopped, and her whole body was still and rigid. Her tail
(50) was stretched straight and tense, and only wagging at the extreme end. Her mouth was slightly open, her ears raised. One ear had been turned wrong side out as she ran up, and she breathed heavily but warily, and still more warily looked round, but more with her eyes than her head, to
(55) her master. He was coming along with the face she knew so well, though the eyes were always terrible to her. He stumbled over the stump as he came, and moved, as she thought, extraordinarily slowly. She thought he came slowly, but he was running.
(60) Noticing Laska's special attitude as she crouched on the ground, as it were, scratching big prints with her hind paws, and with her mouth slightly open, Levin knew she was pointing at grouse, and with an inward prayer for luck, especially with the first bird, he ran up to her. Coming
(65) quite close up to her, he could from his height look be-yond her, and he saw with his eyes what she was seeing with her nose. In a space between two little thickets, to a couple of yards' distance, he could see a grouse. Turning its head, it was listening. Then lightly preening and fold-
(70) ing its wings, it disappeared round a corner with a clumsy wag of its tail.
"Fetch it, fetch it!" shouted Levin, giving Laska a shove from behind.
She darted forward as fast as her legs would carry her
(75) between the thick bushes.
Ten paces from her former place a grouse rose with a guttural cry and the peculiar round sound of its wings. And immediately after the shot it splashed heavily with its white breast on the wet mire. Another bird did not linger,
(80) but rose behind Levin without the dog. When Levin turned towards it, it was already some way off. But his shot caught it. Flying twenty paces further, the second grouse rose upwards, and whirling round like a ball, dropped heavily on a dry place.
(85) When Levin, after loading his gun, moved on, the sun had fully risen, though unseen behind the storm-clouds. The moon had lost all of its luster, and was like a white cloud in the sky. Not a single star could be seen. Crows were flying about the field, and a bare-legged boy was
(90) driving the horses to an old man. The smoke from the gun was white as milk over the green of the grass.
One of the boys ran up to Levin.
"Uncle, there were ducks here yesterday!" he shouted to him, and he walked a little way off behind him.
(95) And Levin was doubly pleased, in sight of the boy, who expressed his approval, at killing three snipe, one after another, straight off.

1. One effect of lines 85–88 is to emphasize

   (A) the author's ability to create a sense of foreboding
   (B) the passage of time explicitly
   (C) the use of specific details to frame the passage
   (D) the impact of the weather on the events
   (E) Levin's desire to seek shelter

2. How is the word "vexation" used in line 42?

   (A) To demonstrate Levin's confusion about Laska's clumsiness
   (B) To underscore the danger of Laska's mission
   (C) To reveal Laska's bewilderment as to why she stumbled
   (D) To emphasize Laska's single-mindedness
   (E) To highlight her irritation toward Levin's command

3. The passage suggests that Levin

   (A) is visiting with family
   (B) is anxious about his ability to provide for his family
   (C) has a strained relationship with Laska
   (D) prefers to spend time alone
   (E) is on familiar terms with those whom he encounters

4. What is the function of lines 64–67 in relation to lines 30–31?

   (A) Levin's hunting skills are superior to Laska's.
   (B) Laska requires Levin's supervision when hunting.
   (C) Laska finds Levin's proximity to her helpful.
   (D) The author highlights the synergistic relationship between Laska and Levin.
   (E) The author underscores Levin's dependence on Laska.

5. Which lines demonstrate Laska's relationship to Levin?

   (A) Lines 20–21
   (B) Lines 37–40
   (C) Lines 55–56
   (D) Lines 70–71
   (E) Lines 72–73

6. The author views Levin

   (A) with impartial objectivity
   (B) with wry optimism
   (C) as a domineering master
   (D) as a boastful hunter
   (E) through a critical lens

7. The passage as a whole is most indebted to which literary tradition?

   (A) Romanticism
   (B) Realism
   (C) Modernism
   (D) Transcendentalism
   (E) Naturalism

8. In context of the passage as a whole, lines 8–23 serve to

   (A) provide a description of the setting
   (B) foreshadow later events
   (C) build anticipation
   (D) establish perspective
   (E) establish the characters' contentment in nature

9. The passage contains which of the following?

   I. Similes and alliteration
   II. Imagery
   III. An omniscient narrator

   (A) I only
   (B) I and II only
   (C) I and III only
   (D) II and III only
   (E) I, II, and III

10. In lines 95–97, the author characterizes Levin as

    (A) proud and content
    (B) pleased and exhausted
    (C) powerful and victorious
    (D) astonished and boastful
    (E) approving and dignified

11. The narrator suggests that the individuals Levin encounters are characterized by

    (A) envious curiosity about Levin's excursion
    (B) exuberant pleasure for Levin's skill
    (C) pious respect for Levin's hunting prowess
    (D) warm regard for Levin
    (E) affectionate approval for his day's accomplishments

12. What dominant technique is the author using in lines 31–40?

   (A) Personification
   (B) Irony
   (C) Anthropomorphism
   (D) Dialogue
   (E) Metaphor

13. The sentence in lines 40–45 contains all of the following EXCEPT

   (A) a character flaw
   (B) alliteration
   (C) suspense
   (D) juxtaposition
   (E) complex syntax

14. Lines 32–37 suggest

   (A) Levin's temperamental nature
   (B) Laska's submissive nature toward Levin
   (C) Laska's ability to speak to Levin
   (D) Laska's inexperience with hunting
   (E) Levin's deftness in hunting

PROSE FICTION ANALYSIS PASSAGE DRILL: ANSWERS AND EXPLANATIONS

Considered one of the greatest writers of all time, Leo Tolstoy was a Russian author, and *Anna Karenina* was his second novel. This novel, along with *War and Peace*, are hallmark examples of realism in literature.

1. **C**   Coming at the end of the passage, this description of the sun bookends the passage nicely (lines 85–88). Therefore, the correct answer is (C). The passage ends on a pleasant note, so the author is not creating a sense of foreboding, so eliminate (A). The effect of these lines is not to highlight the passage of time explicitly or implicitly, so (B) is incorrect. Rather, these lines offer further description of the setting and are written in such a way that they parallel the description provided at the beginning of the passage. The weather is not impacting Levin's hunting—he's done quite well so far—and he does not appear to be seeking shelter at the conclusion of the passage, so (D) and (E) are also incorrect.

2. **D**   *Vexation* means annoyance or irritation, not confusion, so eliminate (A) and (C). This word highlights Laska's desire to find the source of the smell, and she's irritated that the stump got in her way. However, she does not let it or her stumble impede her forward progress for very long. She is focused on the task at hand and does not let this event distract her, making (D) the correct answer. She is not irritated that Levin has asked her to find the bird, (E), nor is there evidence in the passage that she's in danger, (B).

3. **E**   Although Levin refers to the old lady as "granny" (note the lower case g), and the boy calls Levin "Uncle," Levin is not related to either of them. The old woman is the hostess of the place at which he is staying, and he comes across the boy while he is hunting, so eliminate (A) and (B). There is no evidence in the text to support (C) or (D). Since he does speak with the old woman in a friendly way, and the boy addresses him in a casual way, we can infer that Levin treats those whom he encounters in an informal and warm way. Therefore, (E) is the answer.

4. **D**   The first line reference illustrates the advantage Levin's height gives him. From his vantage point, Levin can see what Laska's nose has tracked. The second line reference demonstrates Laska's ability to put the pair in close proximity to the bird—a tracking skill she has but Levin does not. Therefore, these lines emphasize how the combined efforts of the pair allow them to pinpoint the bird's exact location. The correct answer is (D). In (A), the cooperative interaction is minimized. The fact that Levin, not Laska, can actually see the bird makes (E) wrong. Finally, (B) and (C) do not reflect the purpose of these lines, nor are they supported by the text.

5. **B**   Laska is obedient to her master. She follows his commands and seeks to please him. The correct answer is (B). Choice (D) is referring to the grouse, not Laska, and is incorrect. Choice (A) does not answer the question—it asks for Laska's relationship to Levin. This choice is from Levin's perspective. In the context of the whole passage, there is no evidence to support (C) and (E). She does obey Levin, she moves "eagerly" and "joyfully," and she does want to please him. She is not afraid of him or threatened by him.

6. **A** The author shows Levin's friendly exchanges with the people he encounters, his manner toward Laska, and his thoughts as he hunts. The reader is given a wide range of information from which to draw his or her own conclusions about Levin. Therefore, the author provides a neutral view, and (A) is the best answer. Choices (C) and (D) could be inferred at certain parts, but there are moments that undermine both. We see a softer side of Levin, for example, when he pats Laska on the head and allows her to run off leash, both of which would discount (C). There's a moment when he prays for luck on his bird, which undermines (D). The author is not sarcastic, (B), nor is he critical toward Levin, (E) overall.

7. **B** Tolstoy is classified as a writer of realism, so the correct answer is (B). Note that the naturalism movement did not occur until well after Tolstoy wrote *Anna Karenina*. Literature from the realism movement is notable for its use of detail, transparent language, truthfulness, and omniscient narrator. Writers of realism sought to reflect the true, daily reality of life—this passage is a prime example of realism.

8. **A** The last question helps with this question: this passage is representative of the realism movement, so thorough descriptions of the setting and characters will be present in the work. The purpose of this section of the text is to give the reader a vivid description of what the characters are experiencing and doing, so the correct answer is (A). There is no foreshadowing, (B), or rising anticipation, (C). The perspective changes in this passage, thereby eliminating (D), and while the characters may seem content in nature, it is not the purpose of this part of the text, so (E) can be eliminated as well.

9. **E** Examine each item separately. Item (I) is evident throughout the passage. For example, lines 17–18 contain a simile, and lines 42–46 contain an extended example of alliteration. Therefore, eliminate (D). Item (II) is also featured throughout the passage. The reader is provided with a vivid depiction of the scene to appeal to the reader's senses in lines 49–55, for example. Therefore, eliminate (A) and (C). Item (III) is also true, since the narrator knows the thoughts of both Levin and Laska. Since all three are present in the passage, the correct answer is (E).

10. **A** Levin is quite pleased with himself and satisfied with his haul, at what appears to be just the start of his day of hunting. Therefore, the correct answer is (A). There is no evidence in the text that he feels exhausted, (B), powerful, (C), astonished, or boastful, (D). Furthermore, it is the boy who approves of Levin, so eliminate (E) as well.

11. **D** Use the answer to question 3 to help you on this question. His interactions with the old woman and boy are both friendly and cordial. Everyone is getting along nicely and both seem to enjoy Levin's presence, so the correct answer is (D). There is no evidence of envy, (A). The old woman makes no comment regarding Levin's skill, so eliminate (B) and (C). Levin encounters the old woman before he shoots any birds, so there is no way to know whether she approves of his accomplishments, (E).

12. **C** This is a pure definition question, and you need to know the difference between personification and anthropomorphism. When an animal is given human characteristics, behavior, or motivation, anthropomorphism is at work. Personification requires that the nonhuman quality or thing take on a human shape. In this case, Laska seems to have human thoughts (asking him if she had better not go on doing as she had begun) and motivations (pretending she was looking, so as to please him) but never takes on human form. The correct answer is (C). Note that in order for there to be dialogue, both characters would have to be speaking. Since only Levin is actually speaking, (D) cannot be correct.

13. **A** There is evidence of alliteration, (B), since the initial s sound is repeated in stumbling, stump, strong, supple, she, and circle. She has an intense desire to find the bird, and each event presented in this sentence adds a layer of light suspense, (C). The idea of Levin hindering her (sending her off in the wrong direction) and the stump acting as an impediment, presented with her desire to reach the source of the scent, is an example of juxtaposition, (D). Note the use of compound, complex sentence structure—complex syntax is present, (E). Laska stumbling is not a character flaw, nor is Levin hindering her a flaw in his character, so the correct answer is (A).

14. **B** Use the earlier questions to help you here, especially question 5. Laska obeys her master despite not feeling his command is correct, which makes her obedient and submissive, so keep (B). She cannot actually speak to Levin—remember, this is realism—so eliminate (C). There is no evidence that Laska is inexperienced, (D). If anything, there is evidence to the contrary, since she knows she needs to go on doing as she had begun, which could reveal a slight flaw in Levin's skill as a hunter and would thus disprove (E). Choice (A) might be tempting, but this answer has been wrong before—the rest of the passage does not indicate that Levin has an erratic or volatile disposition. The answer that is best supported by the text is (B).

Summary

o When a question seems unclear, the answer choices can help you make sense of it.

o On general questions, you are looking for a choice that accurately describes some facet of the entire passage.

o Learn to focus on key phrases in the answer choices in order to eliminate using the "half bad equals all bad" technique.

o Use Consistency of Answers.

o For line reference questions: Keep the main idea in mind and use Consistency of Answers whenever possible. Also, go back to the passage and reread the lines in question, as well as one full sentence before and after the line reference.

o Pay close attention to the wording of questions. Put questions in your own words if that makes things easier for you. Be careful not to just ignore confusing parts, though.

o Expect a weird question or two. The test writers like to get creative on the AP English Literature and Composition Exam. We can't prepare you for everything, just almost everything.

o Don't be intimidated by Roman numeral questions. POE works wonderfully on them.

o Our glossary of terms has many valuable definitions and will get you some points; flip to the back of this book to brush up on important key terms!

o Don't worry about studying for grammar questions unless you need to re-familiarize yourself with basic grammar terms.

o Use the Seven-Minute Passage technique for the last passage if you have seven minutes or fewer left: don't read the passage, and answer the questions starting with those that require no knowledge of the passage or those that can be answered by referring to specific lines.

REFLECT

Respond to the following questions:

- Of which types of multiple-choice questions discussed in this chapter do you feel you have achieved sufficient mastery to answer correctly?

- On which types of multiple-choice questions discussed in this chapter do you feel you need more work before you can answer correctly?

- What strategies discussed in this chapter do you feel you will be able to apply effectively when taking the exam?

- What parts of this chapter are you going to re-review?

- Will you seek further help, outside of this book (such as from a teacher, tutor, or AP students), on any of the content in this chapter—and, if so, on what content?

Chapter 9
The Idea Machine: Starting Your Essays with a High Score

FROM IDEA TO EXECUTION

We're going to take you through our AP English writing process, one we've designed specifically for AP essays. The most stressful part of writing essays under time pressure is coming up with something to say quickly. In this chapter, we'll show you how to get the ideas that give you something to write about in the first place. We aren't going to teach you how to write; you've already spent years learning to write. However, AP essays are unlike anything you've had to write before, and you probably haven't spent years learning how to write them.

Approximately 90 percent of this chapter is about how to get an overall idea of your essay and create a great first paragraph. If you can get off to a good start, you're more than halfway to a great score.

THE APPROACH

Just as with the multiple-choice section, you want to have a common sense, step-by-step approach to the essay section (and know how to use it). Here it is:

- Bring a watch and note the time. Remember: 40 minutes per essay.
- Pick the essay (prose fiction analysis, poetry analysis, literary argument) you want to write.
- Identify the key words in the essay prompt.
- Skim the passage.
- Work the passage, make notes, and identify quotations you will want to use.
- Use the Idea Machine (explained in this chapter) to plan your first paragraph.
- Support and develop the points you made in your first paragraph in your body paragraphs.
- Get a solid conclusion on the page. Your conclusion can be as important as your introduction, and it usually is.
- Repeat the process with the other essays.

Don't Write a Formal Outline

You don't have time to write an outline. Outlines are for organizing longer, more complex pieces of writing, like research papers, when you have the time to revise and plan. We know you've probably had outlining drummed into you by your teachers. But short essays, like the ones you'll write for the AP Exam, don't call for an outline. You don't even have time to rewrite. Our method shows you how to come up with a solid beginning from which you can build so that you can just write the rest of the essay without an outline.

The Idea Machine

We've developed a method of approaching AP essays that we call the "Idea Machine." Hey, don't get us wrong, the *real* idea machine is in your skull. The point here is to focus your brain, imagination, and analytical skills in a way that's productive for the AP Exam. This approach won't let you down. Use it, and your essays will shine.

The Idea Machine is a series of questions that direct your reading to the material needed to write an essay. Take these questions, apply their answers to the essay question, and in the end you'll find you've written the kind of essay the Readers want to see.

The Idea Machine

1. What is the meaning of the work?
   a. What is the literal, face-value meaning of the work?
   b. What feeling (or feelings) does the work evoke?
2. How does the author get that meaning across?
   a. What are the important images in the work and what do those images suggest?
   b. What specific words or short phrases produce the strongest feelings?
   c. What do the characters, settling, structure, or narrators tell you about the passage?

That may not look like much, but when we put all the pieces together in this chapter and the next, you'll see just how powerful of a tool we're giving you.

The Classic Essay Question

Whether you are working on a prose fiction analysis or poetry analysis passage, there is a classic essay question that you will be asked to address. Here it is in its most basic form:

> Read the following work carefully. Then, in a well-written essay, analyze the manner in which the author conveys ideas and meaning. Discuss the techniques the author uses to make this passage effective. Avoid summary.

The classic essay question actually breaks down into three questions. The first two should look familiar because they're part of the Idea Machine.

1. What does the poem or passage mean?
2. How did the author get you to see that? Were elements like character, setting, structure, narration, and figurative language deployed? Which ones?
3. How do the answers to questions 1 and 2 direct your knowledge to adequately answer the question?

The first question is hidden, but totally important. It's the foundation on which you build the rest of your essay. Your (high-scoring) essay should answer those three questions in that order. Question 2 is the one you'll be asked on the exam; the test writers feel that question 1 is implied.

If the first question is "What does the passage or poem mean?" Well…what does that mean? What is *meaning*?

The Meaning of *Meaning*

For the AP essays, the meaning of a work of prose fiction or poetry is the most basic, flat, literal sense of what is said plus the emotions and passions behind that sense.

The passages and poems they ask you to write about on the AP English Literature and Composition Exam will present some event or situation in the same way a newspaper article presents an event or a situation. But AP essay passages will, of course, do more than that. They will make the event or situation "come alive" by bringing in human emotions and passions in such a way that those emotions and passions are as important as the facts.

Let's consider an example:

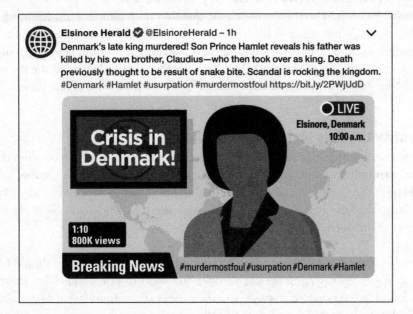

Think of how much will be lost by the Twitter version. Can the tweets really let us know Hamlet's suffering, his frantic (and occasionally crazed) attempts to figure out what is going on with his father and his uncle? Of course not, but those emotions are part of what the story means. They are the most important part of your essay.

Avoid Summary

You must absolutely avoid writing only a newspaper or social media version. Doing that amounts to a summary, something the AP Readers do not want. Discuss the way emotions are involved in the story and focus on the feelings the language produces, and you'll be discussing meaning in the right way. Always identify point of view, tone, and figurative language usage. Discussing these literary elements will ensure that you are moving beyond a summary.

Just Say No...
...to summaries! AP Readers want to see you analyze a literary work, not re-hash what you read.

The Modified Classic Essay Question

Your AP Exam may well have the classic question on it almost word for word, but probably not. What you will likely see is a modified classic essay question. There is an endless number of modifications for the test writers to throw at you. For example, the question might ask you to analyze "the narrator's attitude toward the nature of war," "the speaker's attitude toward society," or "the author's use of repetition."

Identify the Key Words in the Prompt

Of course, the specifics mentioned in the essay prompt are what you should pay close attention to when you read. Just as in the multiple-choice section, where looking at the questions can help you read the passages more actively, identifying precisely what the Readers want you to write about can help you focus on those aspects of the poem or prose fiction.

However, even if you're responding to a modified essay prompt, you should begin just as if you're answering the classic one. You want to talk about what meaning you found in the poem or passage, and then use that as a foundation to discuss the topic about which the question specifically asks.

Let's look at an example. (You don't need the actual passage to understand our discussion of the question here.)

> Read the following passage carefully. Write a well-organized essay that discusses the interrelationship of humor, pity, and horror in the passage.

This seems like a simple enough question—until you try to answer it. How do you go about discussing the interrelationship of humor, pity, and horror? Most students start out something like this:

> The story X by writer Z mixes humor pity and horror in an interesting way. It begins with a father meeting his son. The father seems like a funny guy because of things he does, but then we see that he is actually a person who arouses our pity because he goes too far, so far in fact, that the father becomes almost horrible.

The student who writes this response knows he's basically flailing. He's just trying to answer the question without looking foolish. If the student uses reasonable examples, writes with some organization and only a few grammatical errors, then the student will get a 5, a "limbo" score—not passing, but not failing.

On the other hand, the student who understands that this question is a modified form of the classic question and knows how to use the Idea Machine will break it down.

What does the passage mean? What was I supposed to get from it? What did I get from it? Okay, I got that the passage was about a father and son and that the son feels his father is basically embarrassing. Yeah, that sounds about right. Now, let's see, how does the author get that across using humor, pity, and horror?

Notice how this student has taken the question, turned it into the classic question, and simply used the modification to focus on the point to be developed. The student began by describing the meaning of the story. ("The son feels his father is basically embarrassing" is the meaning. Remember that the meaning doesn't have to be complicated.) Then this student asked herself, *How does the author get that across using humor, pity, and horror?* This student's opening is going to look something like this:

> In story X, writer Z shows us a son confronted by the embarrassing spectacle of his father. By shifting the son's perspective of his father from humor and pity, to horror, we see and feel the son's fluctuating, uncertain responses to his father's vulgarity and ignorance.

This student is writing about something and it shows. She's on the way to a score of at least 7, and if the essay stays this clear and focused, it's going to earn a score of 9. Do you see how slight an alteration has been made between this response and the one that came before it? Yet there's a world of difference. The first student rephrased the question without really saying anything, and then began to work his way through the points, ticking them off…first humor, then pity, then horror. The second student began by answering the implied question in every essay: *What does this story mean?* Then she began to show how the author brought that meaning across.

The best part is that the second essay is easier to write than the first one. It's easier to write an essay about something than nothing. Writing a bogus essay is like trying to wind up a ball of string with nothing to wrap it around. The second essay is going to wrap itself neatly around the core of the story's meaning—the son's uncertain embarrassment at his father's behavior.

No Fear!

Sometimes the questions can be fairly intimidating, but don't let them throw you. Remember to use the Idea Machine. What does the passage mean? How does that meaning come across?

Once you've got that under your belt, you can think about how to focus on the points in a question about a poem. Let's look at an example:

> Read the poem below carefully. Notice that the poem is divided into two stanzas and that the second stanza reapplies much of the first stanza's imagery. Write a well-organized essay in which you discuss how the author's use of language, including his use of repetition, reflects the content and tone of the poem.

You should look at the question and remember that it's just a modified version of the classic essay question. Ask yourself "What is the meaning?" and "How do I know it?," then you can think about how the author uses imagery and figurative language to convey that meaning. In fact, this question almost organizes itself once you break it down. Your first paragraph should talk about what you get from the whole poem, and your subsequent paragraphs should discuss the language and meaning of each stanza. Your conclusion should look at the poem as an entire piece and reiterate your emphasis about why and how repetition is important in understanding the overall tone and theme of the poem.

A Great Start

The key to a great essay is a great start and the key to a great start is having an overall idea of what you're doing. We've shown you how to address the meaning (literal and emotional) of the poem right from the beginning, and that you must then address the "how" of the author's method. Taken together, these things will form your opening and the central idea around which you will write—the idea you will explain and support. If you're already a sharp, sensitive reader, following these instructions will lead you to high-scoring essays.

Sounds easy in principle. But are you ready? Let's go back to that tough, intimidating question we just looked at in the No Fear section, this time along with the poem that goes with it. We'll use our approach to come up with a good first paragraph for a high-scoring essay. Then we'll show you two powerful tools you can use to open up a passage and get the kinds of ideas that blow AP Readers away.

Dylan Thomas's "In My Craft or Sullen Art"

Read the following poem carefully. Notice that the poem is divided into two stanzas and that the second stanza reapplies much of the first stanza's imagery. Write a well-organized essay in which you discuss how the author's use of language, including his use of repetition, reflects the content and tone of the poem.

In My Craft or Sullen Art by Dylan Thomas

In my craft or sullen art
Exercised in the still night
When only the moon rages
Line   And lovers lie abed
(5)   With all their griefs in their arms,
I labor by singing light
Not for ambition or bread
Or the strut and trade of charms
On the ivory stages
(10)   But for the common wages
Of their most secret heart.

Not for the proud man apart
From the raging moon I write
On these spindrift pages
(15)   Nor for the towering dead
With their nightingales and psalms
But for the lovers, their arms
Round the griefs of the ages,
Who pay no praise or wages
(20)   Nor heed my craft or art.

So, where do you begin? Well, before you begin to consider the repetition mentioned in the essay instructions, get the answers to the questions that let you write a classic essay. Use the Idea Machine.

- **What does the poem say, literally?** That shouldn't be too tough to answer, even if you don't know exactly what Dylan Thomas is trying to say. Put it in your own words. What does the poet say about his "craft or sullen art"? Take a moment to think about it, then read on.

You should have come up with something like this: "Dylan Thomas explains that he isn't writing for money or fame but for lovers who don't even care about his writing."

- **Okay, now what is the feel of the poem?** What emotions are conveyed? Is there an overall emotion? Again, think about it a moment before you read on.

It's a tougher question, isn't it? You probably went back to the poem to look at it again, thinking, "Just what emotion was I supposed to get? There's something there, but what?"

You might have picked up on a few aspects of the tone: pride, grief, loneliness, perhaps futility, and also perhaps the opposite of futility—a sense of total purpose. The poem has a truly complex emotional range in it. Don't let that scare you off; it only gives you more to write about.

- **What is the meaning of the poem for your AP essay?** Take your literal sense and your emotional sense, and combine them:

> Dylan Thomas's "In My Craft or Sullen Art" explores the pride, grief, loneliness, futility, and yet sense of total purpose that come from the author's struggle to write not for fame or for wealth but for "the lovers, their arms round the griefs of ages."

So far so good. But don't think we're finished. This sentence is just the answer to question 1 of the Idea Machine—what does the poem mean? If you're particularly astute, you may even notice that we haven't completely answered that question. We've only said what Thomas "explores." We haven't come out and taken a stand on exactly where Thomas's exploration has led him. Don't worry. You don't have to try to pin everything down all at once. If this essay were an assignment due at the end of the week you'd want to write a rough draft that you could revise carefully later. Here on the AP Exam, you don't have the opportunity for careful revision. You don't have to write a perfect essay. The Readers don't expect you to, not even for a score of 9. Just stay with our method: What does the work mean, how does the author achieve his effects, and what does the question ask you to address?

The "Perfect" Essay
No one, not even the AP Readers, expects you to write the perfect essay. But what they DO want you to write is an essay that discusses the meaning of a literary work, how the author conveys that meaning, and how all of that ties into the question you are being asked.

Now you have the second part of our three-part approach to consider:

- **How does the author achieve his effects?** Perhaps in answering that question we can take more of a stand. How does Thomas bring his emotions into his sense of what writing means to him and (because the essay instructions demand we consider it) what does the repetition have to do with it?

How indeed? Thomas gets his message across in so compact a fashion that you may feel a little lost and overwhelmed. Remember, you're just trying to write a 40-minute essay on a poem you've never seen before. The Readers don't expect perfection or profound originality. They want to see you focus on saying *something*, and then say it as clearly as you can. In brief, they want to see you confidently develop your ideas as best you can.

Here's how we'd complete our opening statement and answer the question of how Thomas explores his sense of what, to him, it means to write:

> Dylan Thomas's "In My Craft or Sullen Art" explores the pride, grief, loneliness, futility, and yet sense of total purpose that come from the author's struggle to write not for fame or for wealth but for "the lovers, their arms round the griefs of ages." Thomas gives us an image of himself, laboring alone "by singing light" and contrasts this with an image of self-contained completeness, of lovers wrapped in each other's arms, oblivious to all the world and even to his poetry. By repeating these images, and key words like "moon," "rage," and "grief," he emphasizes the power of his emotions and the intensity of his need to define himself and the purpose of his art.

This opening puts our essay off to a great start. Of course, you might have had different ideas, and you undoubtedly would have phrased your ideas another way, even if you saw exactly what we saw in the poem. You might even have written two or three better sentences—although you wouldn't have had to in order to score well. This brings up our next point.

Have Confidence in Your Answer

Many other insights about Dylan Thomas's poem are waiting between the lines. It all depends on what you got from it. If you ask yourself, "How can I describe the subject of this poem in one word?" You will find that your answer, in this case, reflects the title of the poem. It is his writing. Then, ask yourself: "What is Dylan Thomas saying about the craft of writing?" The answer to this question is the theme of the poem. If you look at the last few lines of the poem, you will discover the answer in those lines. Usually if you look at the title of the poem, the last few lines of the poem, and combine that with the one word that accurately describes the subject of the poem, you are on your way to accurately describing the theme of the poem. You want to make sure that you are on track with your interpretation because the Readers want to see that you have understood the point of the poem and can explain how this understanding helps you answer the essay question.

Use that literary vocabulary you've been building by studying the glossary. The Readers are paying attention to your craft of writing as you address the question. They want to see how the literary work you've been asked to write about acted on your imagination and how well you've managed to convey the impressions you've received.

Imagery and Words

Speaking of *imagination*, notice what we've done in the "how" part of our opening paragraph about the Dylan Thomas poem. We've discussed imagery and part of figurative language. We chose to mention the contrasting images of the author working alone and of the lovers in their self-enclosed togetherness. You might have chosen something else but the point to remember is: *It's always a safe bet to talk about imagery.*

In writing (as opposed to cinema or theater or painting) an image is made of words. Is that obvious? Yes, it is. But just because it's obvious doesn't mean all students pay attention to that important fact. On the AP essays your job is to discuss writing. Remember then that whenever you're discussing the imagery in a passage, you're discussing words. If a word sticks out as unusual or particularly vivid, think about it. Ask yourself, why did the author use *that* word? What effect does that word have? If you can think of something to say about the words an author has used to create an image and the specific effect those words have, by all means put it in your essay. You'll have the AP Readers eating out of your hand. One easy method of discussing imagery is to try to create a short film clip with your words based on what the poet has written.

Notice that in our sample opening we zeroed in on the two most striking word choices in the poem. *Rage* and *grief.* It's odd (and poetic) to say lovers have their arms around their griefs. And when was the last time you saw the moon raging? A lot of students run from unusual language like that. They think that the poet is just being a typical crazy artist who can't really be understood or that they'll misinterpret the phrase anyway and look dumb. But when you see unusual usages like that, consider them. Why that word? What does that word do to the feel of the piece? Thinking this way will jog ideas loose and come up with the material that makes for great AP essays. Notice also that both *rage* and *grief* have strong emotional content. Writing about the emotional content is the best way to let the Reader know you're really reading and not simply enacting some dry, mechanical exercise.

When in Doubt
The most important, most open-ended, most easily discussable aspect of a poem is almost always the imagery.

Opposition

If you've been following our discussion so far, you should see that you need to be able to pull ideas from the text you're working with so that you have ideas for your essay. Considering imagery and word choice is a good start, but there's one more concept we want you to think about as you read, something that should really help you find the ideas that you need to write a great essay.

How can you get to the heart of what you read on the AP English Literature and Composition Exam? How can you find something interesting and important to say about a passage quickly? What do you look for to see what makes a passage or a poem "tick"?

The answer is *opposition*.

Opposition vs. Conflict

Some people call opposition *conflict*, but we think that's too narrow a term. *Conflict* sounds like two people having a fight. Don't be crude. Be subtle. Opposition is everywhere in good writing, and the passages on the AP Exam will always be good sources. Seek it out as you read because opposition leads you to the important parts of a passage or poem.

Attune your reading to seeing opposition and you'll open up AP passages like cans of sardines. You'll have something around which to center your discussion of the way an author uses language and imagery and tone to make her point. If you carefully read the question, you will notice that there is usually a comparison or contrast that it directs you to address. Sometimes it is subtle, but sometimes you are directed to focus your answer on a comparison or contrast noted within the passage or two passages.

So, What's Opposition?

Opposition occurs when any pair of elements contrast sharply. Another way to think about opposition is tension—think of the two opposing elements as if they were magnetized poles, attracting and repelling each other. Opposition provides a structure underneath the surface of the poem, which you will unlock by discovering the oppositional elements. Opposition might be as blatant as night and day. Or it might be less obvious: a character who's naïve and a character who's sophisticated. Opposition might be found in a story that begins with a scene in a parlor but ends with a scene around a campfire, which would be the opposition of indoors and outdoors. It would be easy to miss if you weren't looking for it but it can often be found between the author's style and his subject. For example, a cerebral, intellectual style that's heavy on analysis in a story about a hog farmer would be opposition. Your essay would want to address why the author wrote that way and what effect it has on the story. Keep an eye out for any elements that are in contrast to each other as they'll often lead you to the heart of the story.

Let's look at that Dylan Thomas poem again. Notice what we went after in our opening paragraph: the image of the author working alone and the image of lovers in each other's arms. That's an opposition. Do you see how it's not exactly a conflict? It's a pairing of images whereby each becomes more striking and informative when placed against the other. Doesn't that pair of images seem central to the poem? Doesn't it seem there's something to talk about there? What it means exactly is open to interpretation, and that's exactly what you should do when you see elements opposed to each other: *interpret*. Don't worry about getting it right; there is no single right answer. The AP Reader will see that your searching intelligence has found the complexity of the material and is making sense of it. That's exactly what the Reader wants you to do. (And it's what very few students attempt to do.)

Opposition creates tension and mystery. What's the most mysterious line in "In My Craft or Sullen Art"? We think it's "And lovers lie abed/With all their griefs in their arms." That line alone has an opposition: If they're lovers, why do they have their griefs in their arms?

So your job is to figure out what Thomas means by that. The answer: Nothing simple, but something you can write about. Realize that you don't have to resolve opposition. You don't have to interpret that line (or the poem) in a concrete way that makes absolute perfect sense. It's a poem, not a riddle.

Our opening paragraph mentioned a third opposition: Thomas's sense of futility and his sense of total purpose. The sense of futility in the poem comes from the statements that the lovers "pay no praise or wages," nor do they heed Thomas's "craft or art." Describing how Thomas gets across his deep sense of purpose is more difficult even though it is the stronger of the two impressions. In many ways the entire poem is about conveying the sense of purpose Thomas feels when writing poetry.

We found these things because we looked for the oppositions. Some oppositions are obvious. Like a tiger in a bus station, they catch your attention immediately and make you wonder what's going on. Good writers boldly toss together mismatched concepts, objects, and tones all the time. But good writers also work with quiet oppositions that aren't nearly so easy to spot. If you aren't paying attention, you'll feel what's going on without realizing where it's coming from. Many literary oppositions come from within one character. The character who wants two totally opposite things at the same time is a classic case of opposition, as is the character who badly wants something that he just isn't cut out for. Another important opposition is *tone*. Some writers will write about the silliest thing possible in a deadly serious way. (This is generally done to make a situation funnier.) Still another opposition, one that is often handled with supreme delicacy and with seemingly infinite repercussions, is *time*. Writers will often let the past stand in opposition to the present. The story of a once proud family that has fallen on hard times is an example of a plot that uses the changes time brings to develop oppositions.

We could come up with hundreds of specific examples of oppositions in literature but those examples won't do you any good if you haven't read the works referred to. Our point here is to give you a tool with which to generate ideas for your AP essays.

You're probably still a little unclear as to how to apply this concept of oppositions to a short AP essay, but don't worry. The samples and examples in Chapter 10 will take you through several AP passages and point out how you might use oppositions to find ideas (while also boosting your essay scores into the 8's and 9's).

Opposition in Your Essay
An AP essay won't get to all of these oppositions; it shouldn't try. But you can be sure we'll mention that repetition plays a part.

After the First Paragraph—Do an Essay Check

Looking back at our overall approach to the Essay section, you'll see that the second to last point is the recommendation to do an essay check. That sounds fancy, but all it means is that you should think briefly about the points you need to make in your essay.

The time to do this thinking is after you've written that first paragraph. The first paragraph comes from using the Idea Machine: discussing the meaning of the passage or poem (remember, the newspaper version plus emotion) and beginning to talk about how the author gets her point across. This method gives you a first paragraph that establishes the foundation on which the rest of your essay will be built. If it's hyperfocused, it will already set out the overall points you intend to cover, but even if it just gives you a general platform on which to build, you've got plenty, enough to put you miles ahead of the majority of other (flailing) students. The essay check is just a spot check, a place to pause, make sure you're on the right track, and haven't forgotten anything important. When you finish your first paragraph, stop and ask yourself the following questions:

- What points does my first paragraph indicate I'm going to cover?
- Do those points address the specifics the essay question calls for?
- In what order am I going to put my points?

When you've decided the order in which to put your points, get back to writing. Your check shouldn't take more than a minute. The least important part of the check is deciding the order of your points. It's the closest thing to an outline you need to do, but don't overdo it. As long as you've paused to think about addressing the question it makes sense to form a rough plan of how you'll proceed. But the idea is to make it easier for you to write, not to suffocate your writing. Be flexible. If it's convenient to change the order of your points as you write, change them. If you think of new things to say, say them!

Developing Your Essay

As you write, you'll notice things that you hadn't seen at first, things that will depart from your original ideas and take you in unexpected directions. Should you include these things? YES!

Many, many students are intimidated by the test. They think their writing has to be truly organized and tight and end up writing short, dry, little essays: Essays that receive a score of 5. Go with the flow. As long as your ideas have some connection to the question that was asked, include them. Write a great first paragraph that sets you out in the right direction and then loosen up—you'll score high.

Once you've finished your first paragraph and your essay check, it's time to develop your essay. When it comes to development, each essay is unique. The best way to study development is through examples. The next chapter is devoted to sample essays; we'll show you how to put our method (and your ideas) into practice.

Remember...
It is impossible to write a tight, well-organized essay in 40 minutes—impossible. Style and flair aren't as important here as substance and the clarity of your ideas.

Summary

o   If you can get off to a good start, you're more than halfway to a great score.

o   Use our approach:
- Note the time. Remember, 40 minutes per essay.
- Pick the essay (prose fiction, poetry analysis, literary argument) you want to write.
- Identify the key words in the essay prompt.
- Skim the passage.
- Work the passage, making notes and identifying quotations you will want to use.
- Use the Idea Machine to plan your first paragraph.
- Support and develop the points you made in your first paragraph in your body paragraphs.
- Get a solid conclusion on the page.
- Repeat the process with the other essays.

o   Don't write an outline.

o   Identify key words in the prompt.

o   Understand the question and how to turn the question into an *essay idea*.

o   There is a basic format for the classic essay question on the exam:

    Read the following work carefully. Then, in a well-written essay, analyze how the author conveys ideas and meaning. Discuss the techniques the author uses to make this passage effective. Avoid simple summary.

o   You probably won't see the classic question word for word; you'll see a modified version that asks you to focus on a specific element or two from the passage.

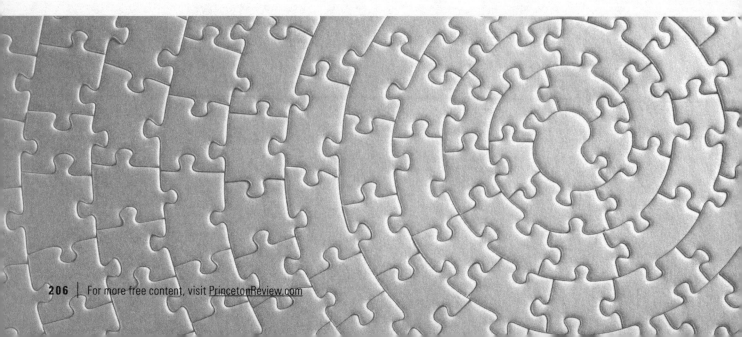

o   Use the Idea Machine:
- What is the meaning of the work? *Meaning* is literal meaning plus the emotions the work evokes.
- How does the author get that meaning across?
  o   important images
  o   specific words or short phrases
  o   opposition

o   The Idea Machine is the tool that will help you apply your skills specifically to a 40-minute essay.

o   Any student who can write an adequate essay can write an AP essay that scores a 7 or higher.

o   Don't worry about being wrong. Have confidence in your interpretation.

o   Unusual language and imagery are great places to find essay ideas.

o   *Opposition* is created when any pair of elements in a story or poem contrast sharply or subtly.

o   Look for elements that are in opposition. They'll lead you to the heart of the passage and give you material for the kinds of ideas that make AP Readers give out nines.

o   Go with the flow. It is impossible to write a tight, well-organized essay in 40 minutes. Write a great first paragraph that sets you out in the right direction, and then loosen up. Don't digress, however, and start talking about irrelevant topics. Always stay focused on the text.

REFLECT

Respond to the following questions:

- Which AP essay-writing strategies discussed in this chapter do you feel you have achieved sufficient mastery to write high-scoring essays?

- On which AP essay-writing strategies discussed in this chapter do you feel you need more work before you can write high-scoring essays?

- What parts of this chapter are you going to re-review?

- Will you seek further help, outside of this book (such as from a teacher, tutor, or AP students), on any of the content in this chapter—and, if so, on what content?

Chapter 10
Sample Poetry
Analysis and Prose
Fiction Analysis

Here's a poem that relies a great deal on irony, similar to Robert Browning's "My Last Duchess," which you worked on back in Chapter 3. This time, the poem we are studying comes with an essay question. Read the question and the poem and think about how you might write a response.

SAMPLE POETRY ANALYSIS ESSAY

William Blake's "The Chimney Sweeper" (Two poems)

Essay (Suggested Time—40 Minutes)

In the following poems by William Blake, the speaker, most likely a small child known as a chimney sweep, has been forced to work inside chimneys cleaning the interiors. Read the poems carefully. Then, in a well-written essay, compare and contrast the two poems and the ways that Blake uses poetic elements and techniques to express the plight of the chimney sweep.

The Chimney Sweeper

When my mother died I was very young,
And my father sold me while yet my tongue
Could scarcely cry " 'weep! 'weep! 'weep! 'weep!"*
So your chimneys I sweep and in soot I sleep.

Line
(5) There's little Tom Dacre, who cried when his head
That curled like a lamb's back, was shaved, so I said,
"Hush, Tom! never mind it, for when your head's bare,
You know that the soot cannot spoil your white hair."

And so he was quiet, and that very night,
(10) As Tom was a-sleeping he had such a sight!
That thousands of sweepers, Dick, Joe, Ned, and Jack,
Were all of them locked up in coffins of black;

And by came an Angel who had a bright key,
And he opened the coffins and set them all free;
(15) Then down a green plain, leaping, laughing they run,
And wash in a river and shine in the Sun.

Then naked and white, all their bags left behind,
They rise upon clouds, and sport in the wind.
And the Angel told Tom, if he'd be a good boy,
(20) He'd have God for his father and never want joy.

And so Tom awoke; and we rose in the dark
And got with our bags and our brushes to work.
Though the morning was cold, Tom was happy and warm;
So if all do their duty, they need not fear harm.

*The child's lisping attempt at the chimney sweep's
street cry, "Sweep! Sweep!"*

(1789)

The Chimney Sweeper

A little black thing among the snow,
Crying "'weep! 'weep!" in notes of woe!
"Where are thy father and mother? say?"
"They are both gone up to the church to pray.

Line
(5) Because I was happy upon the heath,
And smil'd among the winter's snow,
They clothed me in the clothes of death,
And taught me to sing the notes of woe.

And because I am happy and dance and sing,
(10) They think they have done me no injury,
And are gone to praise God and his Priest and King,
Who make up a heaven of our misery."
(1794)

Poetry Analysis Answers in General

Before we delve into this specific poem, we want to discuss some differences between prose fiction and poetry analysis. Poems are special cases because they deal in compressed language. Lyric poems (most of the poems on the AP English Literature Exam are lyric poems) often use a convention, simple on the surface but infinite in its varieties and depth. In this convention, the speaker of the poem (the "I") is addressing the reader directly, as prompted by a certain occasion or dramatic situation. If you pay attention to this lyric convention and its component parts, you may be able to understand a seemingly difficult poem more quickly. Not all poems on the AP Exam will exactly fit into this convention, but most will. The two poems we've chosen to discuss here definitely do.

In the previous chapter, we introduced the Idea Machine; three questions to consider when looking at a work of literature. Do you remember them?

1. What does the poem or passage mean?
2. How did the author get you to see that?
3. How do the answers to questions 1 and 2 direct your knowledge to adequately answer the question?

The same three questions also apply to the poetry analysis essay. Question 2, however, should be considered more like a drop-down kind of menu when you are writing about poetry.

Here are the three Idea Machine questions modified for the poetry analysis essay:

1. What does the poem mean?
2. How did the author get you to see that?
   - What is suggested by the title?
   - Who is the speaker and who is the audience?
   - What is the dramatic situation that prompted the speaker to speak?
   - What problem is being explored in the poem, and does the poem find a solution?
3. How do the answers to the first two questions direct your knowledge to adequately answer the exam question?

You don't have to ask or answer all of the secondary questions under question 2, but the more answers you can find to these questions, the better your essay will be. Let's see how this method works by looking at a specific poem.

Discussion of "The Chimney Sweeper" by William Blake

Like many poems, these two could be the focus of a long discussion. A full class period could be spent analyzing these coupled poems as a group of interested students slowly circled them, discovered small details about them, and found ways to express their discoveries to each other. You don't have that time.

We won't be delving deeply into the many possible interpretations of these poems. The point here is to figure out what you could say about these poems in order to write an essay that answers the question. Let's use the poetry analysis essay Idea Machine—the simple, orderly process that you should apply to every AP English Literature essay.

First, tackle the question.

What's the literal meaning of the poem?

It is the classic AP essay question. That makes our lives a little easier. The Idea Machine will work perfectly here.

Here is some background that may prove helpful to your understanding. The speaker in both poems is a chimney sweep. In the late eighteenth and early nineteenth centuries, boys as young as six were indentured to masters as chimney sweeps by their families, who were too impoverished to keep the children at home. Young children were considered useful as chimney sweeps because they were small

Idea Machine in Action
On the following pages, we break down how to implement the Idea Machine strategy on the day of the exam.

enough to get up into the chimneys to clean them. But the dark, soot-encrusted chimneys were likely terrifying, and the sweeps were subject to a number of hazards, including cancer, broken bones, respiratory diseases, and even suffocation. It was common to see them on the streets of London, as coal-burning fireplaces were perhaps the most common way of heating homes and businesses. The plight of chimney sweeps was the subject of a report to British Parliament in 1817, more than 25 years after Blake's first poem was published. Ultimately, employment of young children in the chimney-sweep trade became illegal.

Both poems are from a larger project by William Blake, *The Songs of Innocence and of Experience*. The first poem is one of innocence; the second one of experience.

If the AP exam writers were to use these poems or others that could benefit from historical background or allusions, the chances are that they wouldn't provide the historical or publication background as we just did. You will be provided with the years of publication (1789 and 1794, respectively), and a note that the poems were written in response to the poor conditions that caused young chimney sweeps to suffer. Most versions of the poem will carry a footnote to the first poem indicating that " 'weep! 'weep! 'weep!" is a child's version of the common chimney-sweep cry, "Sweep! Sweep!" But unless you've read about the plight of the chimney sweeps, the years, brief explanation, and footnote will provide very minimal explication of the historical background.

Fortunately, you don't need to know the background to understand these poems well enough to write a high-scoring essay on the AP exam. Recognizing the importance of the historical background helps, which is why many versions of the published poem include a brief note about it. But the AP exam writers will never choose a poem that relies on knowledge about historical context or allusions to historical events for its very sense.

Here's a quick summary of what you should have in mind after reading the first poem.

In the first three stanzas, a chimney sweeper speaks about how he came to be a sweep. He introduces a fellow chimney sweeper, Tom Dacre, and tells us a dream Tom had. The dream seems to comfort Tom about being a sweep. The poem ends with an injunction that chimney sweeps should do their duty, which will keep them from harm.

Let's look at the first poem in more detail. In its first stanza, the speaker tells us important information: his mother is dead and his father sold him while he, the speaker, was very young (lines 1–2), and that he is a chimney sweeper (line 4). As we saw in the footnote, the chimney sweeper's " 'weep!' 'weep!' 'weep!' 'weep!' "(line 3) resemble his cries of "sweep!"

In the next four stanzas, we receive important information about the chimney sweeper's environment, through the treatment and dream of Tom Dacre. Tom's hair is shaved (line 6), which he finds distressing; Tom cries, which reminds readers of the weeping in the first stanza. Told that a shaved head will at least protect his hair, Tom calms down, falls asleep, and has a dream which is both sinister and comforting. In it, "thousands of sweepers" (line 11) are "locked up in coffins of black" (line 12). In Tom Dacre's dream, the sweeps are released by an "Angel" with a "bright key" (line 13) who "set them all free" (line 14). They run, bathe in a river, and play in the sun (lines 15 and 16).

In the next stanza, they are not just free and playing, but leaving the earth. They leave their bags behind (line 17) and rise on the clouds (line 18). Tom is told, in line 20, that "he'll have God for a father and never want joy."

In the last stanza, we return to earth and to the narrator addressing us directly. Tom wakes up, along with the other chimney sweeps (line 21) and prepares to go to work along with the other boys (line 22). In the last two lines, the narrator's voice shifts to a more omniscient tone, telling us that Tom, in contrast to his fear and tears in the second stanza, was "happy and warm" (line 23). Further, the narrator tells us "if all do their duty, they need not fear harm" (line 24). The line seems comforting. Yet the comfort is conditional; the sweeps must do their duty – work as a sweep without tears or complaint – to be without fear of being hurt.

Now let's look at the second poem. Here's a quick summary of what you should have in mind after reading the second poem. In the first stanza, an unnamed person overhears a chimney sweep crying " 'weep!' " Asked where his parents are, he says they have gone to church. The next two stanzas are the sweep talking: he seems angry that his parents have put him to work and becomes overtly condemnatory in the last stanza.

Now, let's look at the second poem in more detail. The narrator at first seems to be omniscient, talking about "a little black thing among the snow" (line 1) "crying 'weep! weep' " (line 2). Because we are reading this poem in juxtaposition with the 1789 "The Chimney Sweeper" and because the title of this poem is also "The Chimney Sweeper," we might immediately think of the former poem's cry of the chimney sweeps. But, unlike the narrator of the first poem, this chimney sweep seems to have both parents, because when asked where his parents are by an unnamed interlocutor (line 3), he replies that they've gone to church (line 4).

In the next stanza, the sweep speaks, addressing the audience directly. He says that his parents "clothed me in the clothes of death, / And taught me to sing the notes of woe" (lines 7–8). Although readers are not told what the clothes of death and notes of woe are, they can infer from the similarity of titles that they are the chimney sweep's black clothes and the street cry.

Yet in this poem, we are not given direct biographical detail, as we are in the first poem. The "father and mother" in line 3 are not only not dead, we are never told that they have "sold" their children, as line 2 of the first poem tells us. Then the speaker reiterates that his parents are currently in church, "to praise God and his Priest and King" (line 11).

Then there's an abrupt shift in tone in the last line. With "Who make up a heaven of our misery" (line 12), the speaker accuses the authority figures of church and state cited in the penultimate line of creating misery for the chimney sweeps. In fact, the reader is to understand that perhaps those figures' ultimate realm of influence and authority, heaven, is created out of that pain.

The paragraphs preceding this one are a summary of the two poems. They are not an essay. In fact, you can use the paragraphs as a good example of what not to write on your AP essay. A literal reading is only a first step. Nothing is more mechanical or commonplace than a simple retelling of the passage. This kind of essay is going to score in the range of a 4 or 5. If we apply the rest of the Idea Machine to this literal reading, we can move the score much higher. Let's continue with the Idea Machine.

- What is suggested by the title?

- Who is the speaker and who is the audience?

- What is the dramatic situation that prompted the speaker to speak?

- What problem is being explored in the poem, and does the poem have a solution?

- What feelings do you get from the poem?

- What is the overall effect of the poem?

What is suggested by the title? The title is simple on the surface. It's just three words, almost like the title of a painting in a museum. It indicates that the poem will be about a chimney sweeper. In the first poem, it lets the audience know that the "I" of the first stanza is a chimney sweeper. In the second poem, it provides a clue as to who the "little black thing among the snow" is and offers a clue about the "I" in the second stanza. Finally, the fact that the title is the same in both poems unifies them, and suggests that they are to be read in conjunction if readers don't already know that.

Who is the speaker and who is the audience? The answer to this question is crucial for many poems. The primary speaker in both poems is a chimney sweep. He is telling the audience about his life as a chimney sweep, and what came before it. He is also discussing the plight of the chimney sweep with reference to spiritual and authority figures, such as the Angel and God (in the first poem) and God, Priest, and King (in the second poem). The chimney sweep in neither case appeals directly to the audience for sympathy, but makes clear that the life can be a miserable one. The audience is the reader. The audience is also presumed to be sympathetic with the plight of the chimney sweeps, or at least to be susceptible to sympathy.

What is the dramatic situation that prompted the speaker to speak? If you can put the dramatic situation of this poem into your own words, you are off to a good start. While we know from our reading of literature that first-person narrators are not always trustworthy, in this case, they initially seem to be. There is nothing in a surface read of the poem to indicate otherwise. In the first poem, the speaker is talking about his own situation as a chimney sweep and his back story. Then, he discusses a boy presumably new to the trade, Tom Dacre, who is having his head shaved for the first time. The speaker comforts Tom about his hair. Tom's dream, narrated by the speaker, seems partly to be a comforting vision of heaven. The speaker then comes back to offer an adage: if the sweeps do their duty, they needn't fear any harm. In the second poem, the speaker seems also to be discussing his own life as a sweep, but his tone is dark and angry. His parents and other authority figures have seemingly all worked together to take him from the happiness of lines 5 and 9, believing they have not done him injury. But the last line, which directly indicates the sweeps suffer from "their misery," indirectly condemns parents and authority figures for using the sweeps' unhappiness to create "a heaven" from it.

What problem is being explored in these poems, and do the poems find a solution? It's clear that a social problem is being discussed in the poems. First, the chimney sweeps are deprived of parental comfort by being sold into a job in which they sweep chimneys (line 2) and carry bags (line 17, 22), in the first poem. Second, it's a painful existence, in which they sleep in soot (line 4) and cry. In the second poem, they are deprived of happiness as well, and feel misery even more overtly.

The first poem seems initially to find a solution to the problem of their misery: they are presumably to find comfort in dreams of God as a father and doing their duty. Tom, after all, is "happy and warm" after the dream, despite the fact that it's cold outside. But can the reader fully trust this solution? There's disquieting coffin imagery in the third stanza of the first poem. If you follow the thread of metaphor, the later "clouds" they rise on may be heaven. They may be dead, then. So yes, their comfort might still be God, but they find comfort and release in death. Plus, of course, the coffins are black (line 12), a color associated with the sweeps' profession and its discomfort—and also frequently associated with death and mourning.

This might lead the reader to question whether the solution in the first poem— trust God as a father and do one's duty—is actually meant as a solution. Could it be ironic? After all, the last line says the sweeps "need not fear harm," but in the first stanza, the narrator has already suffered harm, in being sold and sleeping in soot.

If the conclusion of the first poem contains some irony, the reader might start to wonder if another problem is being addressed: religion and its role vis-à-vis the social problem. Is it really a comfort?

In the second poem, it clearly is not a comfort, at least to the narrator. The trappings of religion, such as the church, represent parental figures to the sweeps. But the actions of the parents, rather than exhibiting parental concern, endanger their children. His parents "clothed me in clothes of death/ And taught me to sing the notes of woe," the narrator tells us. Not only that, but they are oblivious, believing they have "done him no injury."

As the second poem comes to its final two lines, in fact, the narrator seems to move beyond the parents to higher authorities, the "God and his Priest and King" the parents praise. They, too, exhibit none of the care usually associated with these positions. In fact, the narrator says that these three nouns—collectively referred to by the pronoun "who" in the final line—"make up a heaven of our misery." So God in the second poem definitely isn't the comforting father of the first poem. In fact, if the reader sees the pronoun "our" here as referring to the chimney sweeps, God and his Priest and King may have made up heaven as a comforting fiction for the chimney sweeps or may even be the *cause* of the sweeps' plight. So religion itself is part of the problem being explored.

In neither poem is there a specific solution to the problems explored.

What feelings do you get from the poem? You probably already noticed that the tool of "finding oppositions," which we discussed at great length in the preceding chapter, is coming into play in our discussion of this poem. There are several possible ways to interpret the first poem, for example. One could read it as a religious poem in which God and heaven are offered as a genuine comfort and refuge for Tom Dacre and the other chimney sweeps. Or one could see the ending as ironic—something Tom himself is expected to believe, but that the reader is not expected to find persuasive. Or one could go further, especially when juxtaposed with the second poem, and believe that religion is created as a false comfort by church and other authorities.

Don't let the discovery of two (or more!) possible interpretations to any poem unnerve or confuse you. The AP Exam will feature complex poems full of these kinds of tensions. If they didn't, you'd have nothing to write about.

Readers of these poems sometimes feel that the first does offer a solution. Most think that the second poem is much darker. Some feel that the second poem is very cynical. Readers feel moved by the plight of the chimney sweepers, but some feel that the failure to offer a solution makes the poems unsatisfying.

What is the overall effect of the poem? Many readers have found great depth in these poems because they evoke such sympathy and because they can be so productively analyzed. The speaker in the first poem shows us his life and the life of Tom Dacre and offers a resolution of sorts. The speaker in the second poem shows us his life and offers a bleaker vision. In neither case is a full resolution offered.

We came to all these points by thinking about the answers to the questions and by looking for oppositions. But we also had the time we needed, and we've had some practice at this kind of thing before. So…

> **Relax**
>
> Are you supposed to pick this all up in one or two readings? In between checking your watch to make sure you have time for the next two essays? Not likely. We just wanted to show you how much there is to unearth in a typical AP Exam passage or poem and how much our techniques can dig up for you. All you'd need to see about this poem on the actual test is that the speakers are in some kind of opposition—and that the narrator of the first one might be in opposition with Blake himself. If you saw that and looked for the ways Blake got that across, you'd find enough to write a great essay.

A Strong Beginning

You should be ready to finalize your opening. Here's an example.

> "The Chimney Sweeper" is a pair of poems written in the late eighteenth-century about the plight of young children forced to work as chimney sweeps. Although the narrators in each seem to have profoundly different perspectives, the stylistic unity and similarities in figurative language indicate that William Blake blames social and religious authorities for the fate of the chimney sweeps in both.

Is this great writing? No. It won't win any prizes. But for the AP Exam, such writing is well on its way to a high score. Anything beyond this will impress your Reader. Let's take it apart for a moment, and then we'll finish the essay.

The beginning paragraph is a first pass at writing about meaning. We wanted to start with something more meaningful than "In 'The Chimney Sweeper' by William Blake..." If you start that way, it's okay, and if the rest of your essay is any good, you'll score high. But the readers like to see something more than that. We opened with the idea that it's a pair of poems on a similar topic, but that the narrator's perspectives are very divergent. Then, we link that to an opposition: the author's use of style and imagery, *not* what the narrators say, suggests a unity between the two poems, not a divergence. The Reader will be impressed that you forecast the main point so quickly.

Unfortunately, we ran out of steam before we could satisfy the overall goal of our beginning: to get at the meanings of the poems (literal and emotional) and explain how Blake gets the meanings across (we've barely started this process).

Keep Going

In the next section of our essay, we describe (not summarize!) what Blake's poem is, what it does, and how it does it. This is a poem where the overt statements of the narrator may not reflect what readers are actually to believe with no explanation or what William Blake thinks they should believe. There's a double meaning. On the AP English Lit and Comp Exam, any time you can show that a writer has created a double meaning, you have risen in the estimation of the Reader, who has likely been dealing with single meanings for most of the last hour of her reading assignments. But we can't stop there; we have to say what both meanings are. We chose to talk about the fact that the narrators express very different viewpoints about their lives. So initially these poems seem very different, right? But then we are going to segue to the idea that Blake wants the reader to see that the plights of the sweeps are the same in both.

How do we do this? Let's look at the first two paragraphs. You want to set up the first part of the argument, which is that the narrators differ. We also need to support these assertions with concrete examples from the text. That's our evidence.

While Readers don't have specific checklists to use, one aspect of your writing that every Reader will look for is your fluid use of specific evidence to prove your point. Without evidence, your essay is an empty series of assertions. With evidence, you're building your case. Like this:

> Both narrators are chimney sweeps, but the tone of each contrasts sharply with the other. The first speaker has been cruelly treated, as he was "sold" into work when he was very young. He nonetheless attempts to offer comfort to a fellow chimney sweep, Tom Dacre, who is upset when his hair is shaved. The speaker tells of a dream Tom has, in which an "Angel" tells him "he'd have God for his father, and never want joy." The narrator implies at the end that, not only can Tom be comforted by a vision of heaven, with God and the Angel, but all the hard-working sweeps can be as well, because "if all do their duty, they need not fear harm."

> The second speaker's tone is far more overtly unhappy. He doesn't see God as a beneficent parent, but condemns "God and his Priest and King" for causing the sweeps' plight—they "make up a heaven of our misery." His parents, who have "gone up to the church to pray," are responsible as well.

Ok. We've given evidence that there is contrast. But what about our friend double meaning? Time to introduce that idea. This is not a simple Case of the Two Contrasting Poems, as Nancy Drew might have called it. Let's introduce the opposition. And let's do it by pointing out the forms and shape of the poems, which tell us that the narrators' views aren't all there is.

> On the surface, then, the narrator in each poem expresses quite different beliefs. One is optimistic and one is quite bitter. Yet the poems are not completely different; they are unified by multiple stylistic elements. The first, of course, is the identical title. The unity continues into the first stanza, with both using the "'weep! 'weep!" cry the sweeps employed to announce their services. In each, "'weep!'" reminds the readers of the cry of a child, and thus appeals to their sympathy about the injustice done to the sweeps.

> Through this unity, Blake shows readers that, despite the stark contrast in each narrator's point of view, the poems are in fact a unit, not two widely divergent works of art.

And Going

Okay. We've started to talk about the literary methods that Blake uses to indicate to readers that something is going on beyond the surface of the poem. Let's talk more about those literary methods and tricks! Let's talk imagery and metaphor! Again, let's use abundant examples from the text as evidence for the Reader that we know what we're talking about.

> The imagery of the two poems echo each other as well, with use of contrasting white and black. The sweeps are linked with "soot" and "black coffins" in Poem 1, in vivid contrast to being "naked and white" later on, in Tom's dream. The initial figure in Poem 2, line 1, mirrors this contrasting black and white, as the sweep is "a little black thing among the snow."

Then, we're going to pivot. Why does this imagery matter? Because it's the first indication we have that we are not to believe the narrator of the first poem. Let's hone in on that.

> An analysis of these unified images leads readers to question the first narrator's optimism. The chimney sweeps in Poem 1 are, after all, "locked up in coffins of black" in Tom's dream. Coffins and chimneys are similar: dark rectangles into which the boys' bodies are placed. The coffin is thus a metaphor for the chimneys. While the freedom given by the "Angel who had a bright key" to the coffins is associated with heaven (the boys "rise upon clouds" and go to a place where God is the father), it's also linked to death because of the coffins. The association with dying is repeated and made explicit in Poem 2, where the narrator is "clothed…in the clothes of death" by his parents.

Is the product of our Idea Machine complete? Not quite. We haven't yet fully stated how Blake gets the idea across that the poems are unified, although we're well on the road. We're going to talk further about the shaping of the poem's meaning through irony, which we realize only from our analysis of the imagery above.

Here's the rest.

> Once readers notice this imagery, they realize that Blake intends the first poem's conclusion to be ironic. Regardless of the speaker's attempt to reassure a fellow chimney sweep (and possibly himself) that things will be alright, it's ultimately death the boys in Poem 1 are sold into. The boys in each poem meet a miserable fate.

> But Blake does not intend the ending of Poem 2 to be ironic. The speaker indicts religion, the state ("King"), and parents in the system that condemns him to a bleak life. The end is abrupt—"our misery"—as Blake intends readers to sympathize with that view. Religion and duty are a false comfort in the first poem; in the second, religion and parents help nail the (figurative) coffin shut.

That's the end of our essay. It's not that long and much more could have been written. But that's it. That's all the time we had. So we wrote that and moved on. We checked our watch, and it said that we had used up 40 minutes. Is it the best piece of writing we've ever done? No. But will it earn a high score? Yes, high enough. Why?

First, as we said, the AP Readers are forgiving of some mistakes. The opening of the essay lets the Readers know that we understand some of the main aspects of the poem and are able to put these understandings into fairly clear sentences. Second, our essay continues to make good points. It talks about metaphor and irony and the narrators' trustworthiness. We spread out well-chosen examples from most stanzas throughout each poem. We didn't digress for long, and we weren't overly repetitive. The Readers want to see your ideas. By making these insights clear and obvious to the Reader, you make it easy for the Reader to give you a better score.

Is this a well-organized essay? Not by the standards of the writing process. If you were writing for a take-home essay, this would be more like a free-writing, brain-storming session on the journey to a finished project. But by AP standards, this essay is pretty good. It begins with a clear direction, moves on to a consideration of oppositions, and finishes with specifically developed examples of style, imagery, and irony. For a first draft done in just 40 minutes top to bottom, the essay is admirable and will probably receive a 7.

SAMPLE ESSAY ON PROSE FICTION

Let's look at another sample. If you've got paper and pencil handy, try the question that follows and time yourself. At the very least, before you go to our sample essays (we've written two sample responses to this passage, one great and one fair), think about your first paragraph and try writing it in your head. But you really should practice writing a whole essay under time constraints.

Essay (Suggested Time—40 Minutes)

The following excerpt is from Ultramarine by Malcolm Lowry published in 1933). Read the passage carefully. Then, in a well-written essay, analyze how Lowry uses literary elements and techniques such as imagery and interior monologue to paint a picture of Dana Hilliot, a young lad from a well-off family, as he ventures to sea as a sailor.

From *Ultramarine* by Malcolm Lowry.

This 1933 novel follows Dana Hilliot, a young lad from a well-off family, as he ventures to sea as a sailor.

Puella mea[1]…No, not you, not even my supervisor would recognise me as I sit here upon the number six hatch drinking ship's coffee. Driven out and compelled
Line to be chaste. The whole deep blue day is before me. The
(5) breakfast dishes must be washed up: the forecastle and the latrines must be cleaned and scrubbed—the alleyway too—the brasswork must be polished. For this is what sea life is like now—a domestic servant on a treadmill in hell! Labourers, navvies, scalers rather than sailors. The
(10) firemen[2] are the real boys, and I've heard it said there's not much they can't do that the seamen can. The sea! God, what it may suggest to you! Perhaps you think of a deep gray sailing ship lying over in the seas, with the hail hurling over her: or a bluenose skipper who chewed glass
(15) so that he could spit blood, who could sew a man up alive in a sack and throw him overboard, still groaning! Well, those were the ancient violences, the old heroic days of holystones; and they have gone you say. But the sea is none the less the sea. Man scatters even farther and farther
(20) the footsteps of exile. It is ever the path to some strange land, some magic land of faery, which has its extraordinary and unearthly reward for us after the storms of ocean. But it is not only the nature of our work which has changed, Janet. Instead of being called out on deck at all
(25) hours to shorten sail, we have to rig derricks, or to paint the smokestack: the only thing we have in common with Dauber, besides dungarees, is that we still "mix red lead in many a bouilli[3] tin." We batter the rusty scales off the deck with a carpenter's maul until the skin peels off our hands

(30) like the rust off the deck.…Ah well, but this life has compensations, the days of joy even when the work is most brutalising. At sea, at this time, when the forecastle doesn't need scrubbing, there is a drowsy calm there during the time we may spend between being roused from our bunks
(35) and turning out on deck. Someone throws himself on the floor, another munches a rasher; hear how Horsey's limbs crack in a last sleepy stretch! But when bells have gone on the bridge and we stand by the paintlocker, the blood streams red and cheerful in the fresh morning breeze,
(40) and I feel almost joyful with my chipping hammer and scraper. They will follow me like friends, throughout the endless day. Cleats are knocked out, booms, hatches, and tarpaulins pulled away by brisk hands, and we go down the ladder deep into the hold's night, clamber up along
(45) the boat's side, where plank ends bristle, then we sit down and turn to wildly! Hammers clap nimbly against the iron, the hold quivers, howls, crashes, the speed increases: our scrapers flash and become lightning in our hands. The rust spurts out from the side in a hail of sharp flakes, always
(50) right in front of our eyes, and we rave, but on on! Then all at once the pace slackens, and the avalanche of hewing becomes a firm, measured beat, of an even deliberate force, the arm swings like a rocking machine, and our fist loosens its grip on the slim haft—And so I sit, chipping,
(55) dreaming of you Janet, until the iron facing shows, or until eight bells go, or until the bosun comes and knocks us off. Oh, Janet, I do love you so. But let us have no nonsense about it.

---

[1] My girl (Latin).

[2] The men that tend the steam engines and boilers of the ship.

[3] bouillion

Discussion

Did you practice writing the essay on this passage? Did you time yourself? If so, great; if not, we hope you at least read the passage carefully and thought about how you would go about writing your first paragraph.

Oddly enough, writing about prose fiction can actually be more difficult than writing about poetry. Poetry often presents many difficulties to the reader caused by the density and complexity of poetic language. However, once interpreted, those same difficulties give you material to write about. Prose fiction presents the opposite problem. In general, assimilating the passage is pretty easy; the challenge is finding something worth saying about it. It is useful to remember that the literary devices you look for in poetry can also be pointed out in your essays on prose fiction.

As always, start out with the classic question and let the Idea Machine guide your thinking process. Of course, make sure that you allow the question to focus the development of your essay, and also note the time so that you don't go overboard and come up short on the last essay.

Below you'll find two responses to the passage. One is excellent, the other is mediocre. We'll discuss both responses after the samples are given. By the way, in these two essays we've taken out the annoying errors of diction and spelling that creep into every student's essay. We want you to read the essays for what they say and how they say it without distracting errors. The sentence construction reflects student writing, but in reality, both essays would have more language mistakes.

Sample Response to *Ultramarine*—Essay 1

In the passage, Malcolm Lowry effectively uses the resources of language to create an interior monologue (a mental speech) to dramatize the adventures a young English boy has aboard a ship, and shows the character of the boy, Dana Hilliot, as well. He uses vivid imagery and many details from the boy's life to show who Hilliot is and what he thinks, and captures the different rhythms of life aboard a ship.

First Hilliot thinks that no one, "not even my supervisor would recognise me…" This shows that Hilliot thinks that he has changed and that life at sea has changed him. But he's happy, he likes the change, as he says, "The whole deep blue day is before me." But there are many conflicting feelings in Hilliot as he sits and drinks his coffee. For he quickly screams out, "this is what sea life is like now—a domestic servant on a treadmill in hell!" This shows the conflict that Hilliot undergoes. He doesn't know whether he thinks life at sea is great or a stinking hell. Lowry shows this by switching all the time between images that are pleasant, and images that are full of misery and despair and heartbreak. He really misses Janet and it shows. A sailor's life is lonely, and Lowry shows that. Lonely and boring sometimes, as hard as that may be to believe. But the boredom is broken up by danger and hardship. "We batter the rusty scales off the deck with a carpenter's maul until the skin peels off our hands like the rust off the deck..." is an example of the hardship. But immediately, the conflict shows up again. The very next sentence is, "Ah well, but this life has compensations, the days of joy even when the work is most brutalising."

Through it all though, Hilliot thinks of Janet. He begins thinking of her "Puella mea...," which is Latin for "my girl" and ends saying "Oh, Janet, I do love you so." This tells us a great deal about Hilliot. He misses his girlfriend and is probably homesick for England too. These are normal reactions for the character of a young Englishman far from home, and by framing the story between these statements Lowry shows that the character of Dana Hilliot hasn't changed as much as he thinks it has. Hilliot is still a lonely young man with a great deal to learn.

Sample Response to *Ultramarine*—Essay 2

Who hasn't dreamed of throwing everything away and running off to sea? And yet very few people actually do run off to sea, probably because, at least in part, they realized (around the time they're packing all those wool sweaters into a duffle bag) that life at sea isn't just dropping anchor at exotic ports and gazing at the moon setting over the Indian Ocean. It's a hard, dangerous life. Better unpack the sweaters.

The passage shows the inner thoughts of one young man who actually did run off, and as he sits and thinks of the life he's leading and the life he's left behind, we get a picture of what a young sailor's life is really like. We get something else as well, a detailed portrait of a young, confused man, Dana Hilliot, and all the swirling emotions that he carries in his young heart. Hilliot is lonely, defiant, excited, bored, romantic, and cynical all at once.

The passage begins, "Puella mea..." Although that's Latin for "my girl," the translation isn't so important as the fact that it's Latin. Right from the beginning, Lowry shows us a fish out of water. Dana's educated, but how many of Dana's shipmates speak Latin? Probably none. Dana talks about how unrecognizable he's become. Maybe he really is unrecognizable to his old friends, but it's more likely that he can't recognize himself. He's gotten more than he bargained for, "this is what sea life is like now—a domestic servant on a treadmill in hell!" This is one of the recurring themes of the passage. Hard, dull, work. Polishing brass. Chipping paint. Scrubbing and cleaning. It isn't a very romantic scenario. This theme tells us not just about sea-life, but about Dana. He must have been pretty naïve to not know that a sailor works from daybreak into the night, and it's all manual labor.

Lowry gives us a picture of the wild, terrifying, intense life that Dana thought he was going to lead. He describes it to his girlfriend, to correct her and tell her the truth, but you can be sure that these were Dana's ideas of life at sea before he came to the ship. "Perhaps you think of a deep gray sailing ship lying over in the seas, with the hail hurling over her: or a bluenose skipper who chewed glass so that he could spit blood…" Well, Dana has learned that it isn't anything like that at all. His romantic dreams have been squashed, all except the sea. He still finds poetry in the sea. It is "ever the path to some strange land, some magic land of faery…" This is the beauty that Dana really got on board for.

The passage then takes us even deeper into Dana's character. In the beginning, he talked about how horrible it was to be just a lackey, scrubbing decks. As he thinks deeper though, we see a real change in him. He loves the moments of calm, and is such a sensitive experiencer of the life around him that he even notes the way one of his fellows' joints crack, but the amazing thing is that he's learned to love the work. He describes it with relish, "I feel almost joyful with my chipping hammer and scraper. They will follow me like friends…The rust spurts out from the side in a hail of sharp flakes, always right in front of our eyes, and we rave, but on on!" The work, the hard relentless work, is the real adventure, and in those words "on on!" you can hear almost hear Dana's amazement at the fact that he can do it, he can keep going on.

In the end Dana's loneliness, cut off from his familiar life, returns him to being a moody "Romeo," dreaming of his girlfriend, imagining sweet-talking her. It wells up in him with the line, "Oh, Janet, I do love you so." But then comes the very last line of the passage, another abrupt change, "But let us have no nonsense about it." He's still a young person, pouring out his love to his girlfriend but then a second later he's pretending to be a tough guy, a sailor, who wants "no nonsense." By putting these lines, one after the other, Lowry shows Dana in the midst of growing up, and pretending to be more hardened than he is.

Discussion of Sample Responses 1 and 2

It shouldn't be too difficult to tell which is the better of the two responses. Essay 1 is clearly an average response from an intelligent student struggling to write a response about a passage he didn't get much from. Notice the mechanical repetition of the question and the mechanical, plodding way he works through the passage, not so much interpreting as it is summarizing. He did manage to address the question somewhat and did pull together a few simple insights into the passage. He would receive a score of 5. Not a terrible score by any means, but you can do better.

The biggest mistake the author of the first essay made was to choose to emphasize the life-at-sea aspect of the question. Unless an author is just setting the stage for what is to come, or planting some enormous symbol, almost every sentence in a novel or a story *is intended to reveal character*. This is especially true of the kind of masterful writers you'll be dealing with on the AP Exam. When you read prose fiction on the AP Exam, always ask yourself what the sentences tell you about the people in the passage. In the Lowry passage, everything Dana thinks tells us something about Dana. The first student missed most of the psychological details of the passage and ended up floundering.

The author of the second essay worked with the Idea Machine. She asked herself about both the literal and emotional content of the passage. She kept an eye out for strong imagery and evidence of opposites. In doing so, she saw that the passage was filled with conflicting images. Dana loves Janet, but then wants "no nonsense." Dana thinks the work is beneath him ("domestic servant"—Dana's the kind of kid who's used to having servants, not being one) and makes his shipboard life hell, but at the same time he realizes that when he's lost in the physical frenzy of the labor, he finds the work exhilarating. The author of the second essay tried to put these oppositions together in a meaningful way. Most important, she knew to focus on character. By tying everything back to Dana's character she assured herself of a high score. In fact, the second essay would be scored a 9—the top score.

Also notice that the second passage does not begin with the typical restatement of the question. That doesn't mean that a Reader would look at the beginning of the second sample essay and think, "Oh my, what an original opening—this essay gets a high score." A nice opening isn't enough. You still have to write the essay. But, the Reader would think, "Hmm, this kid isn't writing like a robot...now if she can show me she understood the passage and communicate her understanding with anything like the flair of this opening, I'll give her a high score." In other words, yes, your opening can be a little stiff and dull (yes, you can paraphrase the question if you want to) if you write an otherwise good, insightful essay, but an original, interesting opening is better if you can write one without wasting a lot of time.

Essay Do's and Don'ts to Remember

After reviewing some sample essays, you probably have a good sense of what you need to accomplish to achieve a solid score. Some of this may seem basic and verge on the formulaic. Remember that your good ideas do need to be clear and well-organized. The following are tips for reviewing your own practice essays.

Your first paragraph should

- grab the reader (don't worry if you can't do this, but it helps)
- answer the question in the prompt
- preview the evidence you'll use to support your ideas

Your first paragraph should not

- go off on a tangent
- ignore the prompt
- merely restate the wording of the prompt

Your body paragraphs should

- have clear transitions and topic sentences
- provide evidence, in the form of quotations from the prompt, that supports your opinion
- explain how that evidence supports your point of view

Your body paragraphs should not

- rely on plot summary
- let quotation outweigh analysis
- ramble

Your conclusion should

- exist
- sum up the evidence for the jury
- contain any profound insights about the work that may have occurred to you while writing

Your conclusion should not

- suggest you didn't budget your time
- merely restate the introduction or prompt

Summary

- o   Avoid summary.

- o   Get a feel for the passage.

- o   Notice imagery.

- o   Notice oppositions.

- o   Your essay doesn't have to be great, but you do have to show command of the English language. An AP essay that scores a 9 might not even be an "A" paper in English class. Of course not. It's a 40-minute essay on a story or poem you've never seen before.

- o   Whenever possible, show your verbal flair.

- o   It's okay to establish the foundation of your essay in two or three short opening paragraphs, if necessary.

- o   Your first paragraph should be free of error, but nobody writes an error-free paper. That doesn't mean be careless and sloppy. It means write as well as you can and don't worry about mistakes.

- o   If the question gives you the opportunity, write about character. The writing in AP passages almost always says something about character. This is especially true in the dialogue of a character, or in a first-person narration.

- o   A nice opening is icing on the cake.

- o   Make sure you leave yourself enough time to write a complete conclusion.

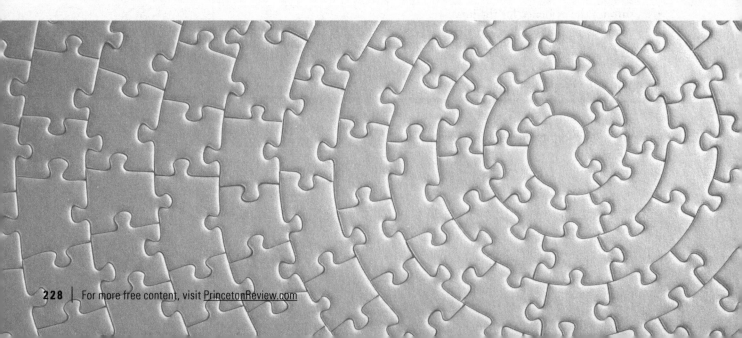

REFLECT

Respond to the following questions:

- Which aspects of poetry analysis essays do you feel you have achieved sufficient mastery of to write a high-scoring essay based on a poem?

- Which aspects of poetry essays do you feel you need more work on before you can write a high-scoring essay based on a poem?

- Which aspects of prose fiction essays do you feel you have achieved sufficient mastery of to write a high-scoring essay based on a work of prose fiction?

- Which aspects of prose fiction essays do you feel you need more work on before you can write a high-scoring essay based on a work of prose fiction?

- What parts of this chapter are you going to re-review?

- Will you seek further help, outside of this book (such as from a teacher, tutor, or AP students), on any of the content in this chapter—and, if so, on what content?

Chapter 11
Literary Argument

HOW DO YOU PREPARE FOR AN ESSAY ON *ANYTHING*?

The literary argument usually appears as the last of the three essays on the AP Exam. Unlike the prose fiction analysis or poetry analysis essays, the literary argument does not give you a text to work with; you must write an essay on a given theme using support drawn from your own reading.

Most people assume that the literary argument is the most difficult of the three essays but this assumption is false. Even though the average score on the literary argument tends to be a little lower than on the other two essays, a close look at the data suggests that students who attempt the literary argument earn higher scores. Many students skip this essay altogether, so there are more scores of 0 here than on the prose fiction analysis and poetry analysis essays. On the other hand, more students earn scores of 8 and 9 on this essay than on the other two. The scores still tend to bunch up around the middle (the mean), but they spread out more across all the score ranges (a greater standard deviation). All the same, the literary argument is the most dreaded and anticipated portion of the AP Exam. It isn't worth any more than the other questions, but unlike the rest of the test, the literary argument question feels like the one you *have to* study for. At the same time, it's the question that most students feel like they *haven't* studied for, at least not enough.

We've shown you that you can and should study for the rest of the test. We *hope* we've shown you that knowing what you're doing on the Essay section is the way to shoot your scores through the roof. Now, what about the literary argument—how do you prepare for it?

The answer is simple. Use all the techniques we've already described for writing the prose fiction analysis and poetry analysis essays. Use the Idea Machine to direct your thoughts and answer the classic question as you go about answering the specifics of the question. The literary argument is no different from the other essays. There's just one more bit of preparation you need for the literary argument: three well-chosen works of literature that you know backward and forward.

WHAT THE TEST WRITERS REALLY WANT FROM YOUR LITERARY ARGUMENT

You can, should, and *must* study a literary work for the literary argument. But what if the literary argument question asks for a theme that the work you've prepared doesn't address? Don't worry. The test writers aren't trying to persecute you (although it does feel that way sometimes). Follow our instructions and you'll be prepared.

What the test writers would really like to do is say, "Write an essay about any major literary work that you enjoyed. We just want to see how well you can write on a longer work that you've read and studied." Unfortunately, they can't ask you that directly because there would be no way to stop students from writing essays ahead of time (or having dear Aunt Toni, the Pulitzer Prize–winning novelist, write an essay ahead of time) and memorizing them. The literary argument question is just a way of making sure that the student hasn't prepared the whole essay in advance.

However, the test writers don't want to ask literary argument questions that are too restrictive, either. They won't ask a question that points to just a handful of literary works, for example. They won't ask for an essay about "a character who may or may not be insane and who sees ghosts that may or may not be there." A few hundred students would get nines by writing about Henry James's *The Turn of the Screw*. A few thousand would struggle to make this question make sense for *Hamlet* or *Macbeth*. The rest would just leave it blank.

The test writers go out of their way to make sure the literary argument question is truly open and provides an opportunity for a student who has read challenging literary works to write a good essay.

Let's look at the types of themes the literary argument question asks about. Remember, you can see real, previously asked essay questions at **https://apcentral.college-board.org/courses/ap-english-literature-and-composition/exam**.

Sample Themes for the Literary Argument

According to The College board, the literary argument question assesses students' ability to do the following:

- Respond to the prompt with a thesis that presents an interpretation and may establish a line of reasoning.

- Select and use evidence to develop and support the line of reasoning.

- Explain the relationship between the evidence and the thesis.

- Use appropriate grammar and punctuation in communicating the argument.

As you can see, these tasks are things that you have been doing in class throughout the year, and can all be applied to thousands of literary works. At the same time, these tasks must be performed on command and you cannot go ahead and write an essay ahead of time. The key to a great literary argument is having the right work for the theme, and knowing it cold.

So what works should you study?

Preparing for the Literary Argument

To be really ready for the literary argument, you should know at least three works very well. Two of them should be longer works that you've studied in class. We'll call these the *primary* works. The third work is a safeguard in case, for some reason, you can't apply your knowledge of the first works to the question at all, or in case you need to back up your points with another example. You have no idea what specific titles will be listed in that tally of potential works just beneath the Literary Argument question, so it's good to be well-versed in at least three important literary works. That way, you may see one of those three listed and it can be your primary work, then you can also discuss another important piece of literature. Trust us, the question stem may say that you need only choose one work to discuss, but a Reader will be hugely impressed if you can adeptly discuss two or three pieces of literature. We'll provide you with a list of short *secondary* works that are useful for the AP Exam.

THE PRIMARY WORK

Have two primary works that you know well. Your primary works should be fairly hefty. One of Shakespeare's plays or a thick, complex novel will do. The full-length works of the following authors are all good choices: Jane Austen, James Joyce, Joseph Conrad, Emily and Charlotte Brontë, Charles Dickens, Nathaniel Hawthorne, Herman Melville, Toni Morrison, Thomas Hardy, George Eliot, Fyodor Dostoyevsky, and Thomas Mann. The object in choosing your primary works is to come up with two novels or plays that are so rich in incident and form that no matter what the literary argument question asks, you have something to say.

Choose a Work You Already Know (and Love)

You've already studied some literary works in school. Pick two and go over your notes. Read the books again or at least spend a few hours looking them over thoroughly. Pick your favorite work. If you fell in love with Shakespeare's *Hamlet*, great; use *Hamlet*. If you felt sleepy every time the word Shakespeare was mentioned but thought Dostoyevsky's *Crime and Punishment* might change your life, then that's the work to use.

There are just a couple of exceptions to the favorite-work rule. Do not pick a short story, a work of nonfiction, or a poem. The literary argument questions, as a rule, say, "Choose a play or a novel: Do not choose a poem or short story." There have been very few exceptions to this rule, and the exception is that they'll allow complete epic poems. Now, if your favorite work of literature is really-honestly-no-I-loved-it Milton's *Paradise Lost* or Spenser's *The Faerie Queene*…well, okay, you could prepare those novel-length poems for the literary argument, but you'd still be better off with a novel. Short stories are wonderful reading material, but they are practically useless for the AP Exam; you're just not allowed to use them. They don't want students preparing to write literary arguments on short stories; they think it's too easy.

If you don't have a usable favorite work or are for some reason undecided about what to choose for your primary work, we highly recommend Shakespeare's plays, particularly *Hamlet*, *A Midsummer Night's Dream*, *King Lear*, *Othello*, and *The Tempest*. All of these plays are intricately plotted, contain elements of comedy and tragedy, and are incredibly rich in the kind of material about which literary arguments are written. The object in choosing your primary work is to find a work that can support any number of questions, and Shakespeare's works fit that bill better than any others of comparable length. As tough as Shakespeare's plays can be to read, they are considerably shorter than say, *Crime and Punishment* or *David Copperfield*. If you decide to go with Shakespeare, you could easily prepare to write about two plays in the time it takes to prepare to write about a longer novel. Just remember, we said we recommend Shakespeare. If you already know the work of another writer better, by all means prepare something else. But remember that we strongly recommend using a book you've already studied in class.

You'll be happy to know that in the past few years many contemporary books have appeared on the list of accepted sources for the literary argument. *The Kite Runner* by Khaled Hosseini, *Life of Pi* by Yann Martel, and *The Bonesetter's Daughter* by Amy Tan are a few contemporary works that fall outside of the traditional primary works list but might be strong choices as one of your primary works.

Suggestions for Primary Works

Here are some other books we think make for good primary works. This list is not even close to complete, but it's a start. If you happen to know and love another long work inside and out, that's fine.

Emma by Jane Austen

Jane Eyre by Charlotte Brontë

Wuthering Heights by Emily Brontë

Don Quixote by Miguel Cervantes

White Noise by Don DeLillo

Bleak House by Charles Dickens

David Copperfield by Charles Dickens

Great Expectations by Charles Dickens

A Tale of Two Cities by Charles Dickens

Crime and Punishment by Fyodor Dostoyevsky

Invisible Man by Ralph Ellison

The Sound and the Fury by William Faulkner

Tess of the D'Urbervilles by Thomas Hardy

The Scarlet Letter by Nathaniel Hawthorne

The Kite Runner by Khaled Hosseini

Their Eyes Were Watching God by Zora Neale Hurston

Sons and Lovers by D. H. Lawrence

The Magic Mountain by Thomas Mann

One Hundred Years of Solitude by Gabriel García Márquez

Moby Dick by Herman Melville

The Catcher in the Rye by J. D. Salinger

The Grapes of Wrath by John Steinbeck

Of Mice and Men by John Steinbeck

The Bonesetter's Daughter by Amy Tan

Anna Karenina by Leo Tolstoy

The Adventures of Huckleberry Finn by Mark Twain

Black Boy by Richard Wright

THE SECONDARY WORK

The secondary work is your just-in-case work and perhaps a bit more. The question just may not fit any aspect of your primary works. This is highly unlikely, but if this happens, you need to have something prepared. You don't want to be stuck trying to remember some book you haven't looked at since ninth grade. The other reason to prepare a secondary work is simply to have more options. If the question fits your secondary work perfectly, you'll want to use it. Prepare your secondary work well and in effect, you have three primary works. With well-chosen and well-prepared primary and secondary works, you would have to be extremely unlucky to find yourself faced with an literary argument question that did not fit any of the works.

Choose Something Different from Your Primary Works

Ideally, you want your secondary work to be as different as possible from your primary works. If you pick *Hamlet* as one of your primary works, you don't want to pick another Shakespearean tragedy starring a messed-up, confused, violent hero. In other words, don't pick *Macbeth*. You'd be much better off picking a comedy such as *A Midsummer Night's Dream*. Even better would be to pick a twentieth-century comic novel like *Catch-22* by Joseph Heller or *A Confederacy of Dunces* by John Kennedy Toole. If you pick an extremely male-oriented work for one of your primary works, say *Invisible Man*, then Kate Chopin's *The Awakening* makes an excellent choice for a secondary work, as would Henry James's *The Turn of the Screw*, both of which feature female main characters.

Suggestions for Secondary Works

We've put together a list of secondary work books. These are all short novels, novellas, and plays which are acceptable to the AP Readers. Some works are not acceptable. Writing about *Family Guy*, episode 56, will result in a low score, as will writing about a Danielle Steele or Stephen King novel. Don't push it. You may think William Gibson's *Neuromancer* is a great book, but the AP committee probably won't be impressed and they'll lower your score.

The books on the following list were chosen according to the following guidelines: They're all recognized classics of which the AP Readers will highly approve. They're all short. Most important, they're all works that have been perfect fits with many literary argument questions.

We strongly recommend studying at least one of the works listed here. If you've read one of these works in class (and there's a good chance you have), by all means look it over again and prepare it for the AP Exam. An asterisk (*) means that the work is most highly recommended reading for the exam. Pick one of these and you won't go wrong.

Finally, if you really don't feel comfortable with any of the longer works that you've studied in class, are thinking of taking the AP Exam without having taken an AP course, or, well, slacked off in class—don't try to prepare a longer work for the AP Exam. Go straight to the list below and knock off two or three or four titles (remember, these are short works). You'll be prepared.

Novellas and Short Novels:

The Stranger by Albert Camus

The Awakening by Kate Chopin*

Heart of Darkness by Joseph Conrad*

Notes from the Underground by Fyodor Dostoyevsky

The Old Man and the Sea by Ernest Hemingway

The Turn of the Screw by Henry James*

Death in Venice by Thomas Mann

Ballad of the Sad Café by Carson McCullers

Billy Budd by Herman Melville

A Sentimental Journey by Lawrence Sterne

The Death of Ivan Ilyich by Leo Tolstoy

Candide by Voltaire

Plays:

Waiting for Godot by Samuel Beckett

A Man for All Seasons by Robert Bolt

The Cherry Orchard by Anton Chekhov

The Seagull by Anton Chekhov

Uncle Vanya by Anton Chekhov

Medea by Euripides*

A Doll's House by Henrik Ibsen*

Hedda Gabler by Henrik Ibsen*

The Crucible by Arthur Miller

Death of a Salesman by Arthur Miller

Emperor Jones by Eugene O'Neill

Hughie by Eugene O'Neill

Long Day's Journey Into Night by Eugene O'Neill

Antigone by Sophocles*

Oedipus Rex by Sophocles*

A Streetcar Named Desire by Tennessee Williams

The Glass Menagerie by Tennessee Williams

What Does "Prepare the Work" Mean?

We keep telling you to *prepare* your primary and secondary works. What does this mean? Two things:

1. Study the work as thoroughly as you can.
2. Write a first paragraph based on the classic question for each work you prepare.

Studying Your Primary and Secondary Works

Study the works you've chosen. Take notes. Record impressions. Map out different themes and examples of these themes within the work. Imagine important scenes as movies in your head. If you're reading this book early in the school year or in the summer before your AP English Lit course begins, you should consider prepping every work you read for class. This strategy will not only give you a broad array of works to select from on test day, but will also improve your study habits. If you have a few months or a few weeks to prepare, then selecting two or three works you have studied will put you in a good place. If it's the week before the test, looking over the books to remind yourself of the plot lines and the names of the main characters might forestall those moments you lose when you're racking your brain, thinking, "Gatsby's girlfriend's name…Rose…Iris…Violet?"

How should you prepare the works?

- **Reread** your primary and secondary works within four weeks of the test. You want to have each one fresh in your mind.
- **Work from critical editions.** The books you should prepare for the AP Exam are the kinds of works that have been studied and restudied over the years. Although you can easily find your chosen texts in small, inexpensive reading editions, you should look for them in larger, critical editions that contain full introductions, notes, annotations, and sometimes appendices containing background material, biographical information, and samplings of past critical commentary. Whenever possible, use these fuller editions. Read as much of the supplementary material as you can stand. If you can put the work in a cultural context and discuss the political or sociological happenings of the time, the Reader's socks will undoubtedly be knocked off. No AP Reader is going to downgrade your essay because the points you make about the novel seem influenced by the opinions of other authors and critics. On the contrary, they'll think you're a genius. One student in a hundred actually bothers to read literary criticism about the book he or she has prepared, but that's about the percentage of students who score a 9 on the literary argument. Coincidence?
- **Write your own study guide.** As much as some teachers might disparage store-bought or online study guides, they can be an invaluable supplement to your own study. (Note that we said "supplement." You still need to read the books.) Even better than a store-bought study guide, however, is one you've written yourself. You'll accomplish a lot of your review just by writing it. Moreover, once you're done, you'll have a study guide that highlights the aspects of a work you find most interesting—and those are the things you're most likely to write about on the exam.

Your custom study guide should be no longer than one page and should contain the following:

12 Is Key
The College Board suggests that AP English Lit teachers have their students read at least 12 works closely in class.

- **Plot**—You want to avoid plot summary in your literary argument, but it's still important to remember what happens—and *why*. Chapter by chapter or scene by scene, note what happens but focus on the major conflicts of the book. The details help you remember the specific chronology of the narrative; thinking about the larger conflicts puts the story into perspective.

- **Character**—Who's who? This list could be as simple as remembering how they spell their names (very useful indeed if a Chekhov play or a Tolstoy novel is one of your works) or it can be as detailed as you want it to be.

- **Themes**—What's the message or moral of the story? Avoid oversimplification.

- **Symbols**—Scarlet letters, green lights, white whales: what do they stand for and how do they help the author achieve his or her purpose?

- **Quotations**—"If you have tears, prepare to shed them now." (That's from *Julius Caesar*, in case you were wondering.) In the literary argument, it's important to provide support for your assertions, and even more important to avoid plot summary. Quoting your chosen work and explaining how the quote relates to the prompt demonstrates to the reader that you know and understand the work. Memorizing the quotes—and understanding what each means—allows you to write with more confidence.

A sample page of your self-made study guide might look like this:

The Seagull by Anton Chekhov

Act I—Lots of complaining (Masha's in mourning for her life, Treplev's mother Arkadina doesn't love him) as preparations are made for Treplev's play, starring Nina. The chain of unrequited lovers is introduced. Treplev loves Nina, Nina has a crush on Trigorin, Arkadina's acknowledged lover. Masha's mother Polina has the hots for Dorn, the local doctor. The play is experimental and a flop. Arkadina laughs at it, and Treplev's feelings are hurt. Trigorin takes an interest in Nina. Masha confesses to Dorn that she loves Treplev.

Act II—Midsummer squabbles on the estate—can Arkadina take the horses out or not. Nina thinks the great actresses' demands are the most important thing. Treplev shoots a seagull and lays it at Nina's feet, threatening that one day he will do the same to himself. Nina dismisses his concerns, and Trigorin promptly begins seducing her. The dead seagull inspires Trigorin—a young girl lives by the lake like a seagull, but one day a man comes along and, for lack of anything better to do, destroys her.

Act III—Three big scenes: Masha tells Trigorin she's going to destroy her love for Treplev by marrying Medvedenko, the schoolmaster who pines for her. Arkadina changes Treplev's bandages (he's attempted suicide offstage between the acts). Arkadina fights with Trigorin, who wants to stay behind and complete his seduction of Nina, but Arkadina wants him out of there. As they're leaving together, Trigorin goes back for his walking stick. Nina goes to him; she's run away from home and heading to Moscow to become an actress. Trigorin gives her his address and asks her to come to him.

Act IV—Two years later. Masha has married Medvedenko, but she's still in love with Treplev and miserable. She's hoping Medvedenko's transfer will tear the love from her heart. Treplev brings Dorn up to date on Nina. She had a child by Trigorin, who managed to stay with Arkadina the whole time, and has returned to her. Meanwhile, Nina's acting career has been a disaster. Trigorin and Arkadina arrive. Trigorin is kind to Treplev's face, but behind his back, disparages his writing. After a quick game of lotto, the party relinquishes the study to Treplev. He struggles with his writing, then is surprised by Nina. He's been trying to see her. They reminisce about old times, and Nina compares herself to a seagull. She leaves as abruptly as she arrived. Treplev tears up his manuscripts and exits, just as Shamreyev shows Trigorin the stuffed seagull. A shot is heard offstage. Treplev has shot himself.

Characters

ARKADINA, an actress. 42 years old. Petty, vain, involved with writer Trigorin.
KONSTANTIN TREPLEV, Arkadina's son, an aspiring writer.
SORIN, Arkadina's brother and the owner of the estate where the play is set.
NINA, a young local girl and aspiring actress. Romantically involved with Treplev at the outset, later falls in love with Trigorin.
SHAMRAYEV, Sorin's estate manager.
POLINA, Shamrayev's wife. In love with Dorn.
MASHA, Shamrayev's daughter. In love with Treplev, but will marry Medvedenko.
TRIGORIN, a writer. Spineless.
DORN, a doctor.
MEDVEDENKO, a schoolteacher. Obsessed with money.

Themes

Unrequited love and lots of it. Idealistic youth spoiled by the corruption of the real world. Struggle to create new art forms (Chekhov creating a new kind of drama in this play).

Symbols

The seagull: symbolic of youth. Trigorin sees it as emblematic of Nina and her innocence, which he will proceed to spoil. Treplev, who has shot a seagull, thinks it represents himself, and he shoots himself at the end of Act IV, just as he threatened when he laid the seagull at Nina's feet in Act II. Nina is a little confused about whether she's the seagull or not, as we see in her Act IV monologue.

Quotations

"I'm in mourning for my life; I'm depressed."—Masha, Act I. Opening lines of play, sets tone for what is to follow.

"I am a seagull; no, that's not it; I am an actress."—Nina, Act IV.

This study guide isn't perfect—it isn't very thorough—but it forces you to think about how the work is structured and how the author achieves his effects. While prepping this, you might note that each act begins with Masha, a minor character. In looking at criticism about the play, you might note that it was a failure when originally produced, possibly because Chekhov's effects are so subtle. Finally, after prepping the work in this way, you'll be certain about the names of the characters and what happens when, which will allow you to write with more clarity.

Prepare for the Literary Argument Ahead of Time

In addition to prepping the works, you should also write the first paragraph of an literary argument a couple of nights before the test. (Remember to use the Idea Machine: What does the work mean? What are the emotional contents of the work?) Writing the first paragraph shouldn't take you longer than 30 minutes, and when you consider how much time and stress it will save you on test day, surely you can see why it's a winning strategy.

While it's true that you have no idea what aspect of the work the prompt will ask you to address, we've supplied you with plenty of sample prompts with which to practice. Once you've seen a few, you'll be familiar with the kind of questions that appear on the exam and should see how altering one or two sentences in your sample introduction will probably save the day. And, even if you do end up writing an entirely new introduction on test day, you'll write with more confidence and skill if you've had some recent practice.

RECENT CHANGES

The literary argument prompt is a little intimidating, but since you've been studying all year for this test, you should have a pretty solid knowledge base regarding various themes in literature. Over the last few decades, this prompt has taken on various forms and it was recently changed by The College Board from the "open prompt" to the "literary argument" prompt. Despite the name change, this prompt remains quite open, so you'll want to be sure that you have read an assortment of books, you have explored the themes, symbolism, and meanings of said books, and you can express your thoughts well. Because we can't see the test in advance, it's impossible to know just how simple or complex the prompt will be; therefore, it might help to consider some previous prompts so that you can prepare yourself with an arsenal of knowledge that will help you to answer appropriately and quickly.

The College Board released a new Course Description for AP English Literature and Composition and they mapped out lots of specifics, thankfully. Here is a sample question that they share:

> Many works of literature feature characters who have been given a literal or figurative gift. The gift may be an object, or it may be a quality such as uncommon beauty, significant social position, great mental or imaginative faculties, or extraordinary physical powers. Yet this gift is often also a burden or a handicap.
>
> Either from your own reading or from the list below, choose a work of fiction in which a character has been given a gift that is both an advantage and a problem. Then, in a well-written essay, analyze how the gift and its complex nature contribute to an interpretation of the work as a whole. Do not merely summarize the plot.

In addition, the College Board has shared the wording that you will see in the Literary Argument question. The text in italics will vary by question, while the remainder of the prompt will be consistently used in all Literary Argument essay questions.

> *[Lead that introduces some concept or idea that students will be asked to apply to a text of their choosing.]*
>
> Either from your own reading or from the list below, choose a work of fiction in which [some aspect of the lead is addressed]. Then, in a well-written essay, analyze how [that same aspect of the lead] contributes to an interpretation of the work as a whole. Do not merely summarize the plot.

Summary

o   When writing the literary argument, use all the techniques we've described for writing the prose fiction analysis and poetry analysis essays.

o   Don't worry about having to face an open question that doesn't apply to the works you've prepared. The test writers try to make the literary argument question broad enough so that you won't be lost—as long as you have *something* prepared.

o   Prepare two primary works and a secondary work.

o   If you've studied Shakespeare's work in class (and enjoyed it), we strongly recommend using a Shakespeare play as one of your primary works. His plays are chock-full of the material that literary arguments call for.

o   Choose a work that you've already studied in class.

o   Our list of secondary works suggests novellas and plays that have proven useful on many AP literary arguments in the past.

o   Your secondary work should be as different as possible from your primary works. For example, if one of your primary works is a Shakespearean tragedy, pick a modern comic novella for your secondary work.

o   If possible, reread your primary and secondary works within four weeks of the test. Otherwise, at least skim the book and look over any class notes you have. Use critical editions if you can find them.

o   Write a sample first paragraph of the literary argument ahead of time. It's great practice for the real thing.

REFLECT

Respond to the following questions:

- Which AP essay-writing strategies discussed in this chapter do you feel you have achieved sufficient mastery of to write a high-scoring literary argument?

- Which AP essay-writing strategies discussed in this chapter do you feel you need more work on before you can write a high-scoring literary argument?

- What parts of this chapter are you going to re-review?

- Will you seek further help, outside of this book (such as from a teacher, tutor, or AP students), on any of the content in this chapter—and, if so, on what content?

Part VI
Practice Test 2

Practice Test 2

The Exam

AP® English Literature and Composition Exam

DO NOT OPEN THIS BOOKLET UNTIL YOU ARE TOLD TO DO SO.

At a Glance

Total Time
1 hour
Number of Questions
55
Percent of Total Grade
45%
Writing Instrument
Pencil required

Instructions

Section I of this examination contains 55 multiple-choice questions. Fill in only the ovals for numbers 1 through 55 on your answer sheet.

Indicate all of your answers to the multiple-choice questions on the answer sheet. No credit will be given for anything written in this exam booklet, but you may use the booklet for notes or scratch work. After you have decided which of the suggested answers is best, completely fill in the corresponding oval on the answer sheet. Give only one answer to each question. If you change an answer, be sure that the previous mark is erased completely. Here is a sample question and answer.

Sample Question   Sample Answer

Chicago is a   Ⓐ ● Ⓒ Ⓓ Ⓔ
(A) state
(B) city
(C) country
(D) continent
(E) village

Use your time effectively, working as quickly as you can without losing accuracy. Do not spend too much time on any one question. Go on to other questions and come back to the ones you have not answered if you have time. It is not expected that everyone will know the answers to all the multiple-choice questions.

About Guessing

Many candidates wonder whether or not to guess the answers to questions about which they are not certain. Multiple choice scores are based on the number of questions answered correctly. Points are not deducted for incorrect answers, and no points are awarded for unanswered questions. Because points are not deducted for incorrect answers, you are encouraged to answer all multiple-choice questions. On any questions you do not know the answer to, you should eliminate as many choices as you can, and then select the best answer among the remaining choices.

GO ON TO THE NEXT PAGE.

ENGLISH LITERATURE AND COMPOSITION

SECTION I

Time—1 hour

Directions: This section consists of selections from literary works and questions on their content, form, and style. After reading each passage or poem, choose the best answer to each question and then completely fill in the corresponding oval on the answer sheet.

Questions 1–15. Choose your answers to questions 1–15 based on a careful reading of the following passage.

An Invective Against Enemies of Poetry

With the enemies of poetry I care not if I have a bout, and those are they that term our best writers but babbling ballad-makers, holding them fantastical fools, that have
Line wit but cannot tell how to use it. I myself have been so
(5) censured among some dull-headed divines, who deem it no more cunning to write an exquisite poem than to preach pure Calvin or distill the juice of a commentary in a quarter sermon. Prove it when you will, you slow-spirited Saturnists, that have nothing but the pilferies of your pen to polish an
(10) exhortation withal; no eloquence but tautologies to tie the ears of your auditory unto you; no invention but "here it is to be noted, I stole this note out of Beza or Marlorat"; no wit to move, no passion to urge, but only an ordinary form of preaching, blown up by use of often hearing and speaking;
(15) and you shall find there goes more exquisite pains and purity of wit to the writing of one such rare poem as "Rosamund" than to a hundred of your dunstical sermons.

Should we (as you) borrow all out of others, and gather nothing of ourselves our names should be baffuld on every
(20) bookseller's stall, and not a chandler's mustard pot but would wipe his mouth with our waste paper. "New herrings, new!" we must cry, every time we make ourselves public, or else we shall be christened with a hundred new titles of idiotism. Nor is poetry an art whereof there is no use in a man's whole life
(25) but to describe discontented thoughts and youthful desires; for there is no study but it doth illustrate and beautify.

To them that demand what fruits the poets of our time bring forth, or wherein they are able to prove themselves necessary to the state, thus I answer: first and foremost, they
(30) have cleansed our language from barbarism and made the vulgar sort here in London (which is the fountain whose rivers flow round about England) to aspire to a richer purity of speech than is communicated with the commonality of any nation under heaven. The virtuous by their praises they
(35) encourage to be more virtuous; to vicious men they are as infernal hags to haunt their ghosts with eternal infamy after death. The soldier, in hope to have his high deeds celebrated by their pens, despiseth a whole army of perils, and acteth wonders exceeding all human conjecture. Those that care
(40) neither for God nor the devil, by their quills are kept in awe.

Let God see what he will, they would be loath to have the shame of the world. What age will not praise immortal Sir Philip Sidney, whom noble Salustius (that thrice singular French poet) hath famoused; together with Sir Nicholas
(45) Bacon, Lord Keeper, and merry Sir Thomas More, for the chief pillars of our English speech. Not so much but Chaucer's host, Bailly in Southwark, and his wife of Bath he keeps such a stir with, in his *Canterbury Tales*, shall be talked of whilst the Bath is used, or there be ever a bad house
(50) in Southwark. Gentles, it is not your lay chronographers, that write of nothing but of mayors and sheriffs and the dear year and the great frost, that can endow your names with never-dated glory; for they want the wings of choice words to fly to heaven, which we have; they cannot sweeten a discourse,
(55) or wrest admiration from men reading, as we can, reporting the meanest accident. Poetry is the honey of all flowers, the quintessence of all sciences, the marrow of wit and the very phrase of angels. How much better is it, then, to have an elegant lawyer to plead one's cause, than a stuttering
(60) townsman that loseth himself in his tale and doth nothing but make legs; so much it is better for a nobleman or gentleman to have his honor's story related, and his deeds emblazoned, by a poet, than a citizen.

—Thomas Nashe

1. In the first paragraph, preachers are accused of all the following EXCEPT

   (A) plagiarism
   (B) stupidity
   (C) dullness
   (D) eloquence
   (E) laziness

2. "Saturnist" (line 8) means

   (A) astrologer
   (B) nymphomaniac
   (C) depressed and depressing person
   (D) pagan
   (E) foolishly optimistic person

GO ON TO THE NEXT PAGE.

3. What are "divines" (line 5)?

   (A) Preachers
   (B) Great writers
   (C) Dead writers
   (D) Fools
   (E) Saturnists

4. "New herrings, new!" (line 21)

   (A) refers to an implied comparison between the writers of new poems and the sellers of fresh fish
   (B) suggests that poetry is slippery and hard to catch the meaning of, like fish
   (C) implies that poetry is just another commodity
   (D) implies that poetry grows stale rapidly, like fish
   (E) compares poetry to rotten fish

5. In lines 29–34 London is described as

   (A) flooded
   (B) a damp, rainy city
   (C) the main influence on the English language
   (D) a cultural garden
   (E) an important port city

6. The main idea of lines 34–40 is which of the following?

   (A) People are motivated by concern for their reputations.
   (B) Poetry is fair to the virtuous and the evil alike.
   (C) Poetry is inspirational.
   (D) Poetry is most attractive to atheists.
   (E) Poets are very judgmental.

7. Who is Salustius (line 43)?

   (A) A French poet
   (B) Sidney's *nom de plume*
   (C) The Roman god of poetry
   (D) The King of England
   (E) The Wife of Bath

8. As it is referred to in line 49, what is Bath?

   (A) A state of sin
   (B) A character in Chaucer
   (C) A married man
   (D) A poet
   (E) A town and spa in England

9. In the last paragraph, poets are said to be like

   (A) lawyers
   (B) mayors
   (C) chronographers
   (D) townsmen
   (E) angels

10. Line 9 is an example of

    (A) metaphor
    (B) onomatopoeia
    (C) paradox
    (D) alliteration
    (E) apostrophe

11. In line 2, what is the referent of "those"?

    (A) Poets
    (B) The author
    (C) Ballads
    (D) Poems
    (E) Poetry's enemies

GO ON TO THE NEXT PAGE.

12. Lines 18–23 argue that

    (A) poets must take second jobs to make a living
    (B) most people don't respect poets
    (C) there are too many poets
    (D) poets have to work hard to present consistently fresh material
    (E) poetry books are never bestsellers

13. The author complains (lines 10–11) that the preachers have no eloquence to hold their audience but only

    (A) repetition
    (B) nonsense
    (C) lies
    (D) irrelevance
    (E) sermons

14. According to the passage, which of the following is NOT a function of poetry?

    (A) To encourage the virtuous
    (B) To purify the language
    (C) To embarrass the villainous
    (D) To illustrate and beautify
    (E) To plagiarize sermons

15. Who first raised the issue of necessity of poetry to the state?

    (A) Nashe
    (B) Sidney
    (C) Salustius
    (D) Plato
    (E) Milton

GO ON TO THE NEXT PAGE.

Questions 16–28. Choose answers to questions 16–28 based on a careful reading of the following poem by John Donne.

Let me pour forth
My tears before thy face whilst I stay here,
For thy face coins them, and thy stamp they bear,
Line And by this mintage they are something worth,
(5)   For thus they be
              Pregnant of thee;
Fruits of much grief they are, emblems of more—
When a tear falls, that Thou falls which it bore,
So thou and I are nothing then, when on a diverse shore.

(10)   On a round ball
A workman that hath copies by can lay
An Europe, Africa, and an Asia,
And quickly make that, which was nothing, all;
              So doth each tear
(15)   Which thee doth wear,
A globe, yea world, by that impression grow,
Till thy tears mixed with mine do overflow This world; by
waters sent from thee, my heaven disolv'd so.

              O more than moon,
(20) Draw not up seas to drown me in thy sphere;
Weep me not dead in thine arms, but forbear
To teach the sea what it may do too soon.
              Let not the wind
              Example find
(25) To do me more harm than it purposeth;
Since thou and I sigh one another's breath,
Whoe'er sighs most is cruelest, and hastes the other's death.

16. The situation described in this poem is

 (A) the end of a romantic relationship
 (B) death
 (C) the separation of lovers
 (D) the end of the world
 (E) a pleasure cruise

17. Lines 10–16 are an example of

 (A) paradox
 (B) dramatic irony
 (C) metaphor
 (D) metaphysical conceit
 (E) dramatic monologue

18. Line 19 is an address to the

 (A) moon
 (B) world
 (C) poet's soul
 (D) workmen
 (E) beloved

19. To what do lines 14 and 15 refer?

 I.   The speaker's tears which reflect the beloved
 II. The beloved's tears
 III. The beloved's clothing, which has been torn as a symbol of her grief

 (A) I
 (B) I and II
 (C) I and III
 (D) II and III
 (E) All of the above

20. Which of the stanzas do NOT include images of roundness?

 (A) Stanza 1
 (B) Stanza 2
 (C) Stanza 3
 (D) Stanzas 1 and 3
 (E) None: All of the stanzas contain images of roundness.

21. The imagery in this poem can most accurately be described as sustained images of

 (A) worthlessness suggesting the hopelessness of the lovers' situation
 (B) the globe suggesting the vast distances of the lovers' separation
 (C) roundness suggesting a perfect circle, and therefore the cosmic and permanent union of the lovers
 (D) water suggesting the shifting faithlessness of the lovers
 (E) water suggesting the bond between the lovers

GO ON TO THE NEXT PAGE.

22. In line 13, to what does the word "which" refer?

    (A) Copies
    (B) The round ball
    (C) The world
    (D) The workman
    (E) The continents

23. Which of the following is NOT an appropriate association for lines 19–20?

    (A) The power of a goddess
    (B) The relationship between the moon and the ocean's tides
    (C) The round shape of the moon
    (D) The folktale of the man in the moon
    (E) The moon as suggestive of unhappy feelings, the opposite of "sunny disposition"

24. What does "diverse shore" (line 9) mean?

    (A) Heaven
    (B) Hell
    (C) Europe
    (D) A different place
    (E) The ground

25. Which of the following types of imagery is sustained throughout the poem?

    (A) Tears
    (B) Globes
    (C) Coins
    (D) Moon
    (E) Ocean

26. Line 4 can best be paraphrased as

    (A) you are not worth the salt of my tears
    (B) my tears are worth something because they reflect your face
    (C) my tears are emotionally refreshing
    (D) my tears are worth something because they are for your sake
    (E) my grief is a valuable feeling

27. What does the speaker ascribe to his beloved in lines 20–25?

    (A) The power to break his heart
    (B) The power to kill him
    (C) The power to influence the natural elements
    (D) The power to restrain her grief
    (E) The right to seek other lovers

28. In the extended metaphors of this poem, the speaker flatters the beloved through the use of

    (A) hyperbole
    (B) sarcasm
    (C) irony
    (D) parallelism
    (E) eschatology

GO ON TO THE NEXT PAGE.

Questions 29–39. Choose answers to questions 29–39 based on a careful reading of the passage below. The passage, an excerpt from a short story by Mary E. Wilkins Freeman, describes a woman about to be married after a long engagement.

Every morning, rising and going about among her neat maidenly possessions, she felt as one looking her last upon the faces of dear friends. It was true that in a measure *Line* she could take them with her, but, robbed of their old
(5) environments, they would appear in such new guises that they would almost cease to be themselves. Then there were some peculiar features of her happy solitary life which she would probably be obliged to relinquish altogether. Sterner tasks than these graceful but half-needless ones would
(10) probably devolve upon her. There would be a large house to care for; there would be company to entertain; there would be Joe's rigours and feeble old mother to wait upon; and it would be contrary to all thrifty village traditions for her to keep more than one servant. Louisa had a little still, and she
(15) used to occupy herself pleasantly in summer weather with distilling the sweet and aromatic essences from roses and peppermint and spearmint. By-and-by her still must be laid away. Her store of essences was already considerable, and there would be no time for her to distil for the mere pleasure
(20) of it. Then Joe's mother would think it foolishness; she had already hinted her opinion in the matter. Louisa dearly loved to sew a linen seam, not always for use, but for the simple, mild pleasure which she took in it. She would have been loath to confess how more than once she had ripped a seam
(25) for the mere delight of sewing it together again. Sitting at her window during long sweet afternoons, drawing her needle gently through the dainty fabric, she was peace itself. But there was small chance of such foolish comfort in the future. Joe's mother, domineering, shrewd old matron that she was
(30) even in her old age, and very likely even Joe himself, with his honest masculine rudeness, would laugh and frown down all these pretty but senseless old maiden ways.

Louisa had almost the enthusiasm of an artist over the mere order and cleanliness of her solitary home. She had
(35) throbs of genuine triumph at the sight of the window-panes which she had polished until they shone like jewels. She gloated gently over her orderly bureau-drawers, with their exquisitely folded contents redolent with lavender and sweet clover and purity. Could she be sure of the endurance of even
(40) this? She had visions, so startling that she half repudiated them as indelicate, of coarse masculine belongings strewn about in endless litter; of dust and disorder arising necessarily from a coarse masculine presence in the midst of all this delicate harmony.
(45) Among her forebodings of disturbance, not the least was with regard to Caesar. Caesar was a veritable hermit of a dog. For the greater part of his life he had dwelt in his secluded hut, shut out from the society of his kind and all innocent canine joys. Never had Caesar since his early youth
(50) watched at a woodchuck's hole; never had he known the

delights of a stray bone at a neighbor's kitchen door. And it was all on account of a sin committed when hardly out of his puppyhood. No one knew the possible depth of remorse of which this mild-visaged, altogether innocent-looking old
(55) dog might be capable; but whether or not he had encountered remorse, he had encountered a full measure of righteous retribution. Old Caesar seldom lifted up his voice in a growl or a bark; he was fat and sleepy; there were yellow rings which looked like spectacles around his dim old eyes; but
(60) there was a neighbor who bore on his hand the imprint of several of Caesar's sharp white youthful teeth, and for that he had lived at the end of a chain, all alone in a little hut, for fourteen years. The neighbor, who was choleric and smarting with the pain of his wound, had demanded either Caesar's
(65) death or complete ostracism. So Louisa's brother, to whom the dog had belonged, had built him his little kennel and tied him up. It was now fourteen years since, in a flood of youthful spirits, he had inflicted that memorable bite and with the exception of short excursions, always at the end of the
(70) chain, under the strict guardianship of his master or Louisa, the old dog had remained a close prisoner. It is doubtful if, with his limited ambition, he took much pride in the fact, but it is certain that he was possessed of considerable cheap fame. He was regarded by all the children in the village
(75) and by many adults as a very monster of ferocity. Mothers charged their children with solemn emphasis not to go too near him, and the children listened and believed greedily, with a fascinated appetite for terror, and ran by Louisa's house stealthily, with many sidelong and backward glances
(80) at the terrible dog. If perchance he sounded a hoarse bark, there was a panic. Wayfarers chancing into Louisa's yard eyed him with respect, and inquired if the chain were stout. Caesar at large might have seemed a very ordinary dog, and excited no comment whatever; chained, his reputation
(85) overshadowed him, so that he lost his own proper outlines and looked darkly vague and enormous. Joe, however, with his good-humored sense and shrewdness, saw him as he was. He strode valiantly up to him and patted him on the head, in spite of Louisa's soft clamor of warning, and even attempted
(90) to set him loose. Louisa grew so alarmed that he desisted, but kept announcing his opinion in the matter quite forcibly at intervals. "There ain't a better-natured dog in town," he would say, "and it's downright cruel to keep him tied up there. Some day I'm going to take him out."
(95) Louisa had very little hope that he would not, one of these days, when their interests and possessions should be more completely fused in one. She pictured to herself Caesar on the rampage through the quiet and unguarded village. She saw innocent children bleeding in his path. She was
(100) herself very fond of the old dog, because he had belonged to her dead brother, and he was always very gentle with her;

GO ON TO THE NEXT PAGE.

still she had great faith in his ferocity. She always warned people not to go too near him. She fed him on ascetic fare of corn-mush and cakes, and never fired his dangerous temper *(105)* with heating and sanguinary diet of flesh and bones. Louisa looked at the old dog munching his simple fare, and thought of her approaching marriage and trembled.

29. In overall terms, how is Louisa characterized?

    (A) As a bitter, domineering woman
    (B) As a naive, childish woman
    (C) As a frightened, foolish woman
    (D) As a sheltered, innocent woman
    (E) As a selfish, cruel woman

30. Which statement best describes Louisa's household activities (paragraphs 1 and 2)?

    (A) They symbolize the timeless rituals of ancient rural harvest deities.
    (B) They demonstrate Louisa's contented absorption in a traditionally feminine cultural sphere.
    (C) They demonstrate Louisa's mental illness.
    (D) They demonstrate Louisa's repressed artistic genius.
    (E) They describe the highest traditional values of Louisa's town.

31. Which of the following statements are TRUE?

    The story of Caesar is used in this passage to reinforce the idea that

    I.   Louisa has grown too accustomed to her circumscribed life to welcome change
    II. cruelty to animals is an indicator of a cruel society
    III. marrying is like being conquered by an invading emperor
    IV. people can be trapped by unchanging and unexamined ideas

    (A) I and IV only
    (B) I, II, and III only
    (C) IV only
    (D) All of the above
    (E) None of the above

32. Caesar's "ascetic" diet (paragraph 4)

    (A) reflects Louisa's poverty
    (B) is part of his punishment
    (C) reflects a nineteenth-century theory that bodily humors are affected by diet and can change disposition
    (D) is part of a religious practice meant to encourage celibacy in hermits
    (E) is typical pet food in nineteenth-century homes

33. The word "purity" in line 39 is an example of

    (A) irony
    (B) metaphor
    (C) simile
    (D) oxymoron
    (E) allusion

34. The tone of the description of Caesar (paragraphs 3 and 4) is

    (A) gently satirical
    (B) indignant
    (C) pensive
    (D) foreboding
    (E) menacing

35. In context, the word "sanguinary" (line 105) most nearly means

    (A) expensive
    (B) feminine
    (C) masculine
    (D) vegetarian
    (E) bloody

36. Judging from this passage, which of the following best describes Louisa's beliefs about gender relations?

    (A) Men and women naturally belong together.
    (B) Men and women should remain separate.
    (C) Men bring chaos and possibly danger to women's lives.
    (D) Women help to civilize men's natural wildness.
    (E) Men are more intelligent than women.

GO ON TO THE NEXT PAGE.

37. In line 41, how is the word "indelicate" used?

    (A) To indicate the differences between Louisa and Joe
    (B) To indicate that Louisa considered her thoughts inappropriately sexual
    (C) To indicate the coarseness of Joe's personality
    (D) To indicate the inferior quality of Joe's belongings
    (E) To foreshadow the vision of Caesar's rampage

38. Which of the following are accomplished by the Caesar vignette?

    (A) It shows us Joe's down-to-earth, kindhearted character.
    (B) It symbolically shows us Louisa's fears of the future.
    (C) It serves as a symbol of what happens to those who refuse change.
    (D) It provides a humorous satire of small-town concerns.
    (E) All of the above

39. In context, "mild-visaged" (line 54) most nearly means

    (A) having a calm temper
    (B) having a gentle face
    (C) having an old face
    (D) being confused
    (E) having a kind mask

GO ON TO THE NEXT PAGE.

Questions 40–55. Read the poem below, entitled "Thou art not lovelier than lilacs—no" by Edna St. Vincent Millay, then choose answers to the questions that follow.

THOU are not lovelier than lilacs,—no,
    Nor honeysuckle; thou are not more fair
    Than small white single poppies,—I can bear
Line Thy beauty; though I bend before thee, though
(5) From left to right, not knowing where to go,
    I turn my troubled eyes, nor here nor there
    Find any refuge from thee, yet I swear
So has it been with mist,—with moonlight so.

Like him who day by day unto his draught
(10)   Of delicate poison adds him one drop more
Till he may drink unharmed the death of ten,
Even so, inured to beauty, who have quaffed
    Each hour more deeply than the hour before,
I drink—and live—what has destroyed some men.

40. The poem is best described as

   (A) a Shakespearean sonnet
   (B) a Petrarchan sonnet
   (C) a sestina
   (D) a ballad
   (E) an ode

41. The speaker's attitude toward the subject's beauty is all of the following EXCEPT

   (A) critical
   (B) tolerant
   (C) assertive
   (D) perplexed
   (E) insouciant

42. In line 10, "delicate poison" is a good example of

   (A) paradox
   (B) juxtaposition
   (C) oxymoron
   (D) truism
   (E) metaphor

43. The subject of the verb "adds" in line 10 is

   (A) him (line 9)
   (B) who (line 9)
   (C) poison (line 10)
   (D) he (line 11)
   (E) I (line 14)

44. Which of the following best describes the tone of the poem?

   (A) Admonishing
   (B) Apologetic
   (C) Ironic
   (D) Sentimental
   (E) Sincere

45. What is the most important thematic point made in lines 1–8 of the poem?

   (A) The speaker cannot escape the subject.
   (B) The speaker believes nothing is more beautiful than flowers.
   (C) The speaker finds nature troublesome.
   (D) The speaker relegates the subject's beauty but recognizes its power over him.
   (E) The speaker desires a refuge.

46. The poem is notable for its use of all of the following EXCEPT

   (A) alliteration
   (B) enjambment
   (C) iambic meter
   (D) refrain
   (E) metaphor

47. The speaker conveys in lines 6–8 that the subject's beauty is

   (A) ethereal
   (B) enveloping
   (C) insignificant
   (D) superficial
   (E) exasperating

48. In context, "inured" (line 12) most nearly means

   (A) hurt
   (B) drunk
   (C) conditioned
   (D) enamored
   (E) drawn

49. In line 8, "it" refers to

   (A) "THOU" (line 1)
   (B) "honeysuckle" (line 2)
   (C) "Thy beauty" (line 4)
   (D) "thee" (line 4)
   (E) "Find any refuge" (line 7)

GO ON TO THE NEXT PAGE.

50. The function of line 14 is best described by which statement?

    (A) The verb "drink" emphasizes the bacchanalian nature of some men.
    (B) It contains the subject of the sentence.
    (C) The verb "destroyed" emphasizes the secret desire of the speaker.
    (D) Its use of punctuation underscores the speaker's desire to live.
    (E) The verb "live" demonstrates the physical superiority of the speaker.

51. In line 9, the poem shifts from

    (A) the speaker feeling engulfed by the subject's beauty to developing immunity from it
    (B) the speaker admiring the subject's beauty to wanting to destroy it
    (C) the speaker being enamored with nature to wanting to poison it
    (D) the speaker criticizing the subject's beauty to disdaining it
    (E) the speaker giving in to desire to trying to resist it

52. How does the first line of this poem function?
    I. It sets up a comparison.
    II. The reference to lilacs makes this poem a pastoral poem.
    III. It establishes the initial tone.
    IV. It states the theme of the poem.

    (A) I only
    (B) I and III only
    (C) II and IV only
    (D) I, III, and IV only
    (E) All of the above

53. Lines 12–14 of the poem function as

    (A) a metaphor
    (B) an allusion
    (C) personification
    (D) a non sequitur
    (E) a metonym

54. Which of the following is true of the rhyme scheme in the second stanza?

    (A) Rhyme is abandoned in the second stanza.
    (B) The final words of lines 9–11 are the basis for the rhyme scheme in the second stanza.
    (C) Line 14 completes a couplet.
    (D) The rhyme scheme is abba.
    (E) Lines 9–12 repeat the rhymes established in lines 5–8.

55. What is the speaker's meaning in lines 10–11?

    (A) The speaker is developing an immunity to poison.
    (B) The speaker wants to protect the subject from harm.
    (C) The speaker is proving his strength over poison.
    (D) The speaker is building a tolerance to the subject's beauty.
    (E) The speaker can drink more than other men.

STOP
END OF SECTION I
**IF YOU FINISH BEFORE TIME IS CALLED, YOU MAY CHECK YOUR WORK ON THIS SECTION.
DO NOT GO ON TO SECTION II UNTIL YOU ARE TOLD TO DO SO.**

SECTION II

Total Time—2 hours

Question 1

(Suggested time—40 minutes. This question counts as one-third of the total essay score.)

In the following poem, "Does It Matter?" by Siegfried Sassoon, the speaker cynically explores the ways that war takes a toll on the former soldier. Read the poem carefully. Then, in a well-written essay, analyze how Sassoon uses bad faith arguments, cynicism, symbolism, and repetition to convey an anti-war message.

Does It Matter?

Does it matter?—losing your legs?...
For people will always be kind,
And you need not show that you mind
When the others come in after hunting
To gobble their muffins and eggs.

Does it matter?—losing your sight?...
There's such splendid work for the blind;
And people will always be kind,
As you sit on the terrace remembering
And turning your face to the light.

Do they matter?—those dreams from the pit?...
You can drink and forget and be glad,
And people won't say that you're mad;
For they'll know you've fought for your country
And no one will worry a bit.

—Siegfried Sassoon

Line
(5)

(10)

(15)

GO ON TO THE NEXT PAGE.

Question 2

(Suggested time—40 minutes. This question counts as one-third of the total essay score.)

The following excerpt is from "The Yellow Wallpaper" by Charlotte Perkins Gilman (1892). In this passage, taken from a work that is regarded as an early feminist literature, the narrator explores her bedroom and her current feelings about her life. Read the passage carefully. Then, in a well-written essay, analyze how Perkins Gilman uses literary elements and techniques to convey a sense of the narrator's mental state and attitude toward her environment and present situation.

The wallpaper, as I said before, is torn off in spots, and it sticketh closer than a brother—they must have had perseverance as well as hatred.

Line
(5) Then the floor is scratched and gouged and splintered, the plaster itself is dug out here and there, and this great heavy bed which is all we found in the room, looks as if it had been through the wars.

But I don't mind a bit—only the paper.

There comes John's sister. Such a dear girl as she is, and
(10) so careful of me! I must not let her find me writing.

She is a perfect and enthusiastic housekeeper, and hopes for no better profession. I verily believe she thinks it is the writing which made me sick!

But I can write when she is out, and see her a long way
(15) off from these windows.

There is one that commands the road, a lovely, shaded, winding road, and one that just looks off over the country. A lovely country, too, full of great elms and velvet meadows.

This wallpaper has a certain kind of sub-pattern in a
(20) different shade, a particularly irritating one, for you can only see it in certain lights, and not clearly then.

But in the places where it isn't faded and where the sun is just so—I can see a strange, provoking, formless sort of figure, that seems to skulk about behind that silly and
(25) conspicuous front design.

There's sister on the stairs!

Well, the Fourth of July is over! The people are gone and I am tired out. John thought it might do me good to see a little company, so we just had mother and Nellie and the children
(30) down for a week. Of course I didn't do a thing. Jennie sees to everything now.

But it tired me all the same.

John says if I don't pick up faster he shall send me to Weir Mitchell in the fall. But I don't want to go there at all.
(35) I had a friend who was in his hands once, and she says he is just like John and my brother, only more so!

Besides, it is such an undertaking to go so far.

I don't feel as if it was worth while to turn my hand over for anything, and I'm getting dreadfully fretful and querulous.
(40) I cry at nothing, and cry most of the time. Of course I don't when John is here, or anybody else, but when I am alone. And I am alone a good deal just now. John is kept in town very often by serious cases, and Jennie is good and lets me alone when I want her to. So I walk a little in the garden
(45) or down that lovely lane, sit on the porch under the roses, and lie down up here a good deal.

I'm getting really fond of the room in spite of the wallpaper. Perhaps *because* of the wallpaper.

It dwells in my mind so!

(50) I lie here on this great immovable bed—it is nailed down, I believe—and follow that pattern about by the hour. It is as good as gymnastics, I assure you. I start, we'll say, at the bottom, down in the corner over there where it has not been touched, and I determine for the thousandth time that I *will*
(55) follow that pointless pattern to some sort of a conclusion.

I know a little of the principles of design, and I know this thing was not arranged on any laws of radiation, or alternation, or repetition, or symmetry, or anything else that I ever heard of.

(60) It is repeated, of course, by the breadths, but not otherwise. Looked at in one way, each breadth stands alone, the bloated curves and flourishes—a kind of "debased Romanesque" with *delirium tremens*—go waddling up and down in isolated columns of fatuity.

(65) But, on the other hand, they connect diagonally, and the sprawling outlines run off in great slanting waves of optic horror, like a lot of wallowing seaweeds in full chase.

The whole thing goes horizontally, too, at least it seems so, and I exhaust myself in trying to distinguish the order of
(70) its going in that direction.

They have used a horizontal breadth for a frieze, and that adds wonderfully to the confusion.

There is one end of the room where it is almost intact, and there, when the cross-lights fade and the low sun shines
(75) directly upon it, I can almost fancy radiation, after all,—the interminable grotesques seem to form around a common center and rush off in head-long plunges of equal distraction.

It makes me tired to follow it. I will take a nap, I guess.

I don't know why I should write this.
(80) I don't want to.

I don't feel able.

And I know John would think it absurd. But I *must* say what I feel and think in some way—it is such a relief!

But the effort is getting to be greater than the relief.

GO ON TO THE NEXT PAGE.

Question 3

(Suggested time—40 minutes. This question counts as one-third of the total essay score.)

In some works of literature, mothers or the concept of motherhood play central roles.

Either from your own reading or from the list below, choose a work of fiction in which motherhood and the maternal interaction between two characters is explored. Then, in a well-written essay, analyze how that exploration of motherhood contributes to an interpretation of the work as a whole. Do not merely summarize the plot.

A Doll's House
The Awakening
As I Lay Dying
Beloved
Black Rain
Bleak House
The Color Purple
Daniel Deronda
Dombey and Son
Fifth Business
The Glass Menagerie
Hamlet

The Joy Luck Club
Medea
Mrs. Warren's Profession
A Room with a View
Pedro Paramo
Pride and Prejudice
The Scarlet Letter
The Seagull
Sons and Lovers
The Sound and the Fury
The Stranger
To the Lighthouse

STOP
END OF EXAM
IF YOU FINISH BEFORE TIME IS CALLED, YOU MAY CHECK YOUR WORK ON THIS SECTION.

Practice Test 2:
Answers and
Explanations

PRACTICE TEST 2 ANSWER KEY

1.	D	21.	C	41.	E
2.	C	22.	B	42.	C
3.	A	23.	D	43.	D
4.	A	24.	D	44.	C
5.	C	25.	A	45.	D
6.	A	26.	B	46.	D
7.	A	27.	C	47.	B
8.	E	28.	A	48.	C
9.	A	29.	D	49.	E
10.	D	30.	B	50.	B
11.	E	31.	A	51.	A
12.	D	32.	C	52.	B
13.	A	33.	B	53.	A
14.	E	34.	A	54.	B
15.	D	35.	E	55.	D
16.	C	36.	C		
17.	D	37.	B		
18.	E	38.	E		
19.	B	39.	B		
20.	E	40.	B		

PRACTICE TEST 2 EXPLANATIONS

Questions 1–15

"An Invective Against Enemies of Poetry" is excerpted from *Pierce Penniless, His Supplication to the Devil*, by English satirist Thomas Nashe (1567–1601). A journalist in London, Nashe published *Pierce Penniless* in about 1592. Although much of his work would now be considered reactionary bigotry, Nashe is admired for his energetic and relatively modern-sounding prose style. In the passage excerpted here, Nashe is defending poetry as a valuable intellectual contribution to society, especially in contrast to the work of preachers and historians.

1. **D** Eloquence, (D), is the answer here, since it runs contrary to the meaning of the passage. (And you remembered you were looking for the contrary, right? This is one of those "EXCEPT" questions.) All the other choices are straightforward accusations in the text except for (E), which is a little obscure. But when Nashe talks about the preachers' "quarter sermon," he means a sermon given once a quarter, only four times a year. The implication is that the preachers really don't work very hard, unlike poets, as the next paragraph goes on to explain.

2. **C** In astrological terms, Saturn was thought to be the planet of depression and gloom, and Saturnists were people ruled by Saturn, hence, depressed, depressing people. Remember that in the sixteenth century, astrology was considered more scientific than it is today. Choice (A) is meant to lure people who recognize that Saturn is a planet and jump to "astrologer" by association. Choice (B), "nymphomaniac," or sex addict, is there to trick people who confuse "Saturnist" with "satyr." Choice (D), "pagan," picks up on the magical associations of astrology, but is certainly the wrong description of a preacher. Choice (E), "foolishly optimistic person" means the opposite of the required definition.

3. **A** Divines are preachers, excoriated here for giving boring rather than poetic sermons. Nashe is opposing divines to writers, whether great, (B), or dead, (C). He does say that the divines are fools, (D), and Saturnists, (E), but those are descriptions rather than definitions. Choice (A) should strike you as the best answer.

4. **A** Nashe is comparing poets to fishmongers, who must constantly keep their product fresh for the marketplace. He is continuing his thought about poets being superior to plagiarizing preachers. You could make arguments in support of (B), the idea that poetry has slippery meanings, but Nashe is not arguing that; he's defending poetry. Choices (C) and (D) are also interesting ideas, but they are not in this passage and are in fact contradicted in other portions of the reading, which praise the special cultural meaning and lasting fame of poetry. Choice (E) is just ridiculous and completely contradicts the meaning of the passage.

5. **C** Nashe is asserting the purity and beauty of the English language and argues that London, as the seat of literary culture, influences how English is spoken all over the country, like the streams of a fountain spreading out beyond the fountain itself. Therefore, poets who improve English in London have a national influence. Choices (A), (B), and (E) are just incorrect associations with the watery imagery of fountains. Choice (D) is tempting because it includes the idea that London is the source of culture, but it does not include the important concept of national influence.

6.   **A**   Lines 34–40 describe how people are motivated by what is said about them, by their longing for fame or their horror of shame, and by fear for their reputations. Nashe might agree with (B), but nothing is said about fairness in these lines. (And despite what he may have thought, Nashe was often considered a slanderer during his lifetime, so his contemporaries didn't think he was fair.) Choice (C) is tempting because the passage does mention that soldiers are inspired by poetry, but the concern in this passage is specifically the personal concerns of individuals for their reputations, not the general idea that poetry is uplifting. Choice (D) might trick people who focus on the reference to "those that care neither for God nor the devil," but Nashe is not interested in atheists except as another category of people with reputations to worry about. Choice (E) doesn't really have anything to do with the passage, except for those who overthink and get caught up in why the poets are writing about everyone in the first place. But that's getting away from the meaning of the specified lines.

7.   **A**   This question is actually pretty straightforward; the parenthetical phrase directly following the name Salustius tells you he is a French poet, actually more familiarly known today as Guillaume de Saluste du Bartas (1544–1590). Choice (B) might confuse people who know what *nom de plume* means (it means "pen name"). Choice (C) is simply incorrect but suggested by the Latinate name. Choice (D) is straight out of left field. Choice (E) is for people whose eyes glazed over while reading this passage and got stuck on the Wife of Bath.

8.   **E**   As used in line 49, Bath is an ancient town and spa in England. This is a general knowledge question that you are just expected to know; the town shows up not only in Chaucer but also in Jane Austen. Choice (B) might be confusing because there is a famous character in Chaucer called the Wife of Bath, because she's from Bath, and she is mentioned in this passage. If you were getting very frazzled, the notion of wife might sucker you into choosing (C), because wives have husbands. Choice (D) is there to confuse you if you were getting overwhelmed by this list of poets. Choice (A) is just irrelevant.

9.   **A**   Nashe says it is better "to have an elegant lawyer to plead one's cause" than a stuttering townsman (lines 58–59), and similarly, it is better to have a poet write your history than a historian. Choice (B) is wrong because mayors are not even compared to anything here; they are just something chronographers write about. Chronographers are local historians and poets are said to be better than chronographers, not like them, so (C) is incorrect. Choice (D) is wrong for the same reason: Lawyers are better than townsmen just as poets are better than chronographers. Choice (E), angels, is a little tricky, because poetry is said to be "the very phrase of angels" (lines 57–58), which might imply that poets are the angels speaking the phrases. But that sentence is talking about poetry as a concept, not about poets as members of society. And even conceited poets don't generally compare themselves to angels, certainly not in the middle of such a satirical piece. Even if you were confused by that, you should be able to see that lawyers is a direct comparison while "angels" requires some overreading and stretching.

10. **D** The phrase "the pilferies of your pen to polish" is an example of alliteration, which means using the same initial consonant sound repeatedly in a line. All the other answer choices are just wrong. A metaphor, (A), is when one thing is described in terms of another, but this is not metaphorical. Onomatopoeia, (B), is when words sound like what they are (for example, "slither"), but pens and pilferies don't make special sounds. A paradox, (C), is something that sounds like a contradiction but turns out to be true in some deeper sense. An apostrophe, (E), is when a poem directly addresses someone or something that can't hear the poem ("O Moon! You orb of wonder!"). If you don't know these terms, you should be sure to read over the glossary in this book before the exam.

11. **E** "Those" refers back to "the enemies of poetry." This is a straightforward grammar question that requires you to parse the complex opening sentence.

12. **D** Unlike the lazy, plagiarizing preachers, poets must have new material all the time or the public won't buy their books. Choice (A) is wrong because the various professions presented in these lines are only implied comparisons for a poet's career, not a list of moonlighting poets. Choice (B) is wrong because Nashe's audience does respect good poets; they only reject bad poets who present stale recycled material. Choices (C) and (E) are completely irrelevant to the passage but might tempt those who think in terms of marketplace competition.

13. **A** This is a pure definition question; you need to know what a tautology is. It's an unnecessary repetition, so (A) is the best answer. Choices (B), (C), and (D) all sound like criticisms, and so seem to fit but do not paraphrase the cited line. Choice (E) merely says that the preachers have sermons, but sermons are not by definition ineloquent, as specified in the sentence cited.

14. **E** The selection specifically mentions all other options as functions of poetry: Choice (A) is in lines 34–35; (B) is in lines 32–33; (C) is in lines 35–37; and (D) is a direct quote from line 26. Choice (E) is not a function of poetry but is mentioned in the selection as a failure of boring preachers.

15. **D** This is a hard question asking for general knowledge. You could have reasoned it out if you realized that people have been questioning the necessity of poetry for millennia; this might have led you to choose the correct answer: Plato. (Actually, Plato decides that poets aren't really necessary in his *Republic*.) Nashe, (A), is the author of this selection. Sidney, (B), and Salustius, (C), are other writers mentioned in the text. Milton, (E), is the famous British poet who wrote *Paradise Lost*.

Questions 16–28

John Donne was a notable metaphysical poet of the seventeenth century and remains one of the greatest English-language poets. His prodigious output of lyrics, satires, sermons, and meditations treat subjects both sacred and profane. He is also, however, notoriously difficult because of his ingeniously figurative language, which is why he tends to show up on English exams frequently.

This poem, "A Valediction: Of Weeping," expresses feelings upon being separated from one's lover. Through kaleidoscopic shifts of perspective, it plays with the paradoxes of presence and absence, distance and proximity.

16. **C** If you are finding it difficult to tell precisely what this poem is about, you can use POE to answer this question. The easiest one to eliminate is (E), because there is far too much crying here for a pleasure cruise. Some of the images sound apocalyptic, so (D) might sound tempting, but you should have realized that this is a love poem and that the end of the world imagery is metaphorical. Likewise, though death is mentioned it is probably also a metaphorical death, so (B) is wrong. That leaves (A) and (C). It is hard to tell whether the relationship is ending or merely being interrupted by distance, but the lovers are definitely being separated. Therefore, (C) is the correct answer.

17. **D** You should know the definition of "metaphysical conceit" because the exam likes to use metaphysical poets. A metaphysical conceit is an elaborate metaphor or simile that occurs in a metaphysical poem. You should have recognized this as a metaphysical poem since it is by John Donne. Check your literary movement overview in Chapter 6. Note that "metaphysical" here has little to do with philosophy and much to do with depth of meaning. The metaphysical conceit in question is the comparison of tears to globes—each tear becomes an entire world once it reflects his beloved, just as round balls become globes once someone pastes images of the continents on them. You may have been tempted to choose (C), recognizing that this is very metaphorical, but in this instance the lines are not literally a metaphor, but a simile: Note the use of "So doth" (line 14) to indicate the comparison.

18. **E** "O more than moon" is an address to the beloved. You should have realized this because the addressed entity has arms (line 21), which narrows down your choices to either (E) or (D), the workmen. It is obviously not the moon, (A). The world, (B), has no arms. And nothing in this poem mentions the poet's soul, (C).

19. **B** The tears in lines 14 and 15 are the speaker's tears, which "wear" the image of his beloved and they are also the beloved's tears "worn" on her face. There is nothing here about clothing. Therefore, the first and second statements are correct, as given in (B). Choice (A) only gives the first statement, and is therefore incorrect. Choices (C), (D), and (E) include the incorrect statement.

20. **E** All of the stanzas contain images of roundness. The first stanza has coins and fruit, and even pregnancy, in a way. The second stanza has globes and worlds. The third stanza has the moon and the word "sphere."

21. **C** Many, many metaphysical poems contain circle imagery because the iconography—or pictorial material—of seventeenth-century poetry interprets the circle as the perfect shape. Circles have no end and therefore indicate perfect wholeness and eternity. These qualities made circles especially popular in love poetry, of which this is an example. Choice (A) is wrong because there isn't any imagery of worthlessness, nor is there a sense of hopelessness. Choice (B) is half right because there are globes and vast distances, but the whole point of the poem is to reduce the vast distances by containing them within the tiny spheres of tears, so choosing (B) is an incomplete reading of the poem. Furthermore, the globe imagery is really only prominent in the second stanza, rather than being sustained throughout the poem. Choice (D) is wrong because there is no suggestion of faithlessness between the lovers. Eliminate (E) because the water is used as a tool to show separation and alienation within the poem, not bonding.

22. **B** This is really a grammar question to see how well you can sort out the sentence structure in this poem. *Which* begins a dependent clause modifying *that*. So *which* refers to whatever *that* is. *That* is the object of the verb *make*. The subject of *make* is the workman. The workman is making globes out of the round balls that are blank in his workshop. Therefore, both *that* and *which* must refer to the round balls. Although the globes are copied from models, the *copies* are models the workman *hath by* in his shop; he refers to the copies but does not make them into anything, so (A) is wrong. *World* does not even show up in this stanza until several lines later when it is a metaphorized tear, so (C) is wrong. The workman is the subject of this independent clause, but the subject is not being modified by *which*, so (D) is wrong. The listed continents are objects of the subject *workman* but are not modified by the dependent clause, so (E) is wrong.

23. **D** This is a tricky question because it requires both interpretation of the poem and some familiarity with the conventions of metaphysical poetry, but POE can help you out here. Remember to read the question carefully; you are looking to identify the *wrong* association here, so you are looking for what *doesn't* fit in the answers. Choice (B) fits the poem because there is an obvious connection between the moon, the sea, and tides. Choice (C) obviously fits because the round imagery has been sustained throughout the entire poem, and you should remember that you have already been asked about round imagery. Remember to keep your answers consistent across questions. Choice (E) probably fits because the poem certainly does describe unhappy feelings. That leaves us with (A) and (D); you must choose between a goddess and the man in the moon. There is no explicit reference to either a goddess or the man in the moon, but at least the idea of a goddess seems flattering to the beloved and fits the poem better. Therefore, (D) is the least likely association and the correct answer.

24. **D** "Diverse" here just means "different"; the phrase means "a different place." Heaven, (A), and hell, (B), have no place in the poem at all. Europe, (C), is listed as a continent in the poem but is not specified as a destination. The ground, (E), is just an answer for the truly desperate.

25. **A** Tears are found throughout all three stanzas although you have to look closely at the final stanza to find the idea in the word "Weep" (line 21). Globes, (B), are only in the second stanza. Coins, (C), are only in the first stanza. The moon, (D), is only in the third stanza. The ocean, (E), is in the second and third stanzas. Ocean is almost suggested by the mention of shores in the first stanza, but it is not as strong a suggestion as that of "Weep" for tears in the third stanza, so tears, (A), remains the best answer.

26. **B** Line 4 is "And by this mintage they are something worth." "They" refers back to "my tears" in line 2. The tears are said to be coined by the beloved's face (line 3), and the coin metaphor is carried forward into the use of "mintage" here; the process of being coined is the mintage that makes the tears worth something. The tears reflect her face the way that coins show a ruler's face. By showing the beloved's face, the tears become valuable, like coins. Therefore, (B) is the best paraphrase. Choice (A) is contrary to the sense of the poem, because it says the beloved is worthless. Choice (C) does not reflect the meaning of the line, although some readers might be confused if they don't know what "mintage" means. Choice (D) is tempting because it sounds nice and fits with the meaning of the poem, but it overstates—it goes beyond what the line means. Paraphrases are supposed to restate, not extend. Choice (E) is both vague and sort of New Age, and it is not the point.

27. **C** The speaker asks the lover to "forbear/To teach the sea what it may do" (lines 21–22) and that she not let the wind "Example find" (line 24) in her behavior. He is saying that the natural elements are watching and learning from her, copying her behavior, an idea that is carried forward from the description of his lover as the moon influencing the tides. In the face of such great love, one would think that she would have the power to break his heart, but that is not mentioned in the specified lines, so you can eliminate (A). He does mention dying in these lines but mostly in the context of her power over the elements; he warns her against teaching the oceans and winds how to kill him, not against killing him herself. Therefore, (B) is incorrect. The lines assume that she has the power to restrain her grief and they do not emphasize this power the way they emphasize her power over nature, so get rid of (D). Nowhere in the poem is there anything mentioned about the right to take other lovers, making (E) incorrect as well. The correct answer is (C).

28. **A** The speaker flatters the beloved by exaggerating her powers over natural elements and by declaring the inestimable value of even the reflections of her image—in other words, through hyperbole.

Questions 29–39

Mary E. Wilkins Freeman (1852–1930) was a New England writer raised in an impoverished and strictly religious household. As an adult, she wrote fiction that portrayed the psychological effects on women of a traditional and repressive culture. She was well-educated, but most profoundly influenced by her discussions with friends of literary classics. She is generally noted as an important early realist and regional writer, but her characters offer a psychological depth unusual in regional writers of her time. Freeman was also one of the few women of her time able to achieve economic independence through her earnings from her writing.

This selection is from the short story "A New England Nun" published in 1891, about a woman who decides after a very long engagement that she really doesn't want to get married after all.

29. **D** This is a tricky question because the portrait of Louisa appeals to many popular stereotypes about women. But this is also a question in which you can use POE. Choice (A) is obviously wrong: Louisa is not bitter or domineering, but that was thrown in there in case you confused Louisa with her fears about her future mother-in-law. Choice (B) is partly right because Louisa is naive, but she is not shown doing anything childish. You might argue that her preconceptions about men are somewhat childish, but that would be overreading the text. Choice (C) is also alluring because "frightened" seems to relate to the end of the passage in which Louisa "trembles," but there are lots of reasons for trembling, and "foolish" doesn't really fit. You might find Louisa's ideas about men foolish, but her contemplation of how her upcoming marriage will change her life is certainly realistic enough, in its way. Choice (E) might also appeal because of our sympathy for Caesar, but Louisa also loves the dog and nothing in her behavior is deliberately cruel. Therefore, the only really acceptable answer is (D). Louisa is certainly sheltered and knows it, and she is also innocent insofar as she believes what she is told about Caesar, Joe, and Joe's mother. But more importantly, she believes in the conventional wisdom regarding the difficulties of married life.

30. **B** Again, you can answer this question through POE and a careful reading of the selection. Choice (A) is almost ridiculous: the only thing that comes close to a reference to farming in this selection is Louisa's distilling of herbs, and that doesn't seem to involve any seasonal harvest ritual. Besides, harvest rituals and their goddesses are usually sexual, which is precisely what Louisa's maidenly activities aren't. Choice (C) is wrong because there is nothing to suggest that Louisa is mentally ill. Choice (D) is wrong because, although Louisa has "almost the enthusiasm of an artist" while cleaning her house, there is nothing to suggest that she is a genius of any kind. Choice (E) is tempting because Louisa is engaged in many traditional tasks, but because she anticipates that her mother-in-law and husband will make her stop many of her less-productive activities, they are probably not the highest values of the town. This leaves (B). Note that (B) uses the phrase *feminine cultural sphere,* which is a term widely used in feminist criticism to indicate traditionally feminine activities. The passage suggests this interpretation by its contrast between Louisa's activities and Joe's more masculine aura.

31. **A** We can examine each statement separately. Statement (I) expresses the main idea of the passage, and is therefore true. Statement (II) is an interesting idea but is not relevant to the passage, because even if you disapprove of Caesar's treatment, there is no suggestion that society is cruel in this passage. Statement (III) is there to confuse people who skimmed the passage and thought Caesar was an ancient Roman. Statement (IV) is a theme suggested by the passage and supported by the reactions of the townspeople and by Louisa's reactions to her own life, and is therefore true. Therefore, (A) is the only possible answer.

32. **C** There was a well-regarded theory for many centuries that said personalities were influenced by "humors" in the body: Warm humors in the body caused angry or passionate personalities, while cold humors caused unemotional or calm personalities. These humors were affected by diet and by environment. This is where you get the stereotype of the hot Latin lover who lives in a tropical region, eats spicy food, and is given to fits of violent temper. It is also where we get the idea of people being "in a good humor." The bitten neighbor is described as "choleric," which is another reference to the theory of humors. Louisa is deliberately feeding her dog bland food to discourage any further attacks on the neighbors. She is not poor or she would not be able to have such nice things in her house, so (A) is false. The passage does speak metaphorically of Caesar's imprisonment, but Louisa is not deliberately punishing her dog, certainly not for a decade, so (B) is also incorrect. There are many references to hermits and nuns in this story, but dogs do not practice celibacy as a religious practice, so (D) is wrong. Choice (E) is wrong just from context, because the passage mentions that other kitchens give bones to dogs.

33. **B** *Redolent* means "smelling of," and because purity doesn't have a smell, its use here must be metaphorical. Choice (A), irony, is tempting, but there is nothing opposed or contradictory here to indicate irony. Eliminate (C), simile, because there is no direct comparison of two things. And because we've already determined that there is no contradiction, there cannot be an oxymoron, so get rid of (D). Nothing is alluded to, so (E) is wrong. If you are not familiar with these terms, study the glossary in this book.

34. **A** The story of Caesar is a gentle satire on the mini-dramas of small-town life, which finds excitement in the vicious reputation of an old dog. Clues to the satirical tone are the many overwritten references to sin and danger, especially Louisa's vision of Caesar on a rampage through the town. Freeman's treatment of this passage is too humorous to be either indignant or pensive, so (B) and (C) are incorrect. Because it is clear to the reader, and even to Joe, that Caesar isn't really dangerous, there is also nothing foreboding or menacing in this passage, so eliminate (D) and (E). The selection does say that Louisa feels many "forebodings of disturbance," including worries about Caesar, but those are Louisa's feelings rather than the tone of the passage, which indicates the attitude of the author. The correct answer is (A).

35. **E** *Sanguinary* means "bloody," both in the sense of containing blood and of liking blood. Choice (D), vegetarian, is obviously wrong because it contradicts the meaning of the sentence. The other answers draw on ideas raised in previous questions on this piece; remember to keep your answers consistent. We have already established that financial concerns do not dominate Caesar's diet, so (A) is wrong. Choices (B) and (C) drag in the ideas of masculine and feminine traits that predominate in this selection, but they really have nothing to do with what the dog eats.

36. **C** This question tests how well you read Louisa's character because the entire passage is about her attitude toward gender relations. Her meditations on the disorder her future husband will bring to her house and on the impending danger of Caesar's release are best summed up in (C). Louisa is living in a society that believes men and women belong together, but her worries show that she is not entirely convinced of this, so you can get rid of (A). On the other hand, she is not explicitly rejecting marriage, so (B) is not the best answer either. Choice (D) introduces the idea of wildness that you might have associated with Caesar, but it is important to note that Louisa does not believe she has tamed Caesar, nor does she think she will have any influence over her husband, so (D) is wrong. Her belief that Joe's decision to release Caesar will prove disastrous shows that she does not think men are more intelligent than women, so (E) is also incorrect.

37. **B** *Indelicate* is a euphemism for "inappropriately sexual." Dirty jokes are indelicate; graphic sexual details are indelicate. The point here is that Louisa's concern about the chaos Joe may bring to her life is connected to her sexual concerns. Although this passage in general ponders the differences between Louisa and Joe, delicacy or lack thereof is not the primary concern of the passage, so (A) is wrong. There is also nothing to suggest that Joe is especially coarse, nor that his belongings are shoddy, so (C) and (D) are incorrect. Choice (E) is another example of overreading the passage. *Indelicate* does not refer to Caesar in any way, and so cannot foreshadow Louisa's vision of a rampaging dog.

38. **E** All of the statements describe the narrative accomplishments of the Caesar vignette. Joe is shown to be kind and practical, (A), when he urges Caesar's release; Louisa's fears, (B), are demonstrated in her vision of Caesar on a rampage; Caesar's sad plight is an example of what happens when people refuse change, (C); and the inflated terror of the townspeople is a satire of small-town life, (D).

39. **B** Caesar has a gentle face; he is mild-visaged. *Visage* means "face." Choice (E) might have misled some people because there is the suggestion that Caesar is vicious, and hence could be "masked," but we see Caesar differently than Louisa does. This adjective is just straightforwardly descriptive, not a clue to hidden depths. Don't overread the passage.

Questions 40–55

A Pulitzer Prize winner, Edna St. Vincent Millay was one of the most skillful sonnet writers of the twentieth century. This sonnet is from her first published book *Renascence and Other Poems* (1917). One issue that comes up in many of Millay's poems, including this sonnet, is gender. The gender of the speaker in this poem has been debated, and it is perhaps deliberately ambiguous. In the explanations that follow, we use the male pronoun when referring to the speaker.

40. **B** The poem is written in the form of a Petrarchan sonnet: the first eight lines form an octave with the rhyme scheme *abbaabba*, and the remaining six lines form a sestet. In this poem, the rhyme scheme for the sestet is *cdecde*. The correct answer is (B). A Shakespearean, or English, sonnet is written in three quatrains of alternating rhyme and a couplet, so eliminate (A). A sestina is a 39-line poem that is comprised of six stanzas of six lines and a final triplet, so eliminate (C). Because of its specific structure and rhyme scheme, this poem is not a ballad, (D), or an ode, (E).

41. **E** Lines 1–3 contain an example of the speaker's critical attitude, so (A) is not the answer you're looking for. Lines 3–4 and the second stanza contain examples of the speaker's tolerant attitude, so eliminate (B). In both stanzas, the speaker speaks his mind and is therefore assertive, so (C) is also not correct. In lines 5–6, the speaker confesses that he does not know where to go and has "troubled eyes." Thus, he seems to be perplexed, and you can eliminate (D). There is no support in the text that he is indifferent or carefree, so the best answer is (E).

42. **C** "Delicate poison" is an oxymoron because it is a figure of speech that combines contradictory terms. Poison's powerful and often lethal effect makes it the opposite of delicate, so the correct answer is (C). The phrase is not a paradox, (A), because a paradox is a statement that contradicts itself.

43. **D** The best way to figure out the construction of this sentence is to rewrite it in a more natural form. This is a little tricky, as the sentence is the entire second stanza. However, notice that lines 9–11 form a subordinate clause. The subject of "adds" will be within this clause. Get rid of the prepositional phrases, and you're left with "Like him who adds." Who is adding one drop more? That's in line 11: he. He is adding drops of poison to his drink so that he may drink unharmed. The correct answer is (D).

44. **C** The speaker begins by stating that the subject is not prettier than various attractive, fragrant flowers. Then the speaker claims that he finds the subject's beauty weakening (I bend before thee), and states that he is unable to escape from the subject's beauty. Since the first stanza is ironic, eliminate (E). In the second stanza, the speaker compares the subject's beauty to poison and reveals that he is developing a tolerance to it, which is also ironic. Therefore, the best answer is (C). The tone is not one of warning, (A). The speaker is not apologizing, (B), nor is he sentimental, (D).

45. **D** The theme of the first stanza is the subject's beauty and its effect on the speaker, so the best answer is (D). The speaker does claim to be seeking refuge (i.e., escape from the subject's beauty), but that is not the theme of these lines, so eliminate (A) and (E). The theme of the first stanza is also not nature or flowers, so eliminate (B) and (C).

46. **D** The only literary device that isn't used in this poem is refrain, (D). A refrain is a line or set of lines repeated several times. Each line of the poem is distinct, so the correct answer must be (D).

47. **B** There is no evidence in the first stanza that the subject's beauty is not of this world or that he is intensely irritated by it, so you can eliminate (A) and (E). The subject's beauty is significant, as the speaker discusses it throughout this entire stanza, so (C) can be eliminated. The speaker also describes the subject's beauty as being like mist and moonlight that surrounds (i.e., envelops) him, indicating that the subject's beauty is not superficial. Therefore, the correct answer (B).

48. **C** To be *inured* means to be accustomed to something. In this case, the speaker has become accustomed to the subject's beauty by "drinking" it in and compares that to someone teaching himself to tolerate poison (think Westley in *The Princess Bride*). In order to inure himself to the subject's beauty, the speaker has trained or conditioned himself to tolerate it. The best answer is (C).

49. **E** In the first stanza, the speaker desires refuge from the subject's beauty but is unable to find it because it is everywhere—just as the mist and the moonlight are all around, so too is the subject's beauty. Therefore, "it" in line 8 refers back to this idea of finding refuge, (E), not the subject's beauty, (C). Note that (A) and (D) both refer to the subject and therefore can be eliminated (there can't be two correct answers here). The speaker is not trying to escape from the honeysuckle, (B).

50. **B** As noted above for question 43, the entire second stanza is one sentence. In line 14, the main subject for the sentence appears, letting the reader know that the speaker is the one who inured himself to the subject's beauty. Therefore, the function of line 14 is (B).

51. **A** In Petrarchan sonnets, the beginning of line 9 indicates not only a change in the rhyme scheme but also a change in subject matter. Lines 1–8 focus on the speaker's feeling of being enveloped by the subject's beauty; he is not able to get away from it. Then in lines 9–14, the focus shifts to the speaker developing an ability to withstand the subject's beauty. The best choice is (A). The speaker does not wish to destroy, (B), or poison, (C), the subject's beauty in the second stanza. The speaker does not have intense hatred toward the subject's beauty, (D), nor is he trying to resist it (E). Rather, he's developed a tolerance for it.

52. **B** Examine each statement separately. Line 1 of the poem does compare the subject's beauty to that of a lilac. Keep (I), which eliminates (C). Statement (II) is incorrect because this is not a pastoral poem. Eliminate (E). For (III), find the initial tone. Question 41 will help. Initially, the speaker does criticize the subject's beauty (lines 1–3), so line 1 does establish this tone. Eliminate (A). For (IV), use question 51 for help. The theme of the poem is not to criticize the subject's beauty but quite the contrary, which eliminates (D) and makes (B) the correct answer.

53. **A** This is a definition question. The speaker is not alluding to anything, so eliminate (B). There is no personification, so (C) is also incorrect. A *non sequitur* is a conclusion or statement that does not logically follow from the previous statement. Although these lines are filled with imagery, they logically follow each other in the context of this poem, so you can eliminate (D). The poem does not contain any metonyms, words that represent something else with which they might be closely associated; (E) is thus incorrect. The idea that the subject's beauty is a drink containing poison that could be ingested is a metaphor, which makes (A) the correct answer.

54. **B** There is a rhyme scheme in the second stanza, which eliminates (A). Lines 9–11 follow the pattern *cde*, which is repeated in lines 12–14. The correct answer is thus (B). Line 14 does not rhyme with line 13, so it is not a couplet, eliminating (C). Note that Petrarchan sonnets do not end in couplets. Eliminate (D), since *abba* is the rhyme scheme for the first stanza, not the second, which eliminates (E) as well.

55. **D** The speaker is not literally developing an immunity to poison or drinking it. Eliminate (A) and (C). The speaker is comparing that idea to what he is actually doing: conditioning himself to the subject's beauty. Therefore, the correct answer is (D). The speaker is not attempting to protect the subject but rather himself, so (B) can be eliminated. Choice (E) is too literal. The speaker is suggesting that he can handle her beauty more so than other men.

Part VII
Glossary

- Glossary of Basic Parts of Speech
- Glossary of Literary Terms for the AP English Literature and Composition Exam

GLOSSARY OF BASIC PARTS OF SPEECH

You need to know the basic parts of speech.

Become a Grammar Guru

Need to brush up on your grammar before exam day? Pick up a copy of *Grammar Smart,* which contains tons of grammar guidance and practice.

- **Noun:** A person, place, thing, or idea (or an abstraction—for example, *strength* and *determination* are nouns).
- **Verb:** An action word or a word that expresses a state of being.
- **Adjective:** A word that modifies, describes, or limits a noun or pronoun.
- **Adverb:** A word that modifies, describes, or limits a verb, an adjective, or another adverb. (In the phrase *the profoundly nasty little poodle,* *nasty* and *little* are adjectives, but *profoundly* is an adverb, as it modifies the adjective *nasty*.)
- **Preposition:** A word that shows the relationship between a noun or pronoun and some other word in the sentence. A preposition should not be the last word in a sentence in formal writing. A preposition is the first word of a prepositional phrase. The phrase will begin with a preposition and end with a noun or pronoun. (Take, for instance, the phrase *in the lake. In* is the preposition and *lake* is the noun that ends the phrase.)
- **Pronoun:** A word that replaces a noun. Words such as *he, she, it, they, them, who,* and *that* can replace a noun. The noun to which a pronoun refers is called the *antecedent.* You find the antecedent by looking back from the pronoun to the part of the passage immediately preceding the pronoun and looking at the nouns that are in those sentences. One of those nouns, either because it is the closest to the pronoun or because it makes the most sense in context, is the noun to which the pronoun refers.
- **Gerund:** A word that serves two functions. It acts like a noun and it acts like a verb. Look at the following sentence. *Swimming across the lake is fun. Swimming* is the gerund.
- **Participle:** A word that serves two functions. It acts like an adjective and it acts like a verb. Look how *swimming* is used in the following sentence. *The girl, swimming across the lake, reminds me of my sister.* In this case the word *swimming* is describing the girl and, therefore, is a participle.
- **Infinitive:** A phrase that begins with the word *to* and is followed by a verb form. *To swim* is an infinitive. In the following sentence, *to swim* is the infinitive: *To swim across the lake is fun.* Infinitives function as verbs, but they can also function as nouns, adjectives, or adverbs.

GLOSSARY OF LITERARY TERMS FOR THE AP ENGLISH LITERATURE AND COMPOSITION EXAM

We've put an asterisk (*) beside the handful of terms that you *absolutely must know*.

abstract

An *abstract* style (in writing) is typically complex, discusses intangible qualities like good and evil, and seldom uses examples to support its points.

academic

As an adjective describing style, this word means dry and theoretical writing. When a piece of writing seems to be sucking all the life out of its subject with analysis, the writing is *academic*.

accent

In poetry, *accent* refers to the stressed portion of a word. In "To be, or not to be," accents fall on the first "be" and "not." It sounds silly any other way. But accent in poetry is also often a matter of opinion. Consider the rest of the first line of Hamlet's famous soliloquy, "That is the question." The stresses in that portion of the line are open to a variety of interpretations.

aesthetic, aesthetics

Aesthetic can be used as an adjective meaning "appealing to the senses." Aesthetic judgment is a phrase synonymous with artistic judgment. As a noun, an aesthetic is a coherent sense of taste. The kid whose room is painted black, who sleeps in a coffin, and listens only to funeral music has an aesthetic. The kid whose room is filled with pictures of kittens and daisies but who sleeps in a coffin and listens to polka music has a confused aesthetic. The plural noun, *aesthetics*, is the study of beauty. Questions like *What is beauty?* or *Is the beautiful always good?* fall into the category of aesthetics.

allegory

An *allegory* is a story in which each aspect of the story has a symbolic meaning outside the tale itself. Many fables have an allegorical quality. For example, Aesop's "The Ant and the Grasshopper" isn't merely the story of a hardworking ant and a carefree grasshopper, but is also a story about different approaches to living—the thrifty and the devil-may-care. It can also be read as a story about the seasons of summer and winter, which represent a time of prosperity and a time of hardship, or even as representing youth and age. True allegories are even more hard and fast. Bunyan's epic poem, *Pilgrim's Progress,* is an allegory of the soul, in which each and every part of the tale represents some feature of the spiritual world and the struggles of an individual to lead a Christian life.

alliteration

The repetition of initial consonant sounds is called *alliteration*. In other words, consonant clusters coming closely cramped and compressed—no coincidence.

allusion

A reference to another work or famous figure is an *allusion*. A classical allusion is a reference to Greek and Roman mythology or literature such as *The Iliad*. Allusions can be topical or popular as well. A topical allusion refers to a current event. A popular allusion refers to something from popular culture, such as a reference to a television show or a hit movie.

anachronism

The word *anachronism* is derived from Greek. It means "misplaced in time." If the actor playing Brutus in a production of *Julius Caesar* forgets to take off his wristwatch, the effect will be anachronistic (and probably comic).

analogy

An *analogy* is a comparison. Usually analogies involve two or more symbolic parts and are employed to clarify an action or a relationship. *Just as the mother eagle shelters her young from the storm by spreading her great wing above their heads, so does Acme Insurers of America spread an umbrella of coverage to protect its policyholders from the storms of life.*

anecdote

An *anecdote* is a short narrative.

antagonist

A character, group, characteristic, or entity that opposes the protagonist.

antecedent

The word, phrase, or clause that a pronoun refers to or replaces. In *The principal asked the children where they were going, they* is the pronoun and *children* is the antecedent.

anthropomorphism

In literature, when inanimate objects, animals, or natural phenomena are given human characteristics, behavior, or motivation, *anthropomorphism* is at work. For example, *In the forest, the darkness waited for me, I could hear its patient breathing...* Anthropomorphism is often confused with personification, which requires that the nonhuman quality or thing take on a human shape.

anticlimax

An *anticlimax* occurs when an action produces far smaller results than one had been led to expect. Anticlimax is frequently comic. *Sir, your snide manner and despicable arrogance have long been a source of disgust to me, but I've overlooked it until now. However, it has come to my attention that you have fallen so disgracefully deep into that mire of filth which is your mind as to attempt to besmirch my wife's honor and my good name. Sir, I challenge you to a game of badminton!*

aphorism

A short and usually witty saying, such as: " 'Classic'? A book which people praise and don't read."—Mark Twain.

*apostrophe
An address to someone not present or to a personified object or idea.

archaism
The use of deliberately old-fashioned language. Authors sometimes use *archaisms* to create a feeling of antiquity. Tourist traps use archaisms with a vengeance, as in "Ye Olde Candle Shoppe"—Yeech!

archetypes
Standard or clichéd character types, such as the drunk, the miser, and the foolish girl.

argumentation
The act or process of analyzing evidence, drawing conclusions, and developing claims. Literary argumentation applies this process to literature.

aside
A speech (usually just a short comment) made by an actor to the audience, as though momentarily stepping outside of the action on stage. (See *soliloquy*.)

aspect
A trait or characteristic, as in "an *aspect* of the dew drop."

assonance
The repeated use of vowel sounds, as in, "*O*ld king C*o*le was a merry *o*ld s*ou*l."

atmosphere
The emotional tone or background that surrounds a scene.

attitude
A speaker's, author's, or character's nature toward or opinion of a subject. (See *tone*.)

ballad
A long, narrative poem usually in very regular meter and rhyme. A *ballad* typically has a naive folksy quality, a characteristic that distinguishes it from epic poetry.

bathos
When writing strains for grandeur it can't support and tries to elicit tears from every little hiccup, that's *bathos*.

black humor
This is the use of disturbing themes in comedy. In Samuel Beckett's *Waiting for Godot*, the two tramps, Didi and Gogo, comically debate over which should commit suicide first and whether the branches of the tree will support their weight. This is *black humor*.

bombast

This is pretentious, exaggeratedly learned language. When one tries to be eloquent by using the largest, most uncommon words, one falls into *bombast*.

burlesque

A *burlesque* is broad parody, one that takes a style or a form such as tragic drama and exaggerates it into ridiculousness. A parody usually takes on a specific work, such as *Hamlet*. For the purposes of the AP Exam, you can think of the terms *parody* and *burlesque* as interchangeable.

cacophony

In poetry, *cacophony* is using deliberately harsh, awkward sounds.

cadence

The beat or rhythm of poetry in a general sense. For example, *iambic pentameter* is the technical name for a rhythm. One sample of predominantly iambic pentameter verse could have a gentle, *pulsing* cadence, whereas another might have a *conversational* cadence, and still another might have a vigorous, *marching* cadence.

canto

The name for a section division in a long work of poetry, similar to the way chapters divide a novel.

*caricature

A portrait (verbal or otherwise) that exaggerates a facet of personality.

catharsis

This is a term drawn from Aristotle's writings on tragedy. *Catharsis* refers to the "cleansing" of emotion an audience member experiences having lived (vicariously) through the experiences presented on stage.

character

In literary terms, description, representations, or discussions of the features that make up an individual and represent who they are. Can also refer to an individual in a play.

chorus

In drama, a *chorus* is the group of citizens who stand outside the main action on stage and comment on it.

classic, classical

What a troublesome word! Don't confuse classic with classical. *Classic* can mean typical, as in *Oh, that was a classic blunder*. It can also mean an accepted masterpiece, for example, *Death of a Salesman*. But, *classical* refers to the arts of ancient Greece and Rome and the qualities of those arts.

coinage (neologism)

A *coinage* is a new word, usually one invented on the spot. People's names often become grist for coinages, as in, *Oh, man, you just pulled a major Wilson.* Of course, you'd have to know Wilson to know what that means, but you can tell it isn't a good thing. The technical term for coinage is *neologism*.

colloquialism

This is a word or phrase used in everyday conversational English that isn't a part of accepted "schoolbook" English. For example, *I'm toast. I'm a crispy-critter man, and now I've got this wicked headache.*

complex, dense

These two terms carry the similar meaning of suggesting that there is more than one possibility in the meaning of words (image, idea, opposition); there are subtleties and variations; there are multiple layers of interpretation; the meaning is both explicit and implicit.

*conceit, controlling image, extended metaphor

In poetry, *conceit* doesn't mean stuck-up. It refers to a startling or unusual metaphor, or one developed and expanded upon over several lines. When the image dominates and shapes the entire work, it's called a *controlling image*. A metaphysical conceit is reserved for metaphysical poems only.

connotation, denotation

The *denotation* of a word is its literal meaning. The *connotations* are everything else that the word suggests or implies. For example, in the phrase *the dark forest, dark* denotes a relative lack of light. The connotation is of danger, or perhaps mystery or quiet; we'd need more information to know for sure, and if we did know with complete certainty that wouldn't be connotation, but denotation. In many cases connotation eventually so overwhelms a word that it takes over the denotation. For example, *livid* is supposed to denote a dark purple-red color like that of a bruise, but it has been used so often in the context of extreme anger that many people have come to use *livid* as a synonym for enraged, rather than a connotative description of it.

consonance

The repetition of consonant sounds within words (rather than at their beginnings, which is alliteration). A flo*ck* of si*ck*, bla*ck*-che*ck*ered du*ck*s.

*couplet

A pair of lines that end in rhyme:

> But at my back I always *hear*
> Time's winged chariot hurrying *near*.
> —from "To His Coy Mistress" by Andrew Marvell

decorum

In order to observe *decorum*, a character's speech must be styled according to her social station and in accordance with the occasion. A bum should speak like a bum about bumly things, while a princess should speak only about higher topics (and in a delicate manner). In Neoclassical and Victorian literature the authors observed decorum, meaning they did not write about the indecorous. The bum wouldn't even appear in this genre of literature.

details, choice of details

The items or parts that make up a larger picture or story. Writers can use *details* to bring their characters to life. Chaucer's "Prologue" to *The Canterbury Tales* is one example of how an author can use *details* to develop a character.

devices of sound

Various techniques used by poets to create sound imagery through specific word choice (e.g., rhyme, alliteration, assonance, consonance, and onomatopoeia) to evoke an emotional response, clarify meaning, enhance the reader's experience, and so on.

diction

Word choice.

dirge

A song for the dead. Its tone is typically slow, heavy, and melancholy.

dissonance

The grating of incompatible sounds.

doggerel

Crude, simplistic verse, often in sing-song rhyme. Limericks are a kind of *doggerel*.

*dramatic irony

When the audience knows something that the characters in the drama do not.

dramatic monologue

When a single speaker in literature says something to a silent audience.

dystopia

A seemingly ideal world where the actual implementation of perfection is unsuccessful and destructive; opposite of utopia (see definition).

elegy

A type of poem that meditates on death or mortality in a serious, thoughtful manner. *Elegies* often use the recent death of a noted person or loved one as a starting point. They also memorialize specific dead people.

elements

This word is used constantly and with the assumption that you know exactly what it means—that is, the basic techniques of each genre of literature. For a quick refresher, here's a short and sweet list for each genre:

elements of fiction
Exposition, conflict, rising action, climax, falling action, resolution, denouement

rhetorical elements
Argument (Ethos, Logos, Pathos), evidence/examples, reason/ explanation

*enjambment

The continuation of a syntactic unit from one line or couplet of a poem to the next with no pause.

epic

In a broad sense, an *epic* is simply a very long narrative poem on a serious theme and in a dignified style. *Epics* typically deal with glorious or profound subject matter: a great war, a heroic journey, the Fall from Eden, a battle with supernatural forces, a trip into the underworld, and so on. The mock-epic is a parody form that deals with mundane events and ironically treats them as being worthy of epic poetry.

epitaph

Lines that commemorate the dead at their burial place. An *epitaph* is usually a line or handful of lines, often serious or religious but sometimes witty and even irreverent.

ethos

The appeal to credibility; establishing common ground and trust with an audience.

euphemism

A word or phrase that takes the place of a harsh, unpleasant, or impolite reality. The use of *passed away* for *died*, and *let go* for *fired* are two examples of *euphemisms*.

euphony

When sounds blend harmoniously, the result is *euphony*.

explicit

Something said or written directly and clearly (this is a rare happening in literature because the whole game is to be "implicit,"—that is, to suggest and imply).

farce

Today we use this word to refer to extremely broad humor. Writers in earlier times used *farce* as a more neutral term, meaning simply a funny play; a comedy. (And you should know that for writers of centuries past, *comedy* was the generic term for any play; it did not imply humor.)

feminine rhyme

Lines rhymed by their final two syllables. A pair of lines ending with *running* and *gunning* would be an example of *feminine rhyme*. Properly, in a *feminine rhyme* (and not simply a double rhyme) the penultimate syllables are stressed and the final syllables are unstressed.

figurative language

Writing that uses words to mean something other than their literal meaning. Examples of *figurative language* include metaphor, simile, and irony.

first-person narrator

See *point of view*.

foil

A secondary character whose purpose is to highlight the characteristics of a main character, usually by contrast. For example, an author will often give a cynical, quick-witted character a docile, naive, sweet-tempered friend to serve as a *foil*. Some classic examples include Benvolio and Tybalt or Gatsby and Tom.

foot

The basic rhythmic unit of a line of poetry. A *foot* is formed by a combination of two or three syllables, either stressed or unstressed.

*foreshadowing

An event or statement in a narrative that suggests, in miniature, a larger event that comes later.

free verse

Poetry written without a regular rhyme scheme or metrical pattern.

genre

A subcategory of literature. Science fiction and detective stories are *genres* of fiction.

gothic, gothic novel

Gothic is the sensibility derived from dark novels. This form first showed up in the mid-18th century and has continued to woo audiences every since. Think in terms of Poe, Shelley, even Stephen King. The dark and twisty stories are considered gothic in nature.

hubris

The excessive pride or ambition that leads to the main character's downfall (another term from Aristotle's discussion of tragedy).

*hyperbole

Exaggeration or deliberate overstatement.

imagery

An author's use of figurative language, images, or sensory details that appeal to the reader's senses (e.g., sight, sound, or touch). *Imagery* coupled with figures of speech (such as similes, metaphors, personification, and onomatopoeia) creates a vivid depiction of a scene that strikes as many of the reader's senses as possible.

implicit

Something said or written that suggests and implies but never says it directly or clearly. "Meaning" is definitely present but it's in the imagery, or "between the lines."

in medias res

Latin for "in the midst of things." One of the conventions of epic poetry is that the action begins *in medias res*. For example, when *The Iliad* begins, the Trojan war has already been going on for seven years.

inversion

Switching the customary order of elements in a sentence or phrase. When done badly it can give a stilted, artificial, look-at-me-I'm-poetry feel to the verse, but poets do it all the time. This type of messing with syntax is called *poetic license. I'll have one large pizza with all the fixins*—presto chango instant poetry: *A pizza large I'll have, one with the fixins all.*

*irony

Three types of irony can be found in literature:

situational irony

The contradiction between what is expected and what actually occurs

dramatic irony

The contradiction between what we as readers know to be true and what characters have yet to discover

verbal irony

The contradiction between what is said and what is meant; sarcasm

juxtaposition

Placing two or more concepts, places, characters, or their actions together for the purpose of comparison or contrast.

lament

A poem of sadness or grief over the death of a loved one or over some other intense loss.

logos

The appeal to logic.

loose and periodic sentences

A *loose* sentence is complete before its end. A *periodic* sentence is not grammatically complete until it has reached its final phrase. (The term *loose* does not in any way imply that the sentences are slack or shoddy.)

> Loose sentence: *Jack loved Barbara despite her irritating snorting laugh, her complaining, and her terrible taste in shoes.*

> Periodic sentence: *Despite Barbara's irritation at Jack's peculiar habit of picking between his toes while watching MTV and his terrible haircut, she loved him.*

lyric

A type of poetry that explores the poet's personal interpretation of and feelings about the world (or the part that his poem is about). When the word *lyric* is used to describe a tone it refers to a sweet, emotional melodiousness.

masculine rhyme

A rhyme ending on the final stressed syllable (aka, regular old rhyme).

means, meaning

This is the big one, the one task you have to do all the time. You are discovering what makes sense, what's important. There is *literal* meaning which is concrete and explicit, and there is *metaphorical* or *abstract* meaning.

melodrama

A form of cheesy theater in which the hero is very, very good, the villain mean and rotten, and the heroine oh-so-pure. (It sounds dumb, but *melodramatic* movies make tons of money every year.)

*metaphor

A comparison between two relatively unlike ideas where you call one thing something it's not (e.g., *the pond was his watery tomb*—he died in the pond, but the pond itself isn't actually a burial place).

metonym

A word that is used to stand for something else that it has attributes of or is associated with. For example, a herd of 50 cows could be called 50 *head* of cattle.

monologue

A speech given by one character alone on stage.

motif

A recurring symbol.

narrative techniques

The methods employed in the telling of a story or an account. Examples of *narrative techniques* include point of view, manipulation of time, dialogue, and internal monologue.

neologism
See *coinage*.

*objectivity
An *objective* treatment of subject matter is an impersonal or outside view of events.

*omniscient narrator
See *point of view*.

onomatopoeia
Words that imitate sounds (e.g., boom, pow, buzz, gargle, babble, splat).

*opposition
One of the most useful concepts in analyzing literature. It means that you have a pair of elements that contrast sharply. It is not necessarily "conflict" but rather a pairing of images (or settings or appeals, for example) whereby each becomes more striking and informative because it's placed in contrast to the other one. This kind of *opposition* creates mystery and tension. Oppositions can be obvious. Oppositions can also lead to irony, but not necessarily so.

oxymoron
A phrase composed of opposites; a contradiction. *Bright black. A calm frenzy. Jumbo shrimp. Dark light. A truthful lie.*

parable
Like a fable or an allegory, a *parable* is a story that instructs.

*paradox
A situation or statement that seems to contradict itself but on closer inspection does not.

parallelism
Repeated syntactical similarities used for effect. For example: I love fishing, swimming, and hiking. All parts of the list are grammatically sound, as opposed to the unparallel version, I love fishing, to swim, and a hike.

paraphrase
To restate phrases and sentences in your own words; to rephrase. Paraphrase is not analysis or interpretation, so don't fall into the thinking that traps so many students. *Paraphrasing* is just a way of showing that you comprehend what you've just read—that you can now put it in your own words. No more, no less.

parenthetical phrase
A phrase set off by commas that interrupts the flow of a sentence with some commentary or added detail. *Jack's three dogs, <u>including that miserable little spaniel</u>, were with him that day.*

parody

A work that makes fun of another work by exaggerating many of its qualities to ridiculousness.

pastoral

A poem set in tranquil nature, or even more specifically, one about shepherds.

pathos

The appeal to emotions.

periodic sentence

See *loose sentence*.

persona

A created personality, reflective of the author; provides insight from a third person, not a first person, point of view.

*personification

Giving an inanimate object human qualities or form. *The darkness of the forest became the figure of a beautiful, pale-skinned woman in night-black clothes.*

plaint

A poem or speech expressing sorrow.

*point of view

The perspective from which the action of a novel (or narrative poem) is presented, whether the action is presented by one character or from different vantage points over the course of the novel. Be sensitive to *point of view*, because the AP Exam writers like to ask questions about it and also like you to mention point of view in your essays.

Related to *point of view* is the narrative form that a novel or story takes. There are a few common narrative positions:

- **Third-person omniscient narrator:** This is a third-person narrator who sees, like God, into each character's mind and understands all the action going on.
- **Third-person limited omniscient narrator:** This is a third-person narrator who generally reports only what one character (usually the main character) sees, and who only reports the thoughts of that one privileged character.
- **Third-person narrator:** This is a third-person narrator who only reports on what would be visible to a camera. The objective narrator does not know what the character is thinking unless the character speaks of it.
- **First-person narrator:** This is a narrator who is a character in the story and tells the tale from his or her point of view. When the first-person narrator is crazy, a liar, very young, or for some other reason not entirely credible, the narrator is *unreliable*.
- **Stream of consciousness:** This method is like first-person narration but instead of the character telling the story, the author places the reader inside the main character's head and makes the reader privy to all of the character's thoughts as they scroll through her consciousness.

prelude
An introductory poem to a longer work of verse.

*protagonist
The main character of a novel or play.

pun
The usually humorous use of a word in such a way to suggest two or more meanings.

refrain
A line or set of lines repeated several times over the course of a poem.

requiem
A song of prayer for the dead.

rhapsody
An intensely passionate verse or section of verse, usually of love or praise.

rhetorical question
A question that suggests an answer. In theory, the effect of a rhetorical question is that it causes the listener to feel she has come up with the answer herself. For example, if someone is eating with their mouth open, smacking loudly, you might ask, "is it good?" You don't actually expect an answer, but you convey your point that the smacking is annoying.

rhetorical techniques
The devices used to create effective or persuasive language. Common examples of these techniques include contrast, repetition, paradox, understatement, sarcasm, and rhetorical questions.

*satire
A form of humor that focuses on making fun of society through witty, sometimes dark social commentary; taking things that should be funny and picking on them in a way that raises awareness to ridiculousness and societal frustrations (think *SNL*, *Family Guy*, and slapstick comedies like *Scary Movie* or *Step Brothers*).

setting
The physical location of a play, story, or novel, which often includes information about time and place. The *setting* can also provide background information to a story.

*simile
A comparison between two relatively unlike ideas using *like* or *as* (e.g., *her hair is as bright as the sun*—we all know that the sun is yellow; therefore, we can deduce that her hair is blonde).

soliloquy

A speech given by one character alone on stage in which the character expresses his/her thoughts or feelings.

*stanza

A group of lines in verse, roughly analogous in function to the paragraph in prose.

stream of consciousness

See *point of view.*

structure

The way in which a work is arranged or divided. *Structure* can also refer to the relationship between the parts of a work and the work as a whole. The most common principles of structure are series (A, B, C, D, E), contrast (A versus B, C versus D, E versus A), and repetition (AA, BB, AB). The most common units of structure in plays are scene and act; in novels, chapter; and in poems, line and stanza.

style

The manner in which an author writes which can distinguish him or her from another writer. Examples of *style* include expository, argumentative, descriptive, persuasive, and narrative. *Style* also refers to the technique(s) writers employ as their mode of expression. Examples of these techniques include diction, syntax, figurative language, imagery, selection of detail, sound effects, tone, and voice.

*subjective

A subjective treatment uses the interior or personal view of a single observer and is typically colored with that observer's emotional responses.

subjunctive mood

If I were you, I'd learn this one! That's a small joke because the grammatical situation involves the words "if" and "were." What you do is set up a hypothetical situation, a kind of wishful thing: *if I were you, if he were honest, if she were rich.* You can also get away from the person and into the "it": *I wish it were true, would it were so* (that even sounds like Shakespeare and poetry). Go to question 15 on page 137 for the perfect example: "Were one not already the Duke…."

suggest

To imply, entail, and/or indicate. This is another one of those basic tools of literature. It goes along with the concept of *implicit.* As the reader, you have to do all the work to pull out the meaning.

summary

A simple retelling of what you've just read. It's mechanical, superficial, and a step beyond the paraphrase in that it covers much more material and is more general. You can summarize a whole chapter or a whole story, whereas you paraphrase word-by-word and line-by-line. *Summary* hits the highlights of a piece without revealing all of the facts.

suspension of disbelief
The demand made of a theater audience to accept the limitations of staging and supply the details with imagination. Also, the acceptance on an audience's or reader's part of the incidents of plot in a play or story. If there are too many coincidences or improbable occurrences, the viewer/reader can no longer suspend disbelief and subsequently loses interest.

symbol/symbolism
Anything that stands for or represents something beyond itself.

syncope
Contracting, or shortening, a word by removing internal sounds, syllables, or letters and inserting an apostrophe; or by dropping unstressed vowels, letters, syllables, or consonants from the middle of a word and replacing with an apostrophe. Examples include "heav'n," "ev'ry," and "fail'd" in Phillis Wheatley's poem "On the Death of J.C. an Infant" (see page 179).

synecdoche
Figure of speech in which a part represents the whole.

syntax
Sentence structure; the way in which words and phrases are structured to create meaning.

technique
The methods, the tools, the "how-she-does-it" ways of the author. The elements are not techniques. In poetry, *onomatopoeia* is a technique within the element of rhythm. In drama, *blocking* is a technique, as is *lighting*. Concrete details are not techniques, but *tone* is. Main idea is not a technique, but *opposition* is.

*theme
The main idea or central insight into life or human nature revealed through a literary work.

thesis
The main position of an argument. The central contention that will be supported. The guiding statement that reveals an argument's purpose/goal; essentially a contract with a reader that lets him/her know exactly what you plan to discuss or prove in an essay.

tone
The manner in which an author expresses his or her attitude about a subject. Writers convey *tone* through the use of many devices, such as word choice/diction. (See *attitude*.)

tragic flaw
In a tragedy, this is the weakness of character in an otherwise good (or even great) individual that ultimately leads to his demise.

travesty

The distortion, corruption, or terribly false representation of something.

truism

A way-too-obvious truth.

unreliable narrator

See *point of view*.

utopia

An idealized place. Imaginary communities in which people are able to live in happiness, prosperity, and peace. Several works of fiction have been written about *utopias*.

verisimilitude

The appearance of being real or true.

zeugma

The use of a word to modify two or more words but used for different meanings. *He closed the door and his heart on his lost love.*

The Princeton Review

YOUR NAME:
(...nt) Last   First   M.I.

...NATURE: _____ **DATE:** _____ / _____ / _____

...ME ADDRESS: _____
(...nt)   Number and Street

_____
City   State   Zip Code

...ONE NO. : _____
(...nt)

...PORTANT: Please fill in these boxes exactly as shown on the back cover of your test book.

5. YOUR NAME

First 4 letters of last name				FIRST INIT	MID INIT
A	A	A	A	A	A
B	B	B	B	B	B
C	C	C	C	C	C
D	D	D	D	D	D
E	E	E	E	E	E
F	F	F	F	F	F
G	G	G	G	G	G
H	H	H	H	H	H
I	I	I	I	I	I
J	J	J	J	J	J
K	K	K	K	K	K
L	L	L	L	L	L
M	M	M	M	M	M
N	N	N	N	N	N
O	O	O	O	O	O
P	P	P	P	P	P
Q	Q	Q	Q	Q	Q
R	R	R	R	R	R
S	S	S	S	S	S
T	T	T	T	T	T
U	U	U	U	U	U
V	V	V	V	V	V
W	W	W	W	W	W
X	X	X	X	X	X
Y	Y	Y	Y	Y	Y
Z	Z	Z	Z	Z	Z

. TEST FORM

3. TEST CODE

4. REGISTRATION NUMBER

(bubbles 0–9 / A–G)

6. DATE OF BIRTH

Month	Day		Year	
JAN				
FEB				
MAR	0	0	0	0
APR	1	1	1	1
MAY	2	2	2	2
JUN	3	3	3	3
JUL		4	4	4
AUG		5	5	5
SEP		6	6	6
OCT		7	7	7
NOV		8	8	8
DEC		9	9	9

7. SEX

- MALE
- FEMALE

The **Princeton Review**®

© TPR Education IP Holdings, LLC
FORM NO. 00001-PR

Practice Test 1

Start with number 1 for each new section.
If a section has fewer questions than answer spaces, leave the extra answer spaces blank.

1. A B C D E
2. A B C D E
3. A B C D E
4. A B C D E
5. A B C D E
6. A B C D E
7. A B C D E
8. A B C D E
9. A B C D E
10. A B C D E
11. A B C D E
12. A B C D E
13. A B C D E
14. A B C D E
15. A B C D E

16. A B C D E
17. A B C D E
18. A B C D E
19. A B C D E
20. A B C D E
21. A B C D E
22. A B C D E
23. A B C D E
24. A B C D E
25. A B C D E
26. A B C D E
27. A B C D E
28. A B C D E
29. A B C D E
30. A B C D E

31. A B C D E
32. A B C D E
33. A B C D E
34. A B C D E
35. A B C D E
36. A B C D E
37. A B C D E
38. A B C D E
39. A B C D E
40. A B C D E
41. A B C D E
42. A B C D E
43. A B C D E
44. A B C D E
45. A B C D E

46. A B C D E
47. A B C D E
48. A B C D E
49. A B C D E
50. A B C D E
51. A B C D E
52. A B C D E
53. A B C D E
54. A B C D E
55. A B C D E

Completely darken bubbles with a No. 2 pencil. If you make a mistake, be sure to erase mark completely. Erase all stray marks.

NR NAME: _____

Last   First   M.I.

TURE: _____ DATE: _____ / _____ / _____

ADDRESS: _____

Number and Street

City   State   Zip Code

E NO. : _____

KANT: Please fill in these boxes exactly as shown on the back cover of your test book.

EST FORM _____

_____

5. YOUR NAME

First 4 letters of last name				FIRST INIT	MID INIT
(A)	(A)	(A)	(A)	(A)	(A)
(B)	(B)	(B)	(B)	(B)	(B)
(C)	(C)	(C)	(C)	(C)	(C)
(D)	(D)	(D)	(D)	(D)	(D)
(E)	(E)	(E)	(E)	(E)	(E)
(F)	(F)	(F)	(F)	(F)	(F)
(G)	(G)	(G)	(G)	(G)	(G)
(H)	(H)	(H)	(H)	(H)	(H)
(I)	(I)	(I)	(I)	(I)	(I)
(J)	(J)	(J)	(J)	(J)	(J)
(K)	(K)	(K)	(K)	(K)	(K)
(L)	(L)	(L)	(L)	(L)	(L)
(M)	(M)	(M)	(M)	(M)	(M)
(N)	(N)	(N)	(N)	(N)	(N)
(O)	(O)	(O)	(O)	(O)	(O)
(P)	(P)	(P)	(P)	(P)	(P)
(Q)	(Q)	(Q)	(Q)	(Q)	(Q)
(R)	(R)	(R)	(R)	(R)	(R)
(S)	(S)	(S)	(S)	(S)	(S)
(T)	(T)	(T)	(T)	(T)	(T)
(U)	(U)	(U)	(U)	(U)	(U)
(V)	(V)	(V)	(V)	(V)	(V)
(W)	(W)	(W)	(W)	(W)	(W)
(X)	(X)	(X)	(X)	(X)	(X)
(Y)	(Y)	(Y)	(Y)	(Y)	(Y)
(Z)	(Z)	(Z)	(Z)	(Z)	(Z)

3. TEST CODE

(0)(A)(0)(0)(0)
(1)(B)(1)(1)(1)
(2)(C)(2)(2)(2)
(3)(D)(3)(3)(3)
(4)(E)(4)(4)(4)
(5)(F)(5)(5)(5)
(6)(G)(6)(6)(6)
(7)   (7)(7)(7)
(8)   (8)(8)(8)
(9)   (9)(9)(9)

4. REGISTRATION NUMBER

(0)(0)(0)(0)(0)(0)(0)(0)
(1)(1)(1)(1)(1)(1)(1)(1)
(2)(2)(2)(2)(2)(2)(2)(2)
(3)(3)(3)(3)(3)(3)(3)(3)
(4)(4)(4)(4)(4)(4)(4)(4)
(5)(5)(5)(5)(5)(5)(5)(5)
(6)(6)(6)(6)(6)(6)(6)(6)
(7)(7)(7)(7)(7)(7)(7)(7)
(8)(8)(8)(8)(8)(8)(8)(8)
(9)(9)(9)(9)(9)(9)(9)(9)

6. DATE OF BIRTH

Month	Day		Year	
○ JAN				
○ FEB				
○ MAR	(0)	(0)	(0)	(0)
○ APR	(1)	(1)	(1)	(1)
○ MAY	(2)	(2)	(2)	(2)
○ JUN	(3)	(3)	(3)	(3)
○ JUL		(4)	(4)	(4)
○ AUG		(5)	(5)	(5)
○ SEP		(6)	(6)	(6)
○ OCT		(7)	(7)	(7)
○ NOV		(8)	(8)	(8)
○ DEC		(9)	(9)	(9)

7. SEX

○ MALE
○ FEMALE

The **Princeton Review**®

© TPR Education IP Holdings, LLC
FORM NO. 00001-PR

actice Test 2

Start with number 1 for each new section.
If a section has fewer questions than answer spaces, leave the extra answer spaces blank.

(A) (B) (C) (D) (E)
(A) (B) (C) (D) (E)
(A) (B) (C) (D) (E)
(A) (B) (C) (D) (E)
(A) (B) (C) (D) (E)
(A) (B) (C) (D) (E)
(A) (B) (C) (D) (E)
(A) (B) (C) (D) (E)
(A) (B) (C) (D) (E)
(A) (B) (C) (D) (E)
(A) (B) (C) (D) (E)
(A) (B) (C) (D) (E)
(A) (B) (C) (D) (E)
(A) (B) (C) (D) (E)
(A) (B) (C) (D) (E)

16. (A) (B) (C) (D) (E)
17. (A) (B) (C) (D) (E)
18. (A) (B) (C) (D) (E)
19. (A) (B) (C) (D) (E)
20. (A) (B) (C) (D) (E)
21. (A) (B) (C) (D) (E)
22. (A) (B) (C) (D) (E)
23. (A) (B) (C) (D) (E)
24. (A) (B) (C) (D) (E)
25. (A) (B) (C) (D) (E)
26. (A) (B) (C) (D) (E)
27. (A) (B) (C) (D) (E)
28. (A) (B) (C) (D) (E)
29. (A) (B) (C) (D) (E)
30. (A) (B) (C) (D) (E)

31. (A) (B) (C) (D) (E)
32. (A) (B) (C) (D) (E)
33. (A) (B) (C) (D) (E)
34. (A) (B) (C) (D) (E)
35. (A) (B) (C) (D) (E)
36. (A) (B) (C) (D) (E)
37. (A) (B) (C) (D) (E)
38. (A) (B) (C) (D) (E)
39. (A) (B) (C) (D) (E)
40. (A) (B) (C) (D) (E)
41. (A) (B) (C) (D) (E)
42. (A) (B) (C) (D) (E)
43. (A) (B) (C) (D) (E)
44. (A) (B) (C) (D) (E)
45. (A) (B) (C) (D) (E)

46. (A) (B) (C) (D) (E)
47. (A) (B) (C) (D) (E)
48. (A) (B) (C) (D) (E)
49. (A) (B) (C) (D) (E)
50. (A) (B) (C) (D) (E)
51. (A) (B) (C) (D) (E)
52. (A) (B) (C) (D) (E)
53. (A) (B) (C) (D) (E)
54. (A) (B) (C) (D) (E)
55. (A) (B) (C) (D) (E)

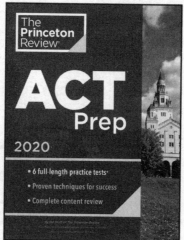
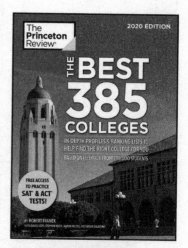